PRAISE FOR
Collateral Stardust

"A dazzling kiss-and-tell that brings vintage Hollywood to life.

(H)er consistent, irreverent voice makes the memoir delightful … her wonderful stories feel like 'remnant[s] of stardust mixed in with a cozy blanket of nostalgia.'"

—*Kirkus Reviews* (starred review)

* * *

"Former Conan O'Brien Show staffer Nash (*72 Raisins*) delivers a gossipy and engrossing account of her life in Hollywood from the 1970s through 2019.

Nash's story…(is a) self-aware, fascinating account of brushing up against the edge of fame. Written with humor, vulnerability, and verve, this satisfies."

—*Publishers Weekly*

* * *

"A cool and entertaining coming-of-age memoir, *Collateral Stardust* relays good times and hard ones with insight and style."

—*Foreword Reviews*

* * *

"Her world of musicians, actors, conspiracy theorists, political fundraisers, and alcohol-fueled parties hosted by her unconventional trombone-playing father and politically radical mother come to life in this work.

This coming-of-age story is a revealing, honest account of the inner workings of Hollywood and is well worthy of top honors."

—Los Angeles Book Festival

"*Collateral Stardust* is a hilarious and brave trek through decades of Hollywood with surprises at every turn."

—Brian Kiley, Emmy-Winning Comedy Writer

* * *

"Eve Babitz's tales are boring compared with what Nikki Nash serves up in this juicy, funny, sexy Hollywood tell-all memoir."

—Neal Pollack, author, *Pothead, Alternadad* and *Stretch*

* * *

"Perfection oozes out at every chance it gets. Best Seller!"

—Robert Hays, Actor

* * *

"*Collateral Stardust*—a powerful and brutally honest memoir—really defines our star-crossed generation, our parents, our business, LA in the latter half of the century, and so much more. I was blown away."

—Rich Hall, TV Producer

* * *

"The title itself is pure genius. In owning her role as a speck in the shimmering Hollywood universe, Nash spotlights the lives of ordinary people consigned forever to live as mere tailings afloat in the wake of superstar luminaries."

—Paul Vandeventer, Social Entrepreneur and Civic Innovator

Collateral Stardust

CHASING WARREN BEATTY
AND OTHER FOOLISH THINGS

NIKKI NASH

Sibylline Press
AN IMPRINT OF ALL THINGS BOOK

Copyright @ 2025 by Nikki Nash

All Rights Reserved. Published in the United States by Sibylline Press, an imprint of All Things Book LLC, California. Sibylline Press is dedicated to publishing the brilliant work of women authors over 50.
www.sibyllinepress.com

Distributed to the trade by Publishers Group West/Ingram Content

Sibylline Press
Paperback ISBN: 9781960573421
eBook ISBN: 9781960573483
Library of Congress Control Number: 2025932901

Book and Cover Design: Alicia Feltman

Author's Note

When my studio musician dad moved to California in 1954, he kept datebooks of every job he booked and every social activity in our family. I not only have his datebooks, but I continued with the tradition and have all my datebooks beginning in 1973. Thus, I was able to document all stories as to time, place, location, and those involved.

Although not all conversations are recreated verbatim, I have recounted them to evoke the meaning, essence, and tone of what was said.

Some names have been changed, but for the most part, my friends were all, "Sure, use my name."

To my brothers, Ted and Bill.

Collateral Stardust

CHASING WARREN BEATTY AND OTHER FOOLISH THINGS

NIKKI NASH

"You will do foolish things, but do them with enthusiasm."

—Colette

Table of Contents

Prologue 1
1. Splendor in the Grass 5
2. Bob Altman and His Magic Tricks 19
3. Malcolm X's Cousin 31
4. The Old World Restaurant 37
5. The Lawyer and The Hummingbirds 53
6. Jesus Christ 59
7. Judo at the YMCA 65
8. A View from the Bridge 77
9. Ding! 93
10. Fetch Ben Stein and Other Odd Requests 97
11. Headshots 105
12. Jules et Jim 109
13. Jack Nicholson and the Skydiving Story 115
14. The Oscars 123
15. How Lovely to Be a Woman 133
16. God Died and Left Me Boss 143
17. Snap Her Little Neck 149
18. Stand Up, Sit Down 163
19. The Groundlings and The Mastery 167
20. An Affair to Remember 177
21. Husbands and Wives 183
22. Mrs. Sonny Barger 193
23. Watching *24* 203
24. The Ring 211
25. Good Evening 221
26. Altered States 225
27. Mulholland Drive 233
28. Last Words 245

Prologue

"Nash. Looking good," Mitch said. Which meant I looked like crap. I had no make-up on, I hadn't washed my hair, and my armpits smelled like cilantro. Thinking about my armpits just made me sweat more, as I was sure Mitch would soon ask: "What's that smell?"

I was wearing corduroy bell-bottoms, a flowered polyester shirt, and platform shoes. Mitch had a mustache, feathered blond hair, and was also wearing platform shoes. We looked like we were going to a 1970s costume party.

Except there was no party. And these weren't costumes.

It *was* the '70s. 1974.

We were at the Old World Restaurant in Beverly Hills, where Mitch was the manager and I was the hostess.

"Shut up," I said. "I think I broke my finger." I'd injured my finger earlier in a judo class at the Y, and although that didn't stop me from showing up for work, I hadn't been able to take a shower, and unfortunately tonight I would come face to face with the man I'd been obsessed with for the last five years.

It was a warm Sunday evening in April. I was nineteen. Listless and longing. *Bennie and the Jets* was the number one song that spring, but what made me swoon was Joni Mitchell's *Help Me*. I was always falling in love.

Although not with Mitch because he was a doofus.

The restaurant was usually slow on Sunday nights. I went to the prep station, got a plastic water glass, filled it mostly with ice, and stuck my index finger in. Holding the cup, my injured finger submerged, I seated a few people. No one asked me about the glass I was carrying around, or maybe no one noticed. It became second nature, and as the pain subsided, I soon forgot about it.

I went into the bathroom, slicked my dirty hair back into a ponytail, pinched my cheeks for color like someone from the 1920s, re-submerged my finger in the plastic glass, and came out of the bathroom.

Mitch stepped in beside me as we walked.

"Your boyfriend's up front," he said. This was his go-to comment about any guy sitting solo—young or old—as if Mitch knew I was perpetually looking for a boyfriend.

"Oh, goody," not getting my hopes up once again.

Mitch didn't reply. He just smiled.

I walked to the front of the restaurant, and holding the glass in my right hand, finger submerged, I grabbed a menu with my left hand and turned to find a man sitting alone at a table in the corner.

Warren Beatty.

I froze. My face flushed.

Dammit! Why tonight?

I had developed my secret obsession with Warren Beatty when I was fourteen—I'd even gotten the damn job at The Old World when I was eighteen as I'd been told he came in occasionally—and tonight, over a year and a half later, he *finally* comes in? I'd had it all mapped out: I would meet him, we would become lovers and eventually friends, and we'd know each other for the rest of our lives. And although I didn't have all the particulars in place, Step One in my plan had been to grow up. Check. Step Two was to meet him.

But not like this.

Warren was reading a newspaper he'd folded into a smaller rectangle, as if he was focused on something important. Or maybe he was tidy and didn't like a lot of paper flapping around. Or maybe he wanted people to see his face.

I sure wanted to see his face. He was beautiful. The most beautiful man I'd ever seen.

Trying to will myself into invisibility, I placed the menu on the table as unobtrusively as I could.

"Your waiter will be right with you," I said blandly.

He looked up. "Thank you."

That voice. I was hearing that voice fifteen inches away from my face. More like my torso, as I was standing, and he was sitting. But he was expelling sounds and molecules in my direction, and they warmed me.

Until I remembered I looked like crap.

He smiled. I half-smiled and turned to walk away. My brain was misfiring all over the place: that's *him*, I'm holding this stupid glass, he'd looked at me, did I say anything to him? Or had I been rendered as mute as I now felt?

I could go upstairs and hide. I'd let Mitch handle things. This was *not* the way I wanted to meet Warren Beatty.

I'd almost met him three years before when my parents dragged me to a party in Westwood. But I knew then I was still too young, so I'd made myself invisible to him. And although I was now old enough, this had *not* been Step Two of my plan: dirty hair, no makeup, smelly armpits. I prayed he had already forgotten me. I almost made it out of the front room and out of his sight.

"Excuse me, miss?" That voice shivered down my back.

Could I just keep walking? *Let me just keep walking.*

But what if this was my only chance? I'd been waiting for Warren Beatty to come into this stupid restaurant for almost two years. I was tired of waiting. And here he was. I couldn't work here for another two years on hope.

I turned around to face him.

1

Splendor in the Grass

In the 1960s, most young girls in Southern California wanted to wear training bras, get their ears pierced, and be allowed to shave their legs. Although I shared these desires and rites of passage on my way to becoming a full-fledged teenager, where I diverged was in the fantasy department. My friends idolized Gidget—innocent and approachable. I wanted to be Ann-Margret—seductive and mysterious. And where other girls had unattainable teen-idol crushes on Paul McCartney or Davy Jones, my secret desire as a young girl was for Warren Beatty.

The other girls grew out of their teenage fantasies and went on to real relationships, but I held onto mine until, well, last month. Although this obsession with Warren Beatty may have manifested when I was fourteen, the undercurrent that fed this obsession was a deep longing that had begun much earlier, growing up in a family of colorful misfits.

My dad, Dick, was a handsome and charming trombone player who flirted with everyone. And the women flirted back. My beautiful mom, Barbara, was more complex, smarter than my dad, and unsuited to being a mother and homemaker. Having a new baby and a handsome husband may have distracted her for a while, but after my brothers were born, she became tired and brittle.

Our first house was a "cracker box"—as my dad called it—on a cul-de-sac in the north end of the San Fernando Valley, beyond which was the wilderness of orange trees and walnut groves, and where the only social activities in the 1950s were having cocktails, playing bridge, and planning for a nuclear war.

Dad was just starting his career as a studio musician, so he was home a lot, and the three of us had fun on laundry day when I'd hide in the pile of dirty clothes. My mom would say, "Where's Nikki?" and when my dad started to pick up the bundle, I'd burst out saying, "Here I am!" with an exuberance I eventually learned to temper when I noticed her responses to my need for attention changed from delight to annoyance. This need for acknowledgment would later take many forms, like being attractive or funny or seemingly smart.

Dad taught me to read, and Mom loved words, so until I could use a dictionary on my own, I turned to my mom for help. When I was five, I'd seen "fuck" and "shit" written on a cinder block wall near the railroad tracks and asked her what those words meant. She was at her sewing machine, and after hearing my question, she took her foot off the machine's pedal but didn't immediately answer. She was a stickler for logic, truth, and grammar, and didn't believe words were either good or bad, except maybe socially, which to her was circumstantial and not definitive.

She took a breath and explained the biological aspects of the words I'd seen, using terms not unfamiliar to me—words we used around the house like *penis, vagina*, and *bowel movement*. "Shit" was easy to explain, but "fuck" gave her pause. She explained the mechanics of the penis and vagina but pulled to do the right thing as a mother by instilling the accepted social morality she may not have believed in, she loosely explained that when a man and a woman got together in this way, they were "most likely" married. Satisfied, I went back outside to play.

That night, my parents were playing bridge and having cocktails with three other couples. I came in and waited politely for a lull in the conversation so I could say goodnight. I heard one couple talking about when they'd gotten married, and another couple mentioned how long they'd been married.

During the lull, I asked, "Mom, how long have you and Daddy been married?"

"Six years."

"So you've been fucking for six years?" I asked.

I didn't know why their friends laughed—I was proud of my conjugation of a new verb—but my mom nodded and simply said, "Goodnight, Nikki."

I said goodnight and went to bed.

This delightful familial attention from both my parents waned after my brothers were born, and I went from only child to oldest child. Mom's moods were inconsistent, which confused me. Some days she seemed fine and some days she seemed mad at me for no reason. I overheard her talking to a neighbor about *The Red Shoes*—a movie she *loved*—and it caught my attention because she didn't talk about love too often. I hadn't seen the movie, but I had a pair of red shoes—scuffed Mary Janes—and I noticed one day while I was wearing them that she seemed to be more attentive. I wore them again the next day. Same thing. Mom was friendlier, happier. She loved me. The third day—feeling I had this figured out—I put on the red shoes, but something had shifted overnight, and when she got up late that morning, she was sullen and didn't look at me. I was confused and then disappointed when I realized the red shoes weren't the secret. They weren't magical. Back to the drawing board.

Whenever I got sick, my mother seemed overwhelmed and became distant. She put me alone in my room, gave me one of my dad's hankies which she'd dabbed with her perfume—Sirocco—put on a recording of the *1812 Overture,* and closed the door. Until, I guess, I felt better. Or the music stopped. I got used to being alone. And so—in an attempt to never be too much for my mom—I started paring down my needs to only the most essential, and in this way, I wouldn't annoy her; I wouldn't risk being disappointed by her absence. Instead, I developed a need to be needless. And a strange love of perfume, which continues to this day.

Dad's career was picking up, as was Mom's drinking. He was getting recording dates with Henry Mancini on movies like *Breakfast at Tiffany's,* and his reputation grew as a studio musician in television as well, working on shows like *Peter Gunn* and *Combat!*

Time for a bigger house.

I was eight and my brothers, Ted and Bill, were three and two when we left the cracker box and bomb-shelter talk and moved to a sprawling Dutch farmhouse in Tarzana, on a street with no sidewalks, as it was zoned for horses. We did not have horses. The house had a lot of brick and wood and came furnished with big sofas and old-timey flourishes like wagon-wheel lighting fixtures, a cobbler's bench coffee table, rag rugs, and flowery flounces on the curtains. It was probably a shock to my mom's esthetics as she preferred the simplicity of 1950s modern (or *moderne* as she referred to it): white walls, one stiff black couch, a slim black slatted coffee table, and one piece of abstract art on a wall.

My brothers and I, however, loved the house, and the best part for me was the canopy bed that was left behind in what would become my bedroom on the second floor. Plus, there was a pool.

Dad didn't care about interior design, or perhaps he didn't notice, but he loved the pool. He loved skimming the leaves; he loved testing the chemicals, checking the vacuum that slunk around at the bottom, sucking up whatever had found its way down there. And he occasionally rescued critters. One time, a lizard had fallen into the pool, and we caught Dad standing on the shallow-end stairs in his plaid boxer shorts, giving the lizard mouth-to-mouth resuscitation, pressing gently on its belly and then blowing into its mouth. He also had about fifteen hummingbird feeders going in the backyard, filled with the sweet liquid he concocted himself. His nicknames—given to him by friends who knew these stories and witnessed his affable good nature—were either Francis of Assisi or The Saint, neither of which my mother called him, as she was otherwise engaged cleaning up all the hummingbird juice-making crap.

As Dad became better known in the music industry, the parties started. There were many drunken nights with directors, musicians, and actors, like Robert Altman (we called him Bob), John Williams (we called him Johnny), and Vic Morrow (we called him, well, Vic). There's a photo—taken at night in the backyard—where I'm wearing a peignoir set: a sheer, blue lacy nightgown and a matching chiffon robe with ruffles and silk ribbons at the neck. I guess the point of these peignoir sets was to present a woman, like on her wedding night, as a gift of sorts. First, untying the silk ribbons, slowly removing the robe to reveal the diaphanous tissue paper-like nightgown, hinting at the ultimate present just beneath the fabric, providing the new bride with the potential for a slow, sexy reveal. Maybe appropriate if you were in your twenties on your honeymoon, but I was *eight*. Why did they even make these for children?

In the peignoir photo, I'm sitting next to Vic Morrow, the star of *Combat!* It was a warm summer night in the Valley, and we were on the small, worn merry-go-round in the backyard by the pool. Vic was very handsome and very drunk, and the merry-go-round was big enough for barely two children, so we were forced to sit close together. Although I was dressed like a child bride ready for bed, it wasn't that late, and I wasn't alone with Vic. I was chaperoned to some extent as my dad was nearby with his camera, silhouetted by the pool behind him, the pool light creating an otherworldly opalescence in the otherwise dark backyard. Dad snapped the photo of me and Vic. I probably said goodnight not long after that because my parents were still strict about my bedtime (if not my attire), although I usually stayed awake a while, listening to the revelry by the pool below my bedroom window.

Bob Altman was an up-and-coming TV director and would eventually, in 1970, go on to direct his first big hit, *M*A*S*H*, followed by other movies, including *The Long Goodbye, McCabe and Mrs. Miller,* and *Nashville*. But in the early '60s it was television, and in addition to directing *Combat!,* he directed three episodes of the *Kraft Suspense*

Theater, from which he was fired for saying their shows were as bland as their cheese, a story my mom loved to retell. She seemed to love Bob for speaking his mind, for his fearlessness, and for saying what he wanted, as opposed to my dad, who was charming and friendly but didn't rock the boat with too many strong opinions. Or maybe he didn't have any strong opinions to express.

Mom was still beautiful and astute, but by 1968, she had started to show a weariness that came from having three kids but no mental stimulation. She still explained things to me when I asked, until her subtle depression took over, and she became less available. Dad was still handsome and charming, and enjoyed the unexpected attention from the occasional jazz jams that took over our living room or the musician groupies that hung around the recording studios. But Mom needed more than the diffused stardust of Dad's success to lift her from the drudgery of being a silent housewife. After her dreams of being a singer were sidelined by polyps on her throat, she found her own mental stimulation and attention with politics. *Radical* politics. And with her new interest came new friends.

We were the only family on the block, as far as I could tell, to have the FBI drive slowly back and forth in front of our house. Not all the time, just when my parents had parties, and we had a lot of parties. I asked my mom why the FBI was driving by, and she explained that the government was watching us, which turned out to be true.

When the black sedan drove past, the men in suits made note of the license plates of the cars parked in our circular drive and on the street in front of our house. There were shiny cars from the wealthier part of the San Fernando Valley belonging to well-meaning, liberal ACLU types; beater cars from a variety of jazz musicians and studio musicians who came from Hollywood; and various old station wagons and vans belonging to the Black Panthers—a militant Black Power organization. There were the cars of actors and reporters, as well as a rogue door-to-door Fuller Brush man on foot who had seen all the cars and rang the doorbell, thinking someone might need some brushes or other household items. He was used to the door being closed in his face, but at our house, he was invited in and stayed for the weekend.

Every couple of weeks, this sprawling house in Tarzana came alive with music, cooking, drinking, and dancing. Everyone singing along: "Grazin' in the grass is a gas, baby, can you dig it." The speakers by the pool were often pulsing with something Brazilian like Sergio Mendes and Brazil '66. My brothers and I could probably still sing along to "Mais Que Nada." Well, not exactly the real words, but a phonetic recreation of Portuguese we'd come up with as children, and belted out with enthusiasm if Mom was in a good mood.

Our adopted family of misfits included Brother Lenny, in a cotton dashiki, who would take over the kitchen with all his loud drinking, Kent-smoking, chitlin-cooking, and storytelling. Brother Lenny also had his hands full playing grab-ass with my mom. Bubba, an afro pick comb embedded in his hair, made jewelry, spreading out all his beads and tools on the coffee table in the living room. Uncle Larry, a tall, beautiful man who may have had an affair with my Gramma Ruth, who was as white as he was Black. The Goldmans came from Woodland Hills, looking like their name, Arnie with his gold chains and gold embellishments on his belt and shoes, Joyce with her gold hair, gold purse, and her gold check-writing pen.

The political conspiracy theorists were a buttoned-down, elbow-patched, cerebral bunch who tended to gather in the backyard to discuss important political conspiracy stuff, despite the music pumping out of the speakers by the pool. They weren't big dancers. There was an old, white-haired dentist who specialized in giving braces to young men so they could avoid the draft. And Humanae, a skinny black guy who always seemed cheerfully drunk. My brothers and I once caught him alone on the living room sofa, making out with a large pink blow-up Easter bunny. This was toward the end of one of these long party weekends when everyone was tired, so maybe the Easter bunny was the recipient of the only sexual energy Humanae could muster at that point before falling asleep. Or passing out.

Various Black Panthers like Huey Newton and Eldridge Cleaver came and went like they were movie stars (often with lawyers or bodyguards in tow), causing a big stir as well as an uptick of FBI drive-bys.

Another frequent sleepover guest was Robby Meeropol, the son of Ethel and Julius Rosenberg, who had been tried and convicted of espionage for passing atomic secrets to the Russians. They were electrocuted in 1953. My mom was on the Rosenberg Committee—a group working to posthumously exonerate the couple. She had a red phone installed in the den in case anyone should call with new evidence on Julius and Ethel Rosenberg's miscarriage of justice. No one was allowed to use this phone. Which never rang. If I had known the number, I would have called it while my brothers were watching TV, just to freak them out.

And at every party was Gil Toff—a skinny, scruffy, white guy—who was everybody's friend and/or an enterprising grifter. He once took me to David Carradine's house, where David and his girlfriend Barbara Seagull (née Hershey) squatted on the floor with Gil to talk about important things. I sat on a chair, as I didn't know them well enough to join the figurative campfire. Plus, I was feeling gassy.

Gil had his own conspiracy theory about the Kennedy Assassination, which centered around then-Vice-President Johnson hiring a special driver to shoot Kennedy while the motorcade drove toward the underpass where there would be fewer onlookers, i.e., witnesses. However, a few stragglers lingered on the grassy knoll. One was Mr. Zapruder, his 8mm camera whirring, catching the end of the motorcade as it passed by, and thus recording the moment President Kennedy was shot in the head. Gil's theory: The driver did it.

Although barely a teenager, I considered myself a free-thinker and therefore I wasn't swayed by the theories swirling around downstairs when the adults were talking and drinking; I wanted to investigate for myself what the "facts" were. I guess some teenagers rebelled by putting on eyeliner, sneaking out at night, and smoking on the corner with friends, but I chose to figure out who killed Kennedy.

Gil gave me an illegal copy of the Zapruder film, so I started there. I took my dad's projector up to my room and watched the twenty-six-second film—over and over—for five hours, meaning I watched it like a billion times. I wrote letters to John Connally, J. Edgar Hoover, and Chief Justice Warren, whose committee produced twenty-six volumes to say Lee Harvey Oswald did it. (The Commission doth protest too much?) I wrote to gun experts. I wrote to the Parkland doctors who had famously tried to keep Kennedy alive. I got responses from everyone.

Dr. Peters' letter was the most personal, and his response sounded like a holiday letter included in Christmas cards, filled with cheery-sounding updates I hadn't asked for: "Mrs. Oswald has remarried and is living in the area with her new husband. She had delivered a baby at Parkland Hospital, I believe Oswald's second child, a few months before the assassination. Mr. John Connally, who was shot along with President Kennedy, is now Secretary of the Treasury and seems to have recovered completely, aside from some wrist pain." Well, Merry Christmas. Only one sentence in his letter seemed out of place in what would have been this otherwise cheery holiday assassination update: "Examination of the brain revealed most of the cerebellum was shot away."

I never was able to determine who shot Kennedy.

Otherwise, we were like any post-'50s suburban family, with a mother who felt trapped and supplemented the adrenaline of her political buzz with the amphetamines she kept under the bathroom sink, and a successful father who liked to swim in the pool naked and taught our mynah bird jazz trombone solos.

During the week, once the parties wound down, we fell into our familiar positions of retreat and solitude, and it was back to just our family at dinner, playing Twenty Questions to avoid anything getting too personal, often going no deeper than: "Is it bigger than a bread box?" Mom wouldn't eat much, preferring to nibble and smoke. I was always back on a start-of-a-new-week diet, and then there was Gramma Ruth, who had her own work-around denial going on. She was tiny, with tiny hands and feet, and a tiny mouth creased from smoking and judgment. When dinner included carbohydrates—which was every night—she'd say, "I've been good all week," as she reached for a baked potato, which exhibited some kind of twisty physics, considering she said this maybe five times a week.

It was disorienting to go from the weekend parties—with all the wild, sexually-charged, alcohol-fueled, unstructured antics—to our small weeknight dinners where sedate parlor games were our only intimacies, and a baked potato became a big adventure. I found it easier to judge Gramma Ruth than look at all of the magical eating, fasting, and diet-chart-making I was doing to try and feel good about myself. Or take control of myself. Or at least not hate myself.

I was probably a normal weight for a teenager, but as with most eating issues, my daily obsession with my body was a distraction from my confusion and loneliness. Better to hate my thighs than hate my mother and better to be thin than hate my thighs. I hadn't yet discovered bulimia, which would later become another tool in my never-ending diet arsenal.

After dinner, Dad hung out with his trombone in the cabaña by the pool when he wasn't taking night gigs as a studio musician. Mom stayed in her bedroom with her cigarettes and brandy. My brother Ted skateboarded around the neighborhood while Bill played with his Hot Wheels in his bedroom upstairs. And I was either alone in my room eating ice cream, or in the den watching TV.

I wouldn't follow in my mother's political footsteps or my father's musical footsteps. I wasn't taking a lot of footsteps, generally. Ted—who was thin and practiced magic tricks—would eventually win two Grammys as a sax player and composer, and Bill—who was chubby and liked biting people—would eventually make amazing guitars that are works of art, coveted by rock musicians near and far. I got straight As in school and was studying acting. And despite all the time I spent trying new diets every week, which involved an endless parade of graphs, colored pencils, and innumerable fresh starts, I mostly watched a lot of TV.

I loved TV.

Occasionally, during one of these quiet, lonely weekdays, I'd come down from my bedroom to watch TV and find my mom in the den—with her bourbon and Pall Malls—watching an old black and white movie. Like *The Shop on Main Street*, where a Czech man takes over a Jewish-run business in a town occupied by Nazis, or *Town Without Pity*, in which four American soldiers rape a German girl. Fun! It wasn't exactly *Mary Poppins,* but I loved sitting next to her on the couch, just the two of us, no matter what she was watching. A movie was usually an hour and a half, so I knew I'd be near her for at least that long. When the movie was over, she usually closed up on herself, got quiet, and left me alone in the den. But I learned to take what I could get.

As I got older, I spent time in my bedroom doing homework and then retreated to the den where I could watch TV. *Secret Agent, Get Smart, Bewitched, The Avengers, I Spy, The Man from U.N.C.L.E., Mission: Impossible, That Girl,* and *The Smothers Brothers.* One night after dinner, on my way to the den to sedate myself with a plate of Oreos and the solace of mind-numbing entertainment, I passed Mom in the kitchen.

She asked why I watched so much TV, and I said in my moody and rebellious teenage voice: "To escape from reality."

She glared at me and said in her moody, hostile voice: "What's wrong with your fucking reality, Miss!?"

Asked and answered.

But there was only so much TV I could watch and only so many cookies I could eat before the gnawing, unsettled feelings of emotional hunger and despair found their way to the surface. My need to be held, to be loved. To be myself. Instead, I kept up with the constant monitoring of my mother's moods until it felt safe to be me, a habit I fine-tuned and employed with others for years, which felt both protective and exhausting.

This unsatisfied longing was a breathless internal cry that came to a head and nearly destroyed me when I saw *Romeo and Juliet* for my fourteenth birthday. My mom dropped me off at the theater near Corbin Bowl on Ventura Boulevard. I sat alone in the dark watching an overwhelming, nearly unbearable love play out on the screen. When the movie ended, I couldn't stop sobbing. I wanted to stay in the dark theater because this tearful heaving felt out of control, but I didn't want to keep my mom waiting. I pulled it together, went out front, and stood in the cool fall weather, intermittently crying and looking for our station wagon. I needed her to explain why I felt so lost. I was also afraid that my crying would be too much for her. I wanted someone to know how sad it was to feel the longing between Romeo and Juliet. I wanted to be consoled. I wanted someone to hold me while I cried. But I had learned as a child that expressing this need for my mother only pushed her away, leaving me frozen and hoping even a soft breeze of her love might come my way.

Once in the car, and between the muffled wet sobbing, I said, "I'm so sad."

"Why?" She lit a Pall Mall.

"They loved each other so much. That's all they wanted, and they couldn't have it. Their love died with them." And I was sobbing again.

"There's Kleenex in the glove compartment," she said, and picked a fleck of tobacco from her tongue.

"Okay." I found the tissues in their Pan Am wrapping, but extracting one was like pulling out a small sheet of dust, and when I blew my nose, the tissue dissolved into a gooey mess.

"It's teenage hormones," she said, as if she had just solved the problem.

But I was left wondering if she meant *my* teenage hormones or Romeo and Juliet's. If nothing else, the wondering distracted me long enough to stop crying.

After that heartfelt exchange, we drove in silence, except for all the sniffling as I pulled myself together. The crying had worn me out. This *could* have been simple teenage hormones, but looking back, I must have sensed that my mother's maternal instincts were waning, and despite appreciating her honest responses, I'd need to find a larger-than-life love to compensate for the gap left by her absence. I knew I needed to find my own great love. That to-the-bone, undying feeling of connection that would fill the deep longing I had. But before I shut the door on any hope for mother love, I needed a substitute that would fill me, comfort me, distract me, delight me.

This is when my obsession took hold. When I found my own reason for living.

I was watching TV and was spellbound when Warren Beatty appeared on the screen in a movie from 1961 called *Splendor in the Grass*. I decided at that moment I would love him, and he would welcome my love, and he would eventually love me back. We would have a secret connection that would start at some undetermined time in the future and would fulfill me for the rest of my life. And knowing this calmed me.

Natalie Wood was also in the movie, playing a vulnerable, psychologically unhinged, and obsessively smitten love interest. I'm guessing most young girls probably saw the movie and aligned with Natalie Wood. But the person who held me in his unknowing thrall was Warren Beatty. The way he looked at her, the subtle, knowing pain behind his eyes, his stunning face that was almost too beautiful to take in. I would rescue him, and he would rescue me. We would love one another forever. Or maybe I'd simply imprinted on him like a duckling to a human, seeing him when I'd felt my most vulnerable, my most alone and bereft. If I'd waited an hour to watch *Bonanza*, I might have fallen head over heels for Lorne Greene.

Any other obsession may have faded naturally with time and the distraction of other interests, but my focus on Warren Beatty was absolute, and with him, I'd find a great love. It wasn't some girly crush that would include posters on my wall or putting his photo in a secret diary. I wanted more. It was my mission to *know* him. Not to meet him, not to get an autograph, but to know him and have him in my life forever. He would see me. Not in that fucked up, what's-the-matter-with-Natalie-Wood way. And he would let me see him. Not in that look-at-me-I'm-a-movie-star way. I would love *him*. I would be his equal.

To an outsider, this may have seemed like an unrealistic or almost pathological longing, like that of women who found comfort in writing to prison inmates. Or the ease of submitting all one's passion to Jesus, who—by his physical absence—is strangely always there for you. Or maybe this was only a way of prolonging disappointment: If I wasn't going to feel love from my mother now, I would create a future where I'd feel seen and heard, like the indirect comfort of dreaming about future fame, of a place where love was abundant. Or maybe I longed for a recipient of the love I had to give. Maybe this was all silliness, but these feelings had to go somewhere. This would be my workaround for my loneliness and longing.

I could live off the fantasy until I made it a reality. Granted, meeting him would have been less likely had I lived in Wisconsin, but I had been born in Hollywood; I lived in the Valley. He wasn't that far away.

And at fourteen, I knew what the first step would be.

I would need to grow up.

2

Bob Altman and His Magic Tricks

In the late 1960s, it was all Nixon and Vietnam. Mom expressed her fury about both by attending local demonstrations and sit-ins. My brothers, although still young, worried about being drafted, but Mom assured them that if the time came, her dentist friend could give them fake braces to avoid the draft. I was almost sixteen and, while waiting to be old enough to put my still-nebulous Warren plan into action, hung out with my best friend Tina, whose brother made us fake IDs to buy alcohol.

The crazy weekend parties continued to a lesser extent but were still counterbalanced by our more sedate weekday family dinners. The only big change was that Twenty Questions was replaced with The Datebook Game which consisted of someone throwing out a date and Dad looking it up in one of his datebooks to report what had happened that day. He'd kept all his datebooks, which detailed his jobs, but also any other pertinent goings-on. The entries included such disparate items like "2p Warner Bros with Mancini," "Boys' therapy with Mrs. B," and "Barb and N (Nikki) to bar with Huey Newton." I still have all those datebooks and found the entries for one day where in the morning, Dad had "Fixed the lawnmower," and in the evening, there was a "Black Panther Fundraiser." Typical family stuff.

The Datebook Game was benign enough until I had a boy over for dinner and, rather than actually talk to him, someone threw out a date, Dad grabbed the appropriate datebook, thumbed through, and found the page. He announced it was from a time two years previous when our family had vacationed in Scituate, Massachusetts. I was expecting something like "Walked on the beach" or "Cooked lobster," but he cleared his throat and blurted out the first entry for that summer day.

"N had messy period."

True, I'd had a messy period that required my getting up before anyone else, hand-washing the sheets, and hanging them on the line outside to dry before remaking the bed. I guess Mom explained to Dad why I was up early, and he felt it was noteworthy enough to go down in the datebooks.

Fine, but could he have maybe *lied* on this night when I had a boy over? Or left that part out?

I was mortified and never invited any boys over for dinner again. Maybe this night would become an entry in the datebook: "N upset for no reason." All those weekend parties with no sexual boundaries, and it was a quiet dinner with my family that left me feeling unsafe. Unprotected. Exposed.

BY 1970, THE WILD WEEKEND parties were subsiding, and Mom started hosting more sedate dinner parties, which felt more like a throwback to a quieter time from the '50s cracker box era. Maybe she was tired, or maybe it gave her a chance to use the dining room, which was usually just a pass-through room to the den. I loved seeing the table come alive with plates and glasses and thin white candles—or tapers, as my mother called them. It was the only room that reflected her more modern tastes: a tiled floor that was cold to bare feet, a white table with six high-backed black dining chairs, and sleek black shelving that displayed dinnerware patterned in a black and white atomic theme, which to me was more Cold War than cozy. Compared to the shag-carpeted living room—with its oversized wooden coffee table, big brick fireplace, colorful glass vases, framed album covers, and pet hair—stepping into the dining room was like entering a cool and unadorned dining room in Sweden.

At one of these dinner parties, Bob Altman sat at the head of the table and held court as his wife, Kathryn, irreverently interjected corrections which Bob both acknowledged and ignored with a wave of his hand as he rambled on, a dynamic that my mother seemed to envy: the intelligence, the banter, the sly humorous equality of their exchanges. I loved how upbeat Mom seemed before and during dinner. Animated, happy. Dressed up and with a purpose, at least for a few hours. The deflation would descend after the guests had gone, and she retreated into a small world that didn't include me.

Bob also liked to do magic tricks at the table, and I dutifully played the part of his young magician's assistant. He'd find me earlier to rehearse with him in the den when the others were in the living room having cocktails. I liked being in on the secret of his magic tricks, and although I usually stayed in my room during Mom's dinner parties, when Bob was over, I lingered nearby until it was—Showtime!

Bob got everyone's attention with his booming voice and called for me to join them in the dining room, where I took my place standing beside him at the head of the table. He turned his empty highball glass upside down, covered it with his napkin, then lifted the glass and napkin combo and held it up to show that the glass was still in his hand and not on the table. Everyone nodded, *Yeah, we get it: you're holding the glass.*

He delivered some snappy patter as he set the glass back down on the table. He grabbed my hand by the wrist and slammed my palm down on top of the glass. Nothing shattered. My hand was fine. The glass had disappeared, leaving the napkin flattened on the table. What the others didn't know was that when he lifted the glass to prove he was still holding it, on the way back to putting it on the table, he'd dropped it onto his lap, with me standing close to make sure it didn't bounce off his leg. During the slight applause, he looked at me like I was his smart, little sidekick, had me take a bow, and seemed to appreciate my playing the innocent.

I wasn't auditioning for him, but I *was* studying acting at Everywoman's Village—which in its early days was called either "a school for bored housewives" or "a cultural center for women," depending on whom you asked—but I'd never mentioned acting to Bob or asked him for help or guidance. I knew there was a separation of church and state, but also, I was never comfortable asking *anyone* for help. Better to keep my needs to myself—and hope someone intuited them—than risk being rejected. Or so I'd learned as a child.

Better to say nothing and then be surprised if something good comes my way by happenstance. And, of course, this meant I'd never ask him if he knew Warren Beatty. Or maybe I didn't want to know; perhaps I only wanted Warren as a fantasy, the bubble of which might burst if I ever actually met him. However, it was too soon to admit that.

After *M*A*S*H* made Bob famous, my parents were invited to a screening of his new movie, followed by a party at his Lionsgate offices in Westwood Village. My parents asked if I wanted to go with them. I wished I had something else to do, but I said yes, if only to keep in touch with Bob while I continued with my acting classes.

Maybe he would intuit my desire for help? He never did.

The movie was *McCabe and Mrs. Miller* and starred Julie Christie and Warren Beatty. What? We were ushered into the screening room, and I wondered if Warren Beatty would be there in person. I'd seen him in *Bonnie and Clyde,* which had only contributed to my obsession. I looked around but didn't see any of the actors and relaxed a little. Once the movie began, I felt a flush on my face and a drop in my belly seeing my beloved on screen.

I had not shared my secret obsession with anyone, including my parents, which was fortunate, as they would have teased me about it after the movie, and Warren was more important to me than just fodder for teasing. I'd seen *Bonnie and Clyde* and wished I was Faye Dunaway, but only to be near Warren Beatty. I knew this was a fantasy. I knew these were movies. I wasn't delusional. But the thing was, I didn't want to be *acting* in a movie with Warren, I wanted to *be* with Warren. In real life.

The party after the movie was boring. Adults standing around talking with Bob in sycophantic tones about the movie, the directing, the acting, the music. I went into the small kitchen in his suite of offices, looking for something to drink, or maybe to take a break from feeling like, at fifteen, the youngest person in a room full of adults. I found the glasses in a cabinet, filled my glass with tap water, and took a sip while staring out the window at the lights of Westwood.

I thought I was alone, but I heard a male voice behind me say, "Where did you find the glass?"

I turned and there was Warren Beatty.

He seemed larger than life, taller than I'd imagined, and was the most gorgeous man I had ever seen. My vision felt blurry. I blushed and worried he'd feel the heat coming from my body.

"In the cabinet here." I set my glass down by the sink, got another glass from the cabinet, and handed it to him. I felt one of his fingers briefly on mine as he took the glass from my hand.

"Thank you," he said with that low, silky voice.

He was looking at me. I nodded and smiled, turned back to the cabinet and quietly closed it, picked up my glass, and with my back to him, I took another sip and again looked out the window, willing my heart to slow down.

He left me alone in the small kitchen.

Which was what I'd wanted.

Meeting him now wasn't in the plan. I was still too young to start our grand love affair, so I avoided any interaction that wasn't going to lead to something more or would color how he would see me once I got older. I didn't want him to see me as a child. Or remember me as a child. I wanted to be a woman and his equal. Darn. So close and yet several years too soon.

I was shaking. I could still feel the touch of his finger, feel the heat of him from where he'd been standing in the kitchen looking at me.

I went back to the party, but Warren had gone, and by then, it was time for my parents to go. I went with them to the valet parking, got in the back seat of the station wagon, and we drove home. Dad drove; Mom talked about the movie and the party. I thought about Warren, replaying every second of our almost non-encounter, knowing I would never forget it and that he most likely had already forgotten.

The parties in Tarzana dwindled.

Mom seemed to be without purpose or distraction. Her dissatisfaction with her life had no outlet, and the house was filled with unspoken tension. Knowing that some mothers occasionally long for the youth they see blossoming in their daughters, I wondered if she was jealous of me. Or maybe her depression was more profound; it was an old habit of mine to try and figure out why she was so distant, always assuming it had something to do with me. It may have had nothing to do with me. Maybe I was just there. A silent witness.

Dad, cheery and oblivious, continued to clean the pool as usual and swim naked when there *was* company. And one day, the "company" enjoying the warm fall weather and perhaps my dad's nudity, were a couple of Catholic nuns—in street clothes—who had left the order to be part of the "revolution," which—when it didn't involve demonstrations and sit-ins—often involved sitting in our backyard waiting for Dad to do another naked swan dive. Their recently discarded habits ended up with my mom who then gave them to me.

You know, for fun.

Finally sixteen and able to drive, I was starting to drink more on the weekends, and since my friend Tina and I were too nervous to try out our fake IDs at the liquor store, we dressed in the nuns' habits to buy alcohol. We did this every weekend, dressing in the habits at my house and then taking my green VW down Ventura Boulevard to the Time To Buy liquor store. It seemed the store clerks didn't have an actual protocol for nuns buying alcohol. Did nuns have a legal drinking age? Were nuns supposed to carry ID, and if so, where would they keep it? Were there pockets somewhere in all that black fabric? Were the clerks even allowed to ask nuns for their ID? They often paused, and I imagined these thoughts cascading through their brains. Or maybe they were simply looking at us for what we were: young girls. As men do. But we'd hand them cash, which broke their reverie, and they'd hand us the bottle.

I didn't have a big religious background (i.e., none) and only a vague idea about wine, but having tasted leftover Manischewitz Concord Grape at one of our parties—not realizing nuns probably didn't drink Manischewitz—that's what we bought. It was sweet and gave us a buzz.

Sometimes we'd put on the nuns' habits and go to Topanga Plaza, approach young guys, and ask if they had any reds—a sleeping pill/downer—just to see their reactions. There may still be some old guy somewhere telling the story of when a nun at the mall asked him if he wanted to get laid. If we saw families, children, or impressionable youth, we bowed our heads and walked solemnly ahead, nun-like. I didn't believe in God, but if others did, I didn't want to spoil it for them.

Now that I could drive, I spent less time hiding out in my bedroom or the den, and when I wasn't with Tina, I hung out with my friend Conny at her house. She was lively and smart, and her parents were doctors. Her family fascinated me. When I stayed over for dinner, I was surprised when they had actual conversations while together at the table. There was talk of someone's day, which might lead to something someone read. Or something philosophical, medical, cultural, or school-related. It seemed so free-form and unstructured—almost dangerous without the boundaries of a controlled parlor game.

I was still studying acting, although not in high school. Maybe I didn't want to be under the seeming scrutiny of my peers or risk exposing myself as either superior or without talent. My tendency to have a secret life kept me from fully engaging in high school, just as the lack of conversation at our dinner table may have reinforced my interpretation that no one was interested in anything I had to say.

Conny wasn't interested in acting and would eventually become a doctor. But in high school, we were innocents and both up for an adventure. She showed me a small blurb she'd found in her sister's *Back Stage* magazine: A movie in Hollywood was looking for extras. Hollywood was just over the hills from where we lived, and even if this wasn't how I imagined my career starting, I figured, why not? My delusionally grand plan was to simply start at the top, but in the meantime, being an extra could be fun, and you never knew. Conny made the arrangements.

On the day of the movie shoot, I grabbed the Thomas Guide from my car, looked up Camrose in the index, found the page with a map of tiny streets and tiny street names, and directed us while she drove over Cahuenga to Highland to Camrose near the Hollywood Bowl. I spotted Broadview Terrace, but it was blocked by vans and trailers.

Conny slowed and I rolled down my window to ask a guy—who had a walkie-talkie and was standing guard at the corner—where we should park. That we were extras. We were directed to a lot near the Hollywood Bowl, and after parking, we walked the few blocks back to Broadview Terrace. It was a small dead-end street with a tall tower at the end and an elevator leading to the terraces of four connected apartments. The sun was setting, and the air felt lush with fuchsia bougainvillea. People were busy with production tables and scripts; lighting equipment was carried to the elevators, and actors and extras were going in and out of trailers. We found someone to ask about the extra work and they pointed to a holding area. We waited, watching the sun slowly set behind the hills, and wondered if we should say something. Or find someone. Had we been forgotten? Or no longer needed? A woman came by and looked us up and down, paying close attention to our jeans and our sandals. She wrote something on a clipboard and left. A few minutes later, someone fetched us and took us to a young, stern guy who explained what we'd be doing. We were revelers at an all-night party on the terrace adjacent to where the main character, played by Elliot Gould, lived.

I resisted the temptation to look around at the mention of his name—I didn't want to seem overly eager, like some neophyte. I was going for more of the seasoned professional. Come on: I'd sat on a small merry-go-round with Vic Morrow!

But Conny, after hearing *Elliot Gould*, looked at me and raised her eyebrows.

The guy continued. We'd do the topless shots first and—

"I'm sorry, what?" I said, maybe too quickly for him to understand.

"What?" he said, surprised he'd been interrupted.

"We weren't told it was topless."

"That's not my problem. I just place the talent."

He continued talking about the particulars of the schedule—it would be an all-night shoot, snacks would be provided during a break, etc.—and we'd be taken up in a few minutes. I looked at Conny but couldn't read her expression.

"I don't think I want to do this," I said to the humorless guy.

"Again, not my problem," he said and walked away.

I thought about how far away the car was. Would they stop us at the end of the street if we simply left? Could they force us to do this? Conny didn't seem as frightened as I was, and when I said I wanted to leave, she said she wanted to stay, at which point the guy returned, followed by—Bob Altman.

"Here's the director," the guy said.

"Bob! It's Nikki." I said my name, knowing how he might be distracted or may not immediately recognize me out of context; I didn't want it to be awkward for him if he needed a moment to process.

"So it is," he said.

I was relieved to see him. My shoulders relaxed. I didn't know he was directing the movie when we'd signed up, and I was excited I could show Conny that I knew important people. That this was Bob, my family friend. It was a good sign. We'd play our very small parts in his movie, and we could keep our tops on.

"How are your parents?" He seemed rushed.

"Fine," I said.

"Listen, this shot is set up and Elliot's in place. We gotta go."

"Okay. But I don't want to take my top off."

"That's the scene." He turned to the others near us and bellowed, "Come on, let's go." Back to me: "It's a wide shot. You're background. No one will even see you."

He walked away. I felt lost. Didn't Bob remember that I was his magician's assistant when I was younger? That I'd refilled his drinks before I was even a teenager?

I didn't know what to do, but Conny shrugged like, *oh well*, and we followed the stern guy to the elevators and up to the apartment.

I was numb when we arrived on set. Rutanya Alda, playing the neighbor, took me under her wing and spoke gently to me. A new guy came over and explained that the scene was later at night when Elliot's character is coming home from getting cat food.

"Places." The new guy looked at us like *Take off your tops*.

The other women easily complied; it seemed easy for them. Maybe because they were older than we were or thought this would help their careers.

We took off our tops as if we were the unwitting participants in another of Bob's magic tricks, conforming to the rules of his game.

There were other extras I hadn't met, and except for the brief kindness from Rutanya Alda, I was among bare-breasted strangers. Conny and I danced around and pretended to laugh like we were at a party and having fun. I guess this was where my ten years of acting classes came in handy. Seeing Conny topless made it seem more natural that I was topless, and so we spent the night on the terrace, take after take, as the night got longer and the air got colder. I fabricated a character who was having fun, who didn't feel exposed, who simply loved the feel of the crisp air on her body and her friends laughing nearby and the lights of Hollywood in the distance.

The movie was *The Long Goodbye*.

I never told my parents what had happened, not wanting to burden them with my vulnerabilities or implicate their director friend for not looking out for me. Johnny Williams ended up scoring the movie, which meant my dad ended up doing the recording session. I doubt my dad even noticed who was in the movie, as the musicians played to a click track and didn't always pay much attention to what was on the screen.

As Bob had said, it was a wide shot, and we were just bodies in the background.

3

Malcolm X's Cousin

My mom found the possibility of happiness in the form of potential new friendships, and our home became a procession of strangers who became family until they were replaced with another procession of strangers. Who became family. As people came and went in our household, my brothers and I grew adept at rolling with the ever-changing allegiances.

Jamal—Hakim Abdullah Jamal—was one of the new friends who passed through the metaphoric revolving doors in Tarzana, Jamal, the man I thumb-wrestled with when I was a teenager, whose kids played in the pool with my brothers. Jamal, who was my dad's best friend. For a while. And then he left us seemingly out of nowhere, as did so many people we grew close to, who then disappeared.

Jamal, who was Malcolm X's cousin, came into our lives when my mom met his wife, Dorothy, at a Black Panther-related activist meeting in South Central. Mom was involved in the Valley chapter of the Panthers, as well as Operation Bootstrap, a job-training program created after the 1965 Watts Riots. My brothers and I had been dragged to Watts for Thursday night "rap sessions," where all the adults were talking about important things, and my brothers just wanted to go home and play with their Legos or Hot Wheels. I was probably fantasizing about my newfound obsession with Warren Beatty.

Mom invited Dorothy and her family to our house to swim. Before their arrival, Dad had made his famous beef jerky on the barbecue in the cabaña. Music pounded out of the big speakers in the backyard. The doorbell rang and in came Dorothy with her six kids. New friends! Dorothy's skin was a deep brown and luminous and her short hair was in a frazzled black afro. Mom's skin was pale and slightly freckled and her short hair was blonde. They looked beautiful together. Mom asked about Jamal, and Dorothy said something about his being in the car.

"Should we wait?" my mom asked. My mother's question had a tone of criticism. Like "What's his problem?"

"Let him be," Dorothy said. "He may not come in at all."

Jamal, having told Dorothy he didn't want anything to do with these "white honkies," stayed in the car the whole day. When everyone left, and we stood at the door to wave goodbye, I caught sight of the man in the front seat of their car, who was wearing a black textured hat like it was winter. The hat had no brim and reminded me of a black sheepskin version of my dad's army cap from Korea. Jamal didn't look our way; he stared straight ahead while his family piled into the car.

Dorothy and the kids came over almost every weekend, and even though Mom and Dorothy were now best friends, Jamal stayed in the car until my dad finally went out to talk to him. Dad could charm pretty much anyone with his perky "Yo, Chief" greeting. "Yo, Chief" worked in almost any situation and also covered the fact that Dad didn't remember names. After a couple of weekends of Dad's guileless visits to Jamal's car, sometimes with beef jerky, sometimes with just his disarming smile, something switched in Jamal, and not only did he follow this chipper white man into the house, but he became a part of our family.

I knew nothing about Jamal (né Allen Donaldson—or as my brother Bill says, "His real name before he got all Muslim-y"), except that he was Dorothy's husband, he was nice to me, and we found our common ground in thumb-wrestling. That and he let me tease him about his hat, which he never took off, even in the summertime when we were all out by the pool in the hot sun.

I loved him in my way. I loved the way he moved, the way his hand felt—warm and dry—and how he took his time before speaking. It relaxed me. There was room to breathe when I was with him. I was too old to play with their kids, so I spent time with Jamal. He was consistently upbeat and had time for everyone. I felt seen by him.

After having spent almost every weekend with the Jamals, our families went on a group vacation. We traveled to the Grand Canyon, the Nashes in our station wagon that never lost the smell of Mom's cigarettes, and the Jamals in their rented RV. In the photo of the thirteen of us, my dad is wearing his dashiki—a loose-fitting African print shirt. Our whole family had dashikis, although we didn't wear them at the same time, as that would have been too much like families who wore matching outfits at Christmas, which my mom mocked for being too sentimental. Some days my brothers would wear their dashikis. Sometimes I would wear mine, which was burgundy and navy blue.

On our trip, we stopped at a Sambo's restaurant (it was a real thing back then) and got wide-eyed stares from the other diners and waitresses as we were seated around the table. It seemed natural to us, but probably not so common in Arizona in the '60s, or anywhere in the '60s, for that matter. After a quick look at the Grand Canyon, a flat tire on the RV, and a few other stops, we went home.

One day, Jamal came to the house with actress Jean Seberg. I asked Mom who she was, and she explained to me that she was discovered in a country-wide talent search to play Joan of Arc and later became part of the French New Wave in a film called *Breathless*. Great, but that didn't explain why she was with Jamal. I didn't know at the time that Jamal was having an affair with Jean Seberg. Nor did my mom, it turned out. It wouldn't be till years later that we'd see the full extent of Jamal's deceptions and fabrications.

To me, he was just Jamal, another asterisk in our life, but years later I would learn the bigger picture of his small infamy when I saw

The Bank Job. In the 2008 movie, Jason Statham and Saffron Burrows assemble their team in '70s London for a heist. Another storyline was revealed that depicted a couple of Black guys from Trinidad and a white woman, Gale Ann Benson, who was the lover of one of the guys, Hakim—who claimed to be Malcolm X's cousin. Something way back in my past came bubbling up as I sat alone in the theater. I knew these names. I realized the man Gale Ann Benson was sleeping with, the man she called Hakim, was our Jamal.

A year after Jamal's first reluctant steps into our Valley house, after the pool parties and our Grand Canyon vacation, the Jamals disappeared from our lives without explanation.

Asking my parents something as benign as "Why don't the Jamals come over anymore?" wasn't an option. My mom took almost any personal question as criticism, and my dad wasn't much help in the illumination department as he summed things up in life with one of his two aphorisms: "If someone hurts you, you write them off and move on," or "If someone dies, you shed a tear and move on."

There was a lot of "moving on," and I would eventually learn that my mom's leaving—the room, the situation, the conversation, a friend—was perhaps not hope for a better, happier tomorrow with new people but her way of avoiding conflict with the current friend, as any conflict-facing conversation was out of the question. I adopted the philosophy that if there's a problem in a relationship, the relationship must be over. I would do a lot of my own leaving over the years to avoid being written off and moved on from, as well as to avoid conflict.

In place of any real answers, my brothers and I accepted the moveable feast of people coming into our lives. There was always a new parade of new best friends, and the Jamals faded away.

But there was more to the story.

Many years later—after our mom had died—my brother Ted found a dusty box of Jamal's stuff in the garage, cassettes my mom had recorded, articles about him, news clippings of his death, and the start of a story she was writing about him. Ted, wanting to make sense of these stories from our childhood—maybe to understand why the Jamals left us—reached out to Jamal's wife, Dorothy, to ask what had happened all those years before. Why had they disappeared from our lives? By now, Dorothy had moved to Atlanta, and her kids were grown. Maybe enough time had passed, and she decided to tell Ted what had happened.

Back then, Dorothy recounted, she had hired a private eye to follow her husband, as she suspected he was having an affair. It was around this time Jean Seberg had become involved with him, and we would learn later he was also seeing Gale Ann Benson, who I remembered from the bank heist movie. Dorothy gave the private eye $500, and he followed Jamal to a motel in the Valley, where he met another woman.

The other woman was my mother.

Looking back, I think my mom was starved for love and Jamal triggered something in her she had never felt with my dad. She was able to live a brief parallel life where she felt alive, mentally stimulated. Seen. Dorothy left Jamal and that was the end of that. No more vacations or pool parties. No more thumb-wrestling. No more hat-teasing.

There was one more deception. Jamal often referred to himself as Malcolm X's cousin. It was the calling card he'd always used, buying him entry into a more radical world, a selling point in the books he wrote and the appearances he made after he moved alone to the East Coast. But it turns out it was *Dorothy* who was Malcolm X's cousin. Not Jamal.

I loved him regardless of his appropriated Malcolm X stardust. Back then, I knew nothing of him outside the world of our house; I only knew him as he was with me. Maybe he sensed that my acceptance and love didn't require charm or dazzle. But I understand now that what he wanted the world to see was a fabrication, picking and choosing the things that would give him credence in the world. Finding lovers to validate him, who could contribute money to his causes.

I suppose we all fabricate occasionally for leverage and acceptance. But for me, Jamal didn't *need* to be Malcolm X's cousin. He didn't do anything to "make" me love him, I just loved him.

I never got to say goodbye to Jamal.

He was dead four years later, shot in Boston by the De Mau Maus, a rival political faction.

4

The Old World Restaurant

After graduating from high school, I was still too young to meet Warren Beatty, so I figured I'd go to college in the meantime, which my father kindly paid for. Not exactly the strongest reason for continuing one's education, but then again, I came from a family of autodidacts, so this college thing must have seemed to my parents like a freakish aberration. I'd chosen Boston University, which was as far away as I could go, and yet it still held for me the glimmer of sweetness from our summer vacations in Scituate.

When the time came, my mom broke a champagne bottle on the hood of the green 1960 VW Gramma Ruth had given me when I received my license the year before. The car was loaded up with a cheap steamer trunk of clothes and the quilt I'd sewn by hand, a shoe box of cassettes and a cassette player, and some egg-salad sandwiches. The car also held a small suitcase belonging to my best friend Tina. A few months earlier, we'd graduated from high school, and now we were about to embark on our drive across the country.

It was midnight. I started the car.

Two seventeen-year-old girls, driving alone into the darkness.

I was concerned about us traveling across the country, not for any practical reason—I knew how to drive, and we had maps from AAA—but I felt an uneasiness driving across the country while still a virgin. Like maybe that was illegal? Would I be allowed to cross borders freely? Did the authorities check? *Were* there authorities? I thought maybe we should have brought the nuns' habits to be safe. Tina had a boyfriend, and they'd had sex, so maybe that was like having an adult in the car when you only have a learner's permit. I was frightened and it was dark out; I didn't feel ready to drive three thousand miles to the unknown world of Boston.

Dad was waving and smiling. Mom was waving and fake-smiling. All the waving didn't leave us much room to change our minds, and I had no choice but to drive out of the driveway and hope for the best as we traveled into the night. But we had sandwiches. Which we ate before we even got to the first freeway onramp.

Tina and I listened to Jethro Tull while speeding across the Midwest. With *Aqualung* on the cassette player, we decided we should swap seats. We didn't want to take the time to pull over, so we traded places going sixty miles an hour. Carefully, but still—the immortality of youth. We slept in crappy motels when we got too tired to continue.

By the time we got to the East Coast, I felt like I'd been holding my breath for days because I wasn't used to being with another human for so long. I was used to having a bedroom to go to where I could exhale and be alone, or a movie theater where I could sit alone in the dark for two hours. I couldn't explain this to Tina; instead, I was grumpy and uncommunicative, much as my mother had been with me when I was younger. Tina was frustrated and probably confused. After driving all night in the rain, I dropped her off at Boston's Logan Airport, and we said our chilly goodbyes.

I wish I had inherited more of the "Yo, Chief" friendliness from my dad, and the ability to express even faux enthusiasm, but I seemed to have gotten the self-laminated defensiveness of my mother, and my discomfort amid conflict led me to shut the other person out. Tina was the unfortunate recipient. Years later, I wrote her an apology letter, but I either didn't have the right address, or she'd "written me off and moved on."

I'd never seen the campus at Boston University, nor did I see the campus when I arrived, as I discovered there was no campus to see. Instead, it was just a lot of buildings along Commonwealth Avenue. I'd seen a brochure with the requisite happy groupings sitting on a lovely expanse of springtime grass. I don't think I'd ever sat on the grass with a happy grouping anywhere, but it was inviting in the abstract. And ultimately non-existent. Maybe a patch of grass existed somewhere between a couple of tall buildings, but I never found it. Nor did I find pockets of happy people laughing, welcoming me to the fold. My dorm was in the West Campus—again, a misnomer, as there was no actual campus. After parking the rickety VW on Babcock, I walked to the dorms with as much stuff as I could carry. The girls around me in the halls of the dorm all seemed giddy and girly and had parents helping them get settled. I found my room, put the quilt on the twin bed, sat down, and that was about it.

The walk from the dorms to classes was all city streets, cars, and a pedestrian overpass that felt like a lonely tundra when the wind hit me. My winter clothes no longer fit as I'd put on weight, soothing myself most nights with midnight french fries. I lived in one of the three high-rise dorms at West Campus, which housed mostly hockey and football players.

I would have felt out of my element had I had an element. I endured Boston University for two semesters, although I have no memory of the classes I took. Maybe I studied some Shakespeare? Maybe American history? Although it wasn't a total loss. I was no longer a virgin, thanks to one of the football players living in the dorm next to mine. And then I made up for lost time with one of the Canadian hockey players who lived in the other dorm at West Campus, at least I think I did, as I woke up in his bed after a night of drinking.

My much smarter high school friend Conny was going to Yale. She invited me to New Haven to visit, and I stayed in her dorm room with her and her boyfriend, Chip. I needed a break from the loneliness of B.U. I spent many weekends at Yale, impressed that they had chocolate milk in fancy chrome dispensers in the dark wood-paneled cafeteria, which looked like a gigantic den for rich men with hunting dogs. Everyone looked smarter than I was. They probably were.

I met a lot of Chip's and Conny's friends, one being a tall, blond guy named Rob who talked about a paper he was writing on the Ouroboros. Chip added his thoughts, and I nodded ambiguously, like I knew what they were talking about. I had to ask Conny later what the hell an Ouroboros was. I slept with Rob in his cold and drafty dorm room. I'd developed an unrelenting cough, and not wanting to wake Rob—my childhood training in needlessness kicking in—I sat in his bathroom, on the cold floor until morning, wrapped in a towel, and using another towel to muffle my coughing.

This was all getting me nowhere. After nearly one year of college, I'd learned two things: what the penalty was in hockey for crossing the blue line and roughly what an Ouroboros was.

Time to head home. Coming from a long line of musicians who never went beyond high school, I wasn't too worried about what my parents would say if I didn't want to go back to college. They may have seen it as more of an anomalous lark—albeit an expensive one.

I checked the bulletin board in the dorm for a driving companion, found a guy who lived in Beverly Hills—which was a few miles from my home in Tarzana—and off we went. He was an oddball, confirmed not by the bad joke he made but by the fact that he kept repeating the same joke.

He sneezed, I said, "Gesundheit."

He says, "What's the definition of a virgin?"

"What," I said, doing my part.

"Goes in tight. Get it? Like *gesundheit*." I got it. We weren't even out of Massachusetts. He did the routine again when he'd sneezed in Ohio and I'd forgotten the dumb joke and had said, "Gesundheit."

By Chicago, I'd decided we no longer needed to split the driving and told him he could sleep if he wanted. I took some amphetamines (and then some more amphetamines), drove forty hours straight to California, and dropped him off in Beverly Hills. My VW was running on three cylinders at this point and could go only twenty miles an hour on the 405 freeway into the Valley, where I puttered along slowly on Ventura Boulevard—people behind me honking—before barely making it to Tarzana. I pulled into the driveway. The engine fell out.

And that was college.

Even if I hadn't had the full rah-rah experience, I'd made an important connection. It wasn't Rob. I never saw Rob again. But I met Rich Hall at Yale. He was the son of Monty Hall, who was the big cheese on the popular game show *Let's Make A Deal*. Rich had finished school and was back in California to begin a writing career. I was back in California to begin—well, I had no idea. Acting? My obsession with Warren didn't include his taking care of me in any way or helping me with any future career. Not to mention, I hadn't yet met him.

Rich introduced me to his actor friend, Victor, and the three of us hung around together while I tried to figure out my next move in life. One night, drinking with them at Monty Hall's Malibu beach house, Victor mentioned he'd recently quit working at the Old World Restaurant in Beverly Hills after getting a part in a small film. We talked about the movie he was doing, and the restaurant, and he mentioned that Hollywood types had often come into the restaurant.

"Like Warren Beatty," he said.

Excuse me—what? Which I didn't say out loud.

He said Mr. Beatty lived in the Beverly Wilshire Hotel—which was a block and a half away from the Old World Restaurant—and had been a frequent patron, usually sitting alone at a corner table near the fireplace.

I tried to keep cool, and although I didn't ask anything about Warren Beatty, I asked about the restaurant and said it might be a good place for me to work while I was studying acting and trying to get an agent. He said it had been a good interim job for him as well, and if I was interested, he'd get in touch with Dr. Franks, the owner, and put in a good word.

Having zero table-waiting experience, I was hired to be a hostess. The primary skills required included smiling, carrying menus, and walking people to their tables. I mastered these quickly. But it was more than just being a hostess, as I was in charge of the cash register and locking up at night if I was on the late shift. Mitch, the manager who set my schedule, was tall, gawky, and blond and treated me like he had a crush on me, but a 4th-grade kind of crush, which involved hitting me on the arm and calling me "Nash." So seductive.

The Old World on Beverly Drive was famous for its Belgian waffles, grilled cheese and bacon sandwiches, and coffee coolers—a coffee ice-cream shake. And sure enough, the restaurant was located just over a block away from the Beverly Wilshire Hotel, an elegant old building with beautiful striped awnings that were changed out every season. On my first day of work, I drove by the hotel and wondered what room Warren Beatty might be in. So close and yet—

I met the waiters, who were mostly actors. The cooks were from Thailand and yelled at the waiters, and I learned enough Thai to ask, "What do you want, darling?" (*Koon tow gon ah rye tee luck*. I have had no occasion to use this.) There were tables in the front near the big windows that looked out on Beverly Drive, a faux fireplace separated the front room from the middle room that was larger but dingy, and beyond that, the kitchen and set-up area, the refrigerated walk-in, and the bathrooms were in the back. Upstairs were the offices, lockers, and supplies. I learned terms like deuce and four-top.

It was at the Old World where I held Angelina Jolie in my arms. Granted, she was a baby at the time. Her father, Jon Voight, and his very pregnant wife, Marcheline, came into the Old World often during the pregnancy, and the three of us had struck up a friendship. They always stopped to talk to me and showed me how big Marcheline's belly was getting. I didn't see them for a couple of months, and when they came in again, Marcheline was holding the new baby and showed her to me.

"We've named her Angelina. Would you like to hold her?"

"Sure." I was cautious. I hadn't held many babies. Had the *National Enquirer* contacted me once Angelina became famous, I could have told them: "She seemed very nice."

My days and nights were energized by the anticipation that any day Warren Beatty might walk in. I was careful with my clothes and makeup. My hair was long and dark, and my eyes were blue, so I didn't use a lot of makeup—basic foundation, mascara, and lipstick—but I put in the effort. I was a little giddy all the time, but it was hard to sustain this daily adrenaline rush of anticipation, even though it was always in the back of my mind: this could be the day.

In the meantime, I struck up a flirtation with one of the waiters, Peter, a wannabe actor who had been in a John Wayne movie as a child, but I guess he hadn't been able to roll that into anything further. Peter was older than I was. He was smart, funny, and had great deep-set eyes and a sly smile. He was also married. But he convinced me the marriage was essentially over and so we sat in his yellow VW and made out after my shift and before his. During one of these make-out sessions, we made plans to have an affair, and for some reason he'd picked out a Holiday Inn on Ventura Boulevard, maybe twenty miles away. We flirted at work, and—in the privacy of his car—we fantasized about the Holiday Inn, waiting for the time when our schedules would sync up for more than an hour. I even went to the drugstore and bought special perfume, which I'd use only for our affair. I don't know if I was channeling some "other woman" from a 1945 tear-jerker, but I bought Ambush. It came in a bottle weirdly encased in a pink rubbery material, making it what, unbreakable? I thought of a commercial: A seedy motel, a couple on the bed, the man's wife shows up, a fight ensues, faces are slapped, lamps are upturned, and the bottle of Ambush is knocked to the floor.

Close-up of the undamaged pink bottle and a voice-over: "Ambush. The perfume that endures even after the affair has ended."

We never made it to the Holiday Inn, and I never got to try out my special perfume because Peter quit one day without telling me. Maybe he had worked things out with his wife.

(Many years later, my dad took me to a recording session for *China Beach*—a show my dad knew I liked. I'd forgotten that Peter was the producer, although I'd wistfully seen his name in the credits. He showed up for the recording session and I was smitten all over again. He was just leaving his fourth marriage, so of course I moved in with him. And then moved out. I was heartbroken, and when I told my mom it was over with Peter, she said, "What the hell am I supposed to do with his Christmas present?" It was a miniature director's chair with Peter's name on it. When I told my brother Bill this story, he said, "It's clear what you should have done. You should have found another Peter to date before Christmas.")

When Peter left the Old World before our affair could even begin, I was disheartened. I was depressed. I was still living at home, I had a dumb job, and although I'd gone on a casting call, the guy told me I needed to lose weight, and it was hard to continue fueling myself with the fabricated excitement that Warren Beatty may one day show up at the restaurant.

Sean, one of the waiters who hadn't been there long (and wouldn't last long), noticed I was depressed and asked, "Can I tell you about Scientology?" I didn't know at the time what this was, and when I asked him, he said it was a way of making your life more goal-directed or better or something.

"What do you mean? How does it work?" I asked.

He said, "Here's an example." He pointed toward the back of the restaurant.

"Walk to the wall."

"No," I said. Sean was sort of an ass, so I wasn't about to go along with this.

"Walk to the wall."

"No."

"Walk to the wall."

"No."

That didn't go anywhere. I would learn later about Scientology and its weird recruiting techniques, so maybe this was the first step in seeing if someone was willing enough. Malleable enough. When I wouldn't walk to the wall, I looked at him and asked, "Now what?'

"Never mind," he said.

"Great. This will be a big help with my career."

Maybe he felt embarrassed at not having recruited me, but he changed direction, asking, "Did you see who's in the restaurant?"

My heart flipped. Was today the day? I forgot about my non-existent career and wondered if I needed lipstick.

"No. Who?" Casual.

He pointed at a large, bald man who'd been in a few times. He was older, looked a bit shabby, and always came in with his pretty daughters, who were about my age.

"Who is he?"

"That's Marty Ransohoff."

It didn't register.

Sean said, "He's a big movie producer. You should get to know him. Be nice to him."

Wasn't I nice to everyone? I wanted to ask. But the wheels were turning, and I realized these were not his daughters. They looked more like models, although they were probably wannabe actresses. The lunch crowd was finishing up, and three people were waiting to hand me their checks and a credit card.

While I was helping the first person, I saw Marty and his girls come to the front of the line as he continued to say possibly witty things to them, and while the girls continued to giggle, he thrust his check in my direction. I stayed focused on the current customer, which got Marty's attention, and he looked my way, like, "Come on. Take this." He was big and sloppy, but the girls behind him were pretty and—I now noticed—had a lot of cleavage going on.

"Excuse me, sir," I said. "I'm helping the people who were here before you and when I'm finished with them, I'll be happy to help you."

I went back to the current customer. I knew exactly what I was doing. It was similar to something I'd read in a book called *Nina's Book,* set in a concentration camp, where the women walked in circles in the cold—as if on parade—in front of the head guard's office, hoping to be picked for what was to be food, but also sex, which at least got them fed and out of the cold for a few hours. The women pinched their cheeks and lips to replicate some kind of vitality and wore padding on their chests to appear shapelier, nubile. Nina did none of these things. She did not thrust out her chest or call attention to herself. She made herself smaller, fragile, knowing this would catch the guard's eye and she would end up warm for the night. Similarly, although working at the Old World Restaurant was hardly as grueling as surviving a WWII prison, I made myself stand out in my difference from the other women Marty Ransohoff was used to. I didn't flirt, and I didn't cater to him. I barely looked at him.

Not to mention, I had very little cleavage to speak of.

"All right," he said, sort of smiling at me. He looked at his girls and raised his palms like this had never happened to him. But he waited.

Eventually, I finished with the other patrons, and when they left, he stepped up. He handed me his check and cash. I smiled nicely, pressed buttons on the register, and turned back with his change.

"Thank you," he said. "And your name is?"

"Nikki."

"And what is it you do?"

"I am the hostess here."

"I mean, what is it you want to do? Beyond this?"

"I've been studying acting," I said, with about the same inflection as if I'd said, "I fold laundry."

"Great. Who are you studying with?"

"Sherman Marx."

"Never heard of him. Why don't you give me your number and I'll see what I can do."

"Are you a teacher?" I was without shame.

He smiled like he was about to give me the greatest gift of my life. "I'm a movie producer."

He told me his name, I gave him my number, thanked him, and off he went with his pretty not-daughters in tow. Sean had seen this encounter unfold and gave me a thumbs up like I'd bagged a big fish.

That night, at home in my bedroom upstairs, my phone rang. My pink princess phone.

"Hello?"

"Hi, it's Marty Ransohoff. May I speak to Nikki?"

"This is she." My mother had drilled good grammar into us at an early age. I used to joke with my brother that if I wrote a suicide note, it would come back with red-penciled corrections.

"Glad to reach you. I wanted to talk more about your acting goals."

"Great. I appreciate it."

"So you're studying?"

"Yes, I have been for about ten years."

"You have a good look about you. I was intrigued."

I didn't know what to say.

He continued. "How important is acting to you?"

"It's very important. It's what I've been studying for since I was little."

"It sounds important to you. That's good. That's the first step. You have to have that drive."

I sat down on the window seat by the window.

"I do," I said.

"I'd like to help you."

"That would be great."

"But first I need to know I wouldn't be wasting my time."

Did he want me to do a monologue from *The Fantasticks* over the phone?

"Okay," I said.

"What I mean is, I'd have to know how willing you were to make this happen. That you'd do just about anything for this chance. My time is valuable."

"I'm sure it is."

"And this sounds very important to you. I have to know how far would you be willing to go to make this dream happen?"

"Well, Mr. Ransohoff," I said, "if it came down to fucking you, I wouldn't go that far."

He stammered a bit, but really, what could he say? I guess we were done chatting.

A FEW WEEKS LATER, A new waiter started. His name was Kurt Wurdeman. He was quiet and efficient, but something more was going on behind his brown eyes. Or maybe less. The other waiters avoided him—maybe he hadn't been working long enough for them to warm up to him—but I was always friendly with him. He seemed a bit of an underdog. He was about my height with short hair and stubby fingers. He never got into any trouble with the owner, Dr. Franks, and Mitch figured he was doing a good enough job, even if he was odd.

After two weeks of awkward hellos, he came up behind me at the cash register, startling me, and spoke in a near whisper, very close to my ear.

"I know you're in the CIA. And you must know I am as well. And I know we were brought together to free Patty Hearst. We'll talk later." He slithered away. Huh? I always thought it would be cool to be a spy, and according to Kurt, I *was* a spy. I knew Patty Hearst had been kidnapped and/or joined a terrorist organization, but I didn't see how it was now my job, with Kurt, to free her.

Days passed before he found another opportunity to speak sideways to me. It was the end of his shift and he explained we'd soon be given our assignments to head up north for the undercover rescue. And to be ready. I was speechless. He left for the night. I was debating whether to talk to Mitch about him, but the next day Kurt didn't show up for work. I couldn't imagine he'd gone to free Patty Hearst without me. I could have let this go, but the following week two Beverly Hills policemen came into the Old World, asking for me.

"Do you know a Kurt Wurdeman?" the first cop asked.

"He was a waiter here for a few weeks."

"When did you first meet him?" the second one asked.

"When he started working here. A few weeks ago."

Mitch had noticed something was going on and came up to the front where I was talking to the two men in uniform.

"Nash," he said. "What did you do this time?" Yeah, that Mitch. So funny.

The first cop turned to him, "And you are?"

"Mitch Wyman. I'm the manager." As if managers never committed crimes. They got his information and excused him as they wanted to speak with me further. They turned back to me.

"And do you know Mr. Robert Evans?"

I knew from the tabloids he'd made the movie *Love Story* with Ryan O'Neal and Ali McGraw and had been married to Ali McGraw, who left him for Steve McQueen. But that was a mouthful, so instead, I simply said, "The producer?"

"Yes. Do you know him?"

"No."

"Mr. Evans has received threatening letters from Mr. Wurdeman. You are copied on all the correspondence. We need to determine your involvement with Mr. Wurdeman and his threats against Mr. Evans."

"No involvement. I think he was delusional."

"Mr. Evans?"

"No. Kurt Wurdeman."

"And why would you think that, Miss Nash?"

I explained about Patty Hearst, they wrote some things down, got my information, said they'd be in touch, and left. I turned around to see many faces looking my way. I smiled and waved meekly and went back to the cash register.

I started getting a lot of correspondence from Kurt. I don't know how he got my parents' address in Tarzana, but every day another stamped manila envelope with my name on it showed up in the mailbox, containing scores of single-spaced, typewritten pages. One letter explained why he'd been in Bellevue—a psychiatric hospital in New York—that it was "to do secret, undercover research."

A week later, I got a call from one of the policemen that I needed to meet with them at Robert Evans' office to clarify what I'd said about my connection to Kurt Wurdeman. I had already told them I had no special relationship with Kurt, but they felt the need for me to come to this meeting. I showed up on the scheduled day and was escorted by an efficient woman into Mr. Evans' office. He was sitting at his big desk, and standing nearby were the two policemen and another man. A lawyer? A detective? They asked me to repeat my story, which I did.

The other man wanted me to go into more detail, like what else was I involved in, where I lived, etc. Maybe they were expecting me to accidentally mention I was part of the Manson family, but I merely said I was studying acting, working at the Old World, and I lived at home with my parents. I added I had been getting weird correspondence from Kurt Wurdeman, but beyond that, I knew nothing more about him.

They seemed to believe me and went on to warn me about any further contact. Turns out Kurt Wurdeman, they said, had been sending threatening letters to not only Mr. Evans but to Richard Nixon, Henry Kissinger, the Secret Service, the Russian KGB, and Warren Beatty. *Warren Beatty? What?*

I recovered and said, "Okay," I said, assuring them I understood.

Warren Beatty? I'd have a good story to tell Mr. Beatty once I finally met him. Or maybe this would lead to my meeting him. Maybe I'd be called to another meeting, and he'd be there and we'd bond over our shared involvement with a sociopath.

The meeting was over, Mr. Evans stood, and we all walked to the front office where Mr. Evans shook hands with the men. He then turned to me.

I put my hand out as if to shake his, but he said, "One minute."

The others left, and he indicated we should go back into his office. I followed him in. He didn't sit, so I didn't sit. He said he was interested in knowing about my acting studies and would I mind if he set up an appointment to talk further.

I said, "Not at all, Mr. Evans."

"Call me Bob."

We went back out to the front office where he told his secretary to set something up for next week and left me standing there.

She went through the book, and we settled on a time. I said thank you, shook her hand and left.

A week later, I showed up a little early for our 5 p.m. appointment. I said hello to the secretary and reintroduced myself and was told Mr. Evans had gone for the day. Before I could register disappointment or ask if I'd gotten the date wrong, she added that he was at his home, which wasn't far away, and gave me a small card on which she'd already typed the address and directions. Like this was a usual thing.

It felt like shades of Marty Ransohoff. But I knew I could take care of myself and liked giving people the benefit of the doubt.

I found his palatial estate, pressed buttons at the gate, a woman's voice asked my name, and the gate opened. I drove my crappy VW in and parked in the big circular drive that could accommodate twenty cars. It was balmy and breezy. I felt glamorous as I approached what looked like a small castle. I knocked on the front door and an older woman answered. Before she could say anything, I heard a male voice from down the hall.

"Nikki, I'm back here."

The woman held the door open for me to come in. I thanked her and headed down a hallway until I found the room where "Bob" was.

"Hello," he said.

He was in bed. It didn't seem grand enough for a master bedroom; it was more like a guest room with sheer curtains and a ficus plant in the corner. Maybe this was the afternoon bedroom. He was wearing pajamas and was under the covers. For a moment I thought he might be ill and this was more of a sick room, but he looked healthy enough. Perky.

"Mr. Evans, are you feeling—"

"Bob." He had a swanky look on his face, like we both knew what was going to happen next.

"Bob. I think you misunderstood. I'm sorry if I gave you the wrong impression but I didn't come here to sleep with you."

"You didn't?" He sounded disappointed, crestfallen, needy. His shoulders slumped and he pushed himself up into a sitting position. This didn't seem to be part of his routine. He had broken character as seduction was no longer on the table. Or in the bed. He seemed sad.

"It's just that—." He patted the bed. "Sit down for a sec."

He looked so forlorn that I sat down on the bed. I looked at his crisp, white pajamas with the thin blue stripes and thought about the beige, oversized T-shirt I wore to bed each night. But then I thought, why is he wearing pajamas in the afternoon? Was this part of the now-abandoned seduction plan? He reached for a silver-framed photo on the nightstand, looked at it wistfully, and then turned the photo so I could look at it as well.

"Isn't she beautiful?" It was Ali McGraw. I'd seen *Love Story* and had loved the movie, even if the schmaltzy Harvard love-and-death story didn't match my own non-preppy East Coast college experience, which was less knit caps and snow angels with a handsome lad and more black-out drinking and waking up in a strange room with some guy missing a few teeth.

"She's very beautiful," I confirmed.

"Why doesn't she love me anymore?"

"I don't know. You seem quite nice."

His eyes were welling up, he went back to looking at the photo, and I gently put a hand on his thigh to indicate comfort, not sexual interest, if he could even feel my hand through the luxurious duvet.

He looked at me and said, "I'm sorry you came all this way."

"That's okay. I hope you feel better."

I stood.

"I'll see myself out," I said, like a scorned woman putting on a brave face in a 1940s melodrama.

And I thought, I may not have met Warren Beatty or freed Patty Hearst, but I did get to see Robert Evans in his snazzy pajamas.

5

The Lawyer and the Hummingbirds

After working at the Old World for over a year with no sign of Warren Beatty, I was feeling pointless and hopeless. Then I was asked on an actual date by an actual person, and I thought: Okay, time to start living a real life. Time to move on from this place-holder of a childhood obsession and into the world of real people. Which made me sad. I would have to forget about Warren Beatty and start dating people I had actually met, although I knew nothing about dating. I almost had a date in high school, but when I told my mom that Jim Starr, the quarterback, had asked me out, she said, "He's probably a fascist." I wasn't entirely sure what a fascist was, but it didn't much matter as he ended up dating a cheerleader.

At nineteen and still living at home, I found that dating was more hanging out with the waiters after work, dancing at discos, doing poppers in a bathroom, all of which was nothing like I'd seen depicted in the movies: a couple goes to a fancy, sedate restaurant where a sophisticated and mysterious man helps the woman into her chair, and after some seductive looks at one another over the menu, the waiter approaches, and the man says, "The lady will have—."

But now I had an actual date with a young lawyer who worked with Charles Garry—my mom's latest new best friend. Charles Garry had been the lawyer for the Black Panther Party. He had defended Huey Newton and Bobby Seale in the '60s and, ten years later, would go on to represent the Peoples Temple, led by Jim Jones of "Drink the Kool-Aid" fame. After several of the Black Panthers were jailed or killed—except Eldridge Cleaver, who went on to invent crotchless pants for men—Mr. Garry had a new set of clients and represented a man and a woman who were in prison for murder or political shenanigans or something—I was never clear on the crime—but I did know Charles's prison visits were a ruse to enable his clients to enjoy a conjugal visit, and he had invited my mom along.

And she'd asked me along. I'd asked her what a conjugal visit was, and she formally explained that married inmates were only permitted to have intercourse with one another if their lawyer was in the cell with them, which meant Charles would turn his back and busy himself with paperwork, or whatever, while his clients had sex. My mother's focus was more on justice, equality, and civil rights, than close-up affection, so her support for this outing was more about her friendship with Charles and his causes than a rally for love. Even loving her own children was indirect, separated by time and space.

My brother Bill and I often reminisced about how every morning growing up, we'd find waiting for us in the kitchen three glasses, three spoons, and the box containing Carnation Instant Breakfast packets. Maybe that's why us kids all ended up with drinking problems. Love in a glass.

Bill said, "She could breastfeed Ethiopia but God forbid she get up and make us breakfast."

"Are *we* in the cell with them when they have sex?" I asked, not at all wanting to be a part of this. I'd agreed to go as it seemed like a fun outing with my mom, and I didn't want to lose the momentum of us doing something together. I'd learned to take what I could get.

"No."

When Charles came to pick us up, I felt a flush on my cheeks as I imagined him in jail with a couple having sex right behind him. This particular trip to the courthouse was for both a hearing and then the conjugal visit, so accompanying Charles was an associate.

We'll call him Todd.

Todd seemed much older than I was, maybe because he had a real adult job and was wearing a suit. He was tall, thin, and had dark hair. After the trip to the courthouse, where I spent most of the time on a bench in a hallway sitting silently with Todd during breaks, he asked me out. He was handsome and smart, and any crumb of attention felt good. I told my mom and figured she'd be happy.

"A date, how fucking provincial," she said.

Jeez, there was no winning with her. Maybe having conjugal sex in a jail cell would have been less provincial. At least he wasn't a fascist, as far as I could tell.

I don't remember much of my date with Todd the lawyer. I don't remember his picking me up, I don't remember where we went, or what we did on our date. But I do remember coming back home with him.

It was after midnight and my parents were up. Usually, it was just my mom who was up at that hour; she was a night owl and did some of her best drinking and thinking when it was late at night, and no one would bug her. There were a lot of things to do late at night when she finally had the quiet house to herself. We weren't sure what these things were, but we'd usually find a small skillet in the sink the next morning with the remnants of a grilled cheese sandwich made with Velveeta cheese. And her empty brandy glass.

My brother Bill and I used to joke that Mom couldn't be an alcoholic because she wasn't a morning drinker—until we realized she didn't usually get up until two in the afternoon.

But this night *both* my parents were in the kitchen. Todd and I joined them, and even though I was tired, it felt festive with the lights on and Dad still up. Like they were hanging out waiting for us. But not in a "look at the clock, young lady" kind of way. More like, *let's keep this party going*.

Mom and Todd talked politics (snooze), and after a couple of their back-and-forths, Dad pointed out the hummingbird feeders outside the kitchen windows. It was too dark to see them, but Dad always got animated when he talked about the hummingbirds and their twilight feeding frenzy. He'd hung several bottles of the sugary red fluid on the eaves in the backyard, and he even made the juice himself, boiling water and sugar and adding the red food coloring. We all looked at the black glass and imagined a feeding frenzy while Dad explained the different personalities. "Buster" would swoop in and scare the others away, while "Tiny" fed on the feeder farthest away. It was a well-worn story my dad relied on when he didn't know what else to talk about.

"There are fifteen feeders," he elaborated.

Todd said, "That's a lot of feeders."

Mom said, "Yeah. St. Francis of Fucking Assisi."

I thought of interjecting with the story about my dad giving mouth-to-mouth to the lizard he'd found in the pool, but I didn't know Todd well enough to start sharing a lot of cute family history, and I didn't want him to think I assumed one date meant anything more, so I simply smiled.

And with that, the conversation dwindled to nothing. We rearranged ourselves from listening positions to wrapping-it-up positions and I felt a surge of adrenaline as I wondered how the goodbye at the door was going to go, but that once he left, I could soothe any anxiety with ice cream and granola alone in my room. I was nervous. I didn't know Todd in any real sense. Would he want to kiss me? In front of my parents? He seemed nice enough, but I didn't know if he would ask for a second date, and if he did so, would my mother blurt out her usual "A date? Jesus. Let me get her dance card." Maybe my mom was envious of the fun I was having being single.

But there'd be no asking for another date, and no time for me to wonder if I would like another date because my dad wrapped up the evening for us with one sentence:

"Well, you kids probably wanna go ball."

I wasn't sure I'd heard right until my mother chimed in.

"The den bed is made up. See you in the morning. Or whenever."

Maybe we'd find Carnation Instant Breakfast laid out for us in the kitchen.

Todd looked at me, confused, and I tried to look neutral, but I felt a combination of shame and embarrassment, as well as repulsion at the word "ball." Looking back, it might not have even been so bad if Dad had said, "screw," or his other go-to, "make it," but "ball" was just gross. I didn't want to go to the den with this guy Todd. It wasn't like Dad was sending me into the woods to get my clitoris removed with a rusty knife by some shaman I didn't know. But still.

Off we went. Todd and I. To the den.

First, the step down into the dining room with its high A-framed ceiling where years before I'd helped Bob Altman do magic tricks at dinner parties, and then another step down into the den with the red Rosenberg Committee phone that never rang, the den that flooded whenever it rained and so it always smelled a little musty. The den where I'd shared the bed every Christmas Eve with Gramma Ruth since I was eight. The first time I'd seen her get into her thin nightgown, I was shocked to see that her pubic hair was entirely gray. I didn't realize pubic hair turned gray.

(As a child, I'd seen my parents' dark pubic hair many times. One time when Mom had to urinate—a stickler for words, she always said "urinate"—Dad thought it would be funny to have a three-way bathroom session. I was five or six. I sat on Mom's lap and Dad peed through both our legs. This didn't seem particularly abnormal at the time, but then again, I had no objective frame of reference.)

I'd always loved the den at Christmas with its subterranean coziness and the bright Christmas lights winking and shimmering just outside the glass of the low windows. The lights I'd helped my dad drape around the house and on the bushes every year since I was little. He had a box of loose bulbs and each year, during this ritual, it was my job to follow him around from ladder spot to ladder spot, ready for him to call out for a replacement bulb.

"Green bulb."

"Yep," and I'd hand him up the bulb.

But now it was time "to ball." And I'm guessing, that's what Todd and

I did. I don't remember much beyond going into the den where he and I found the sleeper bed unfolded, already made up with sheets and a blanket, one corner turned down. Welcoming. Like a nice hotel room but with a lumpy mattress and an old decorative trombone hanging on the wall.

I've remembered the people I've slept with because there was usually enough lead time for me to conjure up a potential romantic future that heightened the whole experience and gave it meaning and became a memory even before the experience itself (even if I unexpectedly never saw the person again). But with Todd, I experienced absolutely no emotional self-fluffing beforehand and combined with the shock of being unwittingly used as a pawn to make my Dad look "with-it," or maybe still reeling from the shock of being verbally escorted to the den to have sex with a stranger, there was no memory bank in which to store this experience. And therefore, the rest of the night was a blank.

Why couldn't I have said, "No, thank you"? Why did I go along with it? Maybe I'd adopted the learned behavior of not making waves or simply rationalized that my parents were conforming to some new norm of hip parenting. Whatever it was, it felt shitty.

I don't remember the next morning.

I don't remember if anyone was up when we got up. I don't remember even getting up. I don't remember seeing Todd, so I guess he was gone early. There's a wrinkle in time from "the den bed is made up," to my getting ready for work.

I knew almost nothing about Todd, but I'm pretty sure he wasn't a fascist. So that's good.

And if my mom had had any concerns at all the next day, I would have told her not to worry: she hadn't missed any important calls on the red Rosenberg phone as it hadn't rung once during the night, so there was still a chance their conviction could be overturned.

Although I'm pretty sure the Rosenbergs themselves would remain dead.

6

Jesus Christ

Jesus kissed me.

At first, I hadn't noticed Jesus standing there in the near-dark as he was up against a burgundy velvet curtain. When my eyes adjusted, I could see he had shoulder-length brown hair and a thin beard. His eyes settled on mine, and he implored me over to him. I was tentative but stepped forward. He handed me a gift, leaned closer until our warm faces were inches from one another, and kissed me on the cheek. He held the kiss for a few moments. His lips felt firm yet soft.

I was not delusional.

I was not participating in a religious re-enactment.

I was probably a little drunk.

The gift he'd given me was the soundtrack album for *The Rocky Horror Show*.

It was Halloween night, 1974. I'd been sitting in the dark at one of the small cocktail tables, along with all the others in the audience, when I heard this announcement:

"And the award goes to—Nikki Nash!"

My heart raced as I took the three small stairs to the stage. There was a spotlight on me, and the people in the room were applauding. I'd always wanted to win an award. I imagined an Oscar.

This was not an Oscar.

I crossed the stage. From the waist up I was wearing a black blouse that buttoned up the back, with long sleeves and a white, starched collar. Covering my head was black fabric with a starched band of white framing my face, i.e., the top half of the nun's habit I'd held onto since my teens. From the waist down I was wearing black panties, a black garter belt, black fishnets, my cigarettes and lighter tucked into the band of the left stocking. Black platform shoes. Over this, I wore a black cape, for modesty's sake. I'd just won first prize in the costume contest.

I was at The Roxy Theater on Sunset to see Paul Jabara play Frank-N-Furter in *The Rocky Horror Show*. I'd gone with my mom, and I had no idea the evening would conclude with a costume contest. I had dressed up for the occasion—it being Halloween and all—with no expectation of glory. But there I was on stage. The winner.

Jesus beckoned me over, and that's when he kissed me on the cheek.

It was, in fact, Ted Neeley—one of the judges—who kissed me.

He'd played Jesus in *Jesus Christ Superstar*, in both the stage version at the Universal Studios Amphitheater (back when it was an actual amphitheater) and in the movie version, which I'd seen at the Cinerama Dome in Hollywood.

But to me, Ted Neeley *was* Jesus.

I wasn't religious. My mom was a non-believer and my dad—maybe not wanting to contradict my mom's beliefs—didn't say much either way, although he had been fostered by Christian Scientists after being orphaned as a child. He once mentioned, with fondness, the founder, Mary Baker Eddy, but was shot down by my mom who made fun of idolatry. Or maybe it was the sentimentality she objected to.

When I was little, all I knew was that on Sunday morning, there wasn't anything good on TV. No cartoons. No *Captain Kangaroo*. No *Engineer Bill*. Sitting under a card table covered with a sheet, I made the best of what TV there was while eating bowls of graham crackers and milk—a soggy light brown mess of sweet delight—but I was confused by all the weird churchy things going on. Men with black poofy hair speaking in unfamiliar cadences of enthusiasm. I could go outside to play but the kids on my street weren't around, having gone to "church."

I asked my mom when she got up where everyone went on Sundays, and she explained something about Church and Sunday school. To her credit, when I'd expressed interest in going—in finding out what church was, or where all my friends were—she made no sarcastic comments and instead found a place to take me the following weekend, where kids I didn't know were painting pictures of sheep on empty cardboard ice cream containers. A smiling adult pinned something on me with a picture of a guy with a beard and talked in over-sweet tones to me about Jesus. As much as I would later be attracted to cults that might provide a relaxing freedom from choice, I didn't want my art projects limited to sheep. I like sheep, but still.

"How was it?" My mom asked when she picked me up.

"I don't need to go back."

I did love Christmas and Christmas music and the Bah Humbug stencil my dad used every year on the mirror over the sofa. I loved all the festivity and the feeling of potential family closeness. I didn't, however, know anything about Jesus. Not that I needed to understand Jesus to enjoy the holidays, but a lot of people mentioned him and/or God, and I was clueless.

As I got older, Jesus continued to be a murky mystery I didn't want to investigate. If I didn't know about something, I didn't want to look silly by asking. I presumed I'd learn what I needed to learn on the planet through osmosis. Or magic. In the meantime, I'd fake it.

And thus, Jesus remained a mystery. Until I was a teenager.

I learned about Jesus in the back of a car, which could be a country-western song or a lyric from something by Meat Loaf, as if I'd learned about Jesus rolling around with a super-religious boy who conflated spiritual fervor and sexual fervor. But I wasn't with some boy when I learned about Jesus, but alone in the way back of the family station wagon on a road trip through Idaho. My education came at the hands of Andrew Lloyd Webber. I had a cassette player and a cassette of *Jesus Christ Superstar*, and it all started to make sense. The dinner party. The donkeys. Mary. Well, there were two Marys, which was confusing and maybe something for Jesus to talk about in therapy. Then the whole dying on a cross and the coming back to life part. Although I still wasn't clear on where the sheep fit in.

Perhaps, as a teenager, I was at the confused and vulnerable age where there's a need for connection, for purpose, for exaltation, or perhaps I simply longed to fall in love, which is its own—yet similar—brain chemical, and was something I did regularly. This longing could have gone either way. I could have fallen into religious commitment, a straight and narrow path of goodness, good deeds, and good works, followed by the comforting acceptance from others who followed the same path. Or I could have latched onto Jesus. I already had the outfit.

Instead, I latched on to Ted Neeley, who played Jesus in the movie and was, therefore, the voice on the cassette I listened to day and night. I wonder if I'd had a cassette of *The Sound of Music*, I would have been obsessed with cute Nazis and being a governess, or had it been *Oklahoma*, would it have been cute farmers and agriculture? Would it have mattered? Obsession—no matter the object—is a good alternative to investigating the source of pain or developing tools for self-reflection and acceptance. Plus, obsession takes less work.

I've seen many productions of the musical, including a version set in Germany in the 1940s and a production in Orange County with rocker Sebastian Bach as Jesus. But I was in high school the first time I saw *Jesus Christ Superstar*, it was Ted Neeley who captivated me. Who would one day kiss me on the cheek.

I went with a guy I met while I was working at a dry cleaner on Ventura Boulevard. It was my first job, if you don't count working at a strip club in Van Nuys. My friend Tina got me the job at the strip club after she'd been working there a week. We had gone from dressing as nuns to buy alcohol to wearing bikinis and serving Near Beer to grimy, sad men who were more interested in me and Tina because we were *not* naked, followed by their requests for us to *get* naked—although they were very nice about it. Tina and I quit after two weeks as the job was icky and depressing.

The job at the dry cleaner was merely boring—hardly anyone came in as it was a drop-off/pick-up location only (i.e., "No plant on premises")—but at least I didn't have to wear a bikini to work. The building was a long, thin structure on Ventura Boulevard, with parking and an entrance in the back. The counter faced the parking lot, and besides taking in dirty clothes, I was in charge of putting the clean clothes on the conveyor belt alphabetically.

When alone, which was often, I created my own excitement to counter the boredom. I had a radio and one afternoon "Layla" came on and I had to dance. I sang along and pleaded and got on my knees, pounding the carpeted floor. Embodying the music. I was weaving in and out of the clothes like my own dance of the seven veils. Twirling and twirling to the music. Seducing myself, seducing imagined lovers. The song ended and I turned around to see Arthur, a thin older man with gray hair, standing at the counter, his clothes in a pile in front of him. I emerged from my secret garden of the hanging clothes.

"Hi, Arthur," I said. Casual. I could feel my face was red. He'd just witnessed a teenager's full and unbridled commitment to the rapture of music and solitude and dance.

"I didn't see a thing," he said.

"You're very kind." I labeled his garments, put them in a bag, and handed him his slip. He nodded and left.

Other than that, not much happened at the dry cleaner.

Until a young guy came in. He was tall with dark wavy hair and porcelain skin, more like a very big doll than a flesh-and-blood man. He seemed oblivious to things around him. Or maybe he was shy. I was completely taken by him. He filled out the slip with his name and address, said thank you, and left. His name was Jeffrey.

The next night, Tina and I got in my VW and drove to the address on the slip. I was cunning and didn't want to appear desperate, so the plan was to drive around the block as many times as it took until we ran out of gas. Tina agreed to this possibly boring and pointless venture, but then again, it was her idea we work at a strip club, so I figured we were even. We drove and drove and drove, and then, having gotten spooked by what we thought was a ghost at a construction site we'd passed maybe twenty times, I said, the hell with this, and pulled over in front of Jeffrey's house.

When he came to the door, I explained to him in an adrenalized rush of words how I'd planned to meet him and how it had backfired. He laughed at me, or at something, and we stood in the doorway chatting. I'd forgotten about Tina, who was still sitting in my VW on the street. I turned and waved. She waved back and took another drag off her cigarette. I figured she was fine.

A week later, Jeffrey called and invited me to see *Jesus Christ Superstar* at the Universal Amphitheater.

Suddenly I was in love. Not with Jeffrey (we never even kissed), but with Ted Neeley. Admittedly, it was perhaps more rapture than love, but Ted Neeley filled me with a blissful enchantment that gave me a better understanding of the full, spiritual surrender that consumed some people in their love of Jesus.

Maybe it was all the same feeling. Maybe loving Jesus was the same as any obsessive love but without all the mess and inconsistencies of actual contact. Spiritual. Other-worldly. Although I ultimately didn't know how to live continuously in that place of rapture.

Jesus may have kissed me, but I didn't see us going to Disneyland anytime soon.

7

Judo at the YMCA

Having given up on actual dating and yet still working at the Old World Restaurant, I felt an overall lack of enthusiasm about the now seemingly unattainable goal of meeting Warren Beatty. Feeling bereft, I imagined myself seventy years old, still at the Old World, escorting people to their seats. I didn't know how to shake off this malaise, so I started taking judo. The classes were at the YMCA, not far from the restaurant, and if I was working an evening shift, I'd take a judo class in the afternoon, shower at the Y, put on some makeup, and go straight to work.

For class, we had to buy a *gi*—a thick, canvas-like pants and robe combo, with a thick belt. It wasn't very slimming, but I was happy to wear it; to feel I was part of this new group. Week after week I showed up, feeling powerful when I took someone down, even if it was pretend. Slapping the mat and yelling was fun. One of the maneuvers we had to practice over and over was like doing a leaping sideways somersault, landing on your back with more slapping and yelling. This was to teach us how to land when thrown by someone else, which was strangely like hitting yourself in the face so you would be prepared for when you invited someone else to hit you in the face. But whatever.

My forearms were already bruised from the blocking moves we'd been working on, so one more potential injury didn't worry me. Then

I landed on my hand and felt something snap on the tip of my right index finger, and that was it for the day. I wasn't sure if it was broken or sprained or how to tell the difference. It was a Sunday afternoon, and I didn't know how to find a doctor or what to do. I asked around at the Y and they suggested ice, but they also said I should see a doctor the next day. Crap.

I was frustrated and in pain and I didn't have time to shower, but I had inherited a strong work ethic from my dad—which included keeping one's commitments—so calling in sick was not an option. Plus, I wasn't sick. Only injured. I'd show up in my unkempt and unwashed state and make it through the evening. Fortunately, Sundays were usually slow. I pulled my hair back into a ponytail, awkwardly avoiding the use of my finger, and drove to work.

And of course, this was the night that Warren Beatty finally came in. This was *not* the way I wanted to meet him. This had not been Step Two of my plan: dirty hair, no makeup, smelly armpits.

I'd been in the bathroom when he came in. With my finger submerged in a drinking glass full of ice water, I saw him sitting there alone. My face felt hot. I grabbed a menu with my left hand and placed the menu on his table as unobtrusively as possible.

"Your waiter will be right with you," I said blandly.

He looked up. "Thank you."

I turned around, and I prayed he had already forgotten me. This is not how I wanted it to happen. I almost made it out of the front room and out of his line of sight.

"Excuse me, Miss?" That voice shivered down my back.

I wondered if I could just keep walking.

Then I turned back, holding my arms tightly at my sides to keep the cilantro armpit smell from wafting toward him.

"What's your name?"

"Nikki."

"I'm Warren."

"Hi," I said, thinking, *biggest DUH in the world*.

"What have you done to your finger?"

"It seems I broke it in my judo class," I said. "This afternoon," I added so he'd understand why I looked like crap.

He nodded. He seemed to think about this rather deeply. "I hope you mend quickly," he said as if his words had the power to make it so. He smiled and went back to his newspaper. I walked away, carrying my dumb plastic glass of ice with me.

I felt adrenalized, foolish, and devastated all at the same time.

I could feel my cheeks were legitimately red on their own—no pinching needed—as I approached the register where Mitch was looking out the window and drinking his coffee cooler. I stepped behind the counter all nonchalant, and I hoped he hadn't been paying attention to my encounter with the man of my dreams. I was overcome by such a mix of feelings that if he teased me, I thought I might cry.

"Did you blow your big chance with a movie star?" He didn't know about my nearly seven-year obsession with Warren Beatty, or my plan to have him in my life. No one did. He certainly didn't know this was the only reason I was working at the Old World.

Steve came up to the front. He was a handsome older waiter, meaning late twenties, and had gotten the job through Mitch because they were pals.

"I need another book," Steve said. I was in charge of the receipt books so when a waiter ran out, I had to go upstairs and get another, keeping track of the check numbers. I grabbed the keys. I was going to stop in the bathroom, but I didn't want to see what I looked like. Plus, I didn't like to keep anyone waiting, and Steve was waiting at the foot of the stairs. I handed him the book and I walked back to the front, happy to be strolling with Steve. If Mr. Beatty was watching, he'd realize I was friendly and popular and not at all interested in him. But when I glanced over, I saw an empty table and a few bills under the salt shaker.

Was that it? Had that been my big chance? I'd been at the Old World for a year and a half and now I'd have to cut my losses? Shed a tear and move on with my life, whatever that looked like. But now there'd been this dose, this jolt, like a drug. Warren Beatty. Would I get a second chance? Should I spend any more time on this? I was almost twenty. Was I going to work at The Old World and keep hoping for another chance?

Like a gambler chasing a loss—or perhaps more like a hostess with no plan for the future—I decided to keep working at the Old World, and from then on—or until I figured out what to do with my life—I was sure to wash my hair. Just in case. I had electric curlers, but they hadn't worked for a couple of years, and I couldn't afford new ones, and—learning from my dad to not be wasteful—I put the hard plastic curlers in boiling water to heat them up and pulled them out of the water with the tongs mom used when boiling hot dogs for dinner. This worked pretty well.

Every day after that Sunday evening when Warren Beatty had asked me my name, I came to work perky and expectant, but I was unable to keep these feelings afloat. I could replay meeting Warren Beatty only so many times before it started to seem like a dream and no longer released serotonin in my brain. Like I'd sucked the marrow dry from that memory bone. The reality was, all we'd done was exchange names. That wasn't like really meeting someone. At least by my standards. However, he had asked about my finger.

After a couple of weeks of nothing, I fell into a sad state of resignation. I had some laughs with the waiters, I was nice to people who came in, and I sometimes hung out after work with Mitch and Steve, but I felt adrift and often ended my evening shifts standing in the refrigerated walk-in eating cheesecake that was going to be tossed the next day.

The next night was busy for a Monday. Steve, Mitch, and I made plans to have a drink after closing. Two more hours and then I'd be off for a couple of days, which I'd usually look forward to, but I was now worried Warren might return on my days off. And I'd miss him. Steve was waiting for a group of ten and had pushed a couple of tables together in the middle room and had placed menus and ice water at each seat, along with a few ashtrays. We hoped they weren't going to linger because it was a late reservation and we'd have to stay at least as long as they wanted to stay; we weren't going to give them the keys and say, "We're going out for drinks. Lock up when you're done."

Finally, I noticed activity on the sidewalk and several smiley, shiny, pretty people came through the door, trailing the cold air in behind them. At the back of the group was Warren Beatty. Steve took charge and led them back to their table. Mitch went to the kitchen, probably to talk to the cooks, and I stood against the wall by the register. Unseen.

The group sat. They ordered. They seemed to all talk at once and I stayed up front forcing myself to look anywhere but at Warren. Eventually, I went to the bathroom, keeping my eyes forward, and on my way back I passed the table.

"Nikki!"

I stopped and looked around like any number of people might be calling my name. But I knew who it was. I knew his voice. I stopped walking but only turned in his direction, resisting the pull he had on me.

"Hi." I feigned a calm that probably came off more as bored.

He waved me over, took my wrist, and held up my hand. The one with the splint on the index finger.

"Are you mending?"

"Yes."

"Good." He said, releasing my wrist.

"Are you enjoying your dinner?" I tried to make it sound like I was a polite and concerned employee. Nothing more.

"Yes."

"Good," I said, mimicking his "good." Like we'd concluded a business interview. "And thank you for asking about my finger."

I smiled in the group's direction although no one was paying much attention to this exchange. They were probably used to this. He wasn't exactly hitting on me, but I'm sure they'd seen him engage plenty of women in conversation. I was most likely just another in a long line. And a nobody at that. I went back up to the register and could still feel his hand on my wrist. This was pathetic. But wonderful.

After an hour or so, Steve came up to the register with the check and a credit card. I ran it on the machine, but it wasn't Warren Beatty's name on the card. When Steve came back with the signed slip I put the carbon in the drawer, and the big group headed past as they were leaving. I felt hopeful; maybe Warren was in town for a while and might be in again for another Sunday night solo tea. Or maybe I could trade shifts with someone and work the next day. I was imagining what I'd wear next Sunday—as if Sunday night was his night—when someone in the group stopped at the register. I looked up.

Warren was looking straight into my eyes.

"What are you doing later?" he said.

A girl can't look too eager. "I'm going for a drink with Mitch and Steve."

"Do I know Mitch and Steve?" Like I should have asked his permission.

"They work here."

"Where are you going?"

"The Luau." I didn't tell him we usually went there because they served food, and I wasn't legally old enough to drink.

"What are you doing after a drink with Mitch and Steve at The Luau?"

"Going home?" Why did I make it a question, dammit?!

"I'll call you," he said.

"Great," I said like we discussed plans all the time. He went out without looking back and I realized he didn't have my number. It was an empty promise but nice anyway. Nice to hear those words coming out of his mouth. That beautiful mouth. He remembered my name. He remembered my broken finger. He'd held my wrist. I could swirl this into something if I tried hard enough.

Mitch came up and said, "Don't tell me you're falling for that."

"For what?"

"You're still going with us tonight, right?"

"Of course."

Mitch took the cash drawer upstairs, I wrapped the receipts in the evening's register tape, and Steve turned in his order book and took off his apron. We got our coats, locked up the Old World, and walked around the corner to The Luau. I was trying to act normal but was still adrenalized by my second encounter—in less than two weeks—with *Warren Beatty*, who was my reason for living. I couldn't think it through in any realistic way, so I simply vibrated internally as I walked with the guys, hoping they wouldn't notice. The cold air felt fantastic on my face.

The Luau was a garish mélange of tiki stuff—bamboo and red walls and green leather booths. We weren't eating so we sat at the long, curvy bar. I ordered tonic water, Steve got a beer, and Mitch ordered two red wines, sliding one of the wines over to me. We gossiped about the waiters, the cooks, the difficult customers. The bartender, who was on the phone, looked over at me and when he looked away, I pushed the red wine back to Mitch in case I was about to get carded, but the bartender came over anyway, the phone still in his hand.

I took a sip of my water to fool him.

"Are you Nikki?"

"Yes." Was I being arrested?

He handed me the receiver.

"For me?"

"If you're Nikki," he said, and walked away. I looked at Mitch and Steve and took the call.

"Hello?"

"Good evening," said the deep voice that of course could only belong to *him*. In two words he could seduce. He'd found me. At The Luau. He'd gotten the number, he'd dialed the number, he'd talked to the bartender, he'd described me and given my name. A lot of effort went into this.

"Hi," I said.

"Come over."

"Okay."

He told me which room at the Beverly Wilshire, I said okay, and handed the phone back to the bartender.

I looked at the guys. "I have to go."

Steve said, "Is something wrong?"

"No," I assured him, trying to temper the excitement I was feeling.

Mitch rolled his eyes. "Christ, Nash. Bailing for a better offer?"

Steve looked at Mitch, "What better offer?"

"She can tell you."

"He can tell you," I said. I put money on the bar, slid off the stool, grabbed my coat, and left.

Walking to the Beverly Wilshire Hotel, which took about two-and-a-half minutes, I thought about my powerlessness to say no to Warren Beatty, wondering if it came from years of imagining this, or if I had some instinct this would be the start of something important. More likely it was the start and end of something foolish.

But one thing I knew, I had no choice in the matter. Unlike with the smarmy producer Marty Ransohoff, who'd asked me if I'd "do anything" for him, I knew for Warren, I *would* do anything. And I wasn't bothered by this at all. I was excited. I was nervous. But I didn't doubt myself. I knew what I wanted. What I had wanted for years.

The hotel had two buildings with a small valet area between them. The buildings were stately and beautiful, with their festive striped awnings dotting the windows, all of which I'd seen during my eighteen months of working nearly across the street. I entered the lobby, found the elevators, and went up to Warren's suite. He answered the door wearing what he'd been wearing in the restaurant. At least he wasn't in pajamas. The room had two sofas with a large coffee table between them. The bedroom was separated from the living room by a partial wall, and beyond that was a bathroom. There was a bottle of champagne chilling in a silver urn on the coffee table. We sat down together on the dark brocade sofa. Warren didn't drink, but he poured me a glass which I sipped like a lady. As much as I liked drinking, I didn't think champagne could touch the buzz I had at the moment just sitting there with him.

Warren asked me if I liked working at the Old World and I told him it served a purpose and explained that I'd gotten the job there to meet him.

"Really." He seemed surprised.

"Yes."

"I'm flattered."

"I thought we should know one another."

"And so we do."

"But I'm not a stalker. Or not a very good one."

I reminded him of the night he'd come in alone and my finger was in the cup of ice, holding up my finger to show him I was still wearing the splint like it was proof.

"Oh, I remember." He seemed amused by the whole story.

Sitting there next to him, hearing my own voice—which sounded confident and fun—my perspective got woozy: *Here I am with Warren Beatty.* After all these years. It was both familiar and heady.

He asked about my background, and I gave him some of the nutty childhood highlights; the Huey Newton and the Black Panthers story was always a crowd-pleaser. I asked about his, which seemed to surprise him, but he recounted his own story of being a virgin until he was twenty. Maybe this too was a well-worn story, but it still felt like he was sharing an intimacy. I tried to stop staring at his beautiful face and just hear his words. His voice calmed me down.

I told him about the encounter at the Bob Altman screening but that I was too young to meet him back then.

"And you're old enough now?"

"I am."

There was a pause, and he said, "I want to lie down next to you."

I realized I had no actual Step Three to my plan, but I knew it didn't involve my saying "No" and leaving.

We went into the bedroom and lay down. I wanted to blurt out something like, "Now what," to break the tension, but I trusted him, and I remained quiet. He stroked my hand, and we turned to face one another. The room was just the two of us, quiet, except for our breathing. Clothes slowly came off and we made love; he was slow and attentive, and it all felt natural and good. Warm. Then hot. Then cool. And we were quiet.

I loved being with Warren, although I wasn't deluded in thinking I was someone important to him. Yet. I accepted that there were many women in his life—at least according to the tabloids—and I didn't need to be a star player; I'd be happy to be on the roster. I didn't think this was a one-time-only thing, which may have been due to Warren's ability to make me feel like I was the only person who mattered in the moment. Maybe I was—for that moment.

Of course, I had no way to know, so I abandoned this pointless, circular thinking and returned to where I was. In bed with Warren Beatty. That's all I needed to know for now.

We lounged in bed, his skin warm against mine, and I could feel myself dozing. When I opened my eyes, I saw that his were closed. I didn't know if he was sleeping or what the protocol was here: Should I slip out and get dressed and leave? Should I let myself fall asleep and if I did would I be embarrassed when he woke me up with some expected evening-ender like "I'll call you a cab." But sleep took over before I could figure it out.

In the morning, he seemed delighted to see me. He walked to the bathroom naked, and I loved seeing the back of him, his dark hair tousled. I felt shy. I got up and got dressed and he came back out wearing a robe.

"That was lovely," he said. "You're lovely."

He asked for my number, which I gave him. He didn't write it down, which seemed odd. I would have let it go—my training in needlessness always on the ready—but I spoke up for what felt like the first time.

"Either you have a good memory," I said, "or you don't really want my number."

"I wouldn't have asked had I not wanted it." He chose his words carefully, as if hearing them in his head before speaking them. Like he was being interviewed, his words recorded for posterity. I felt slightly reprimanded. He added, as if letting me in on a secret of why he hadn't written my number down, "I remember phone numbers by imagining the corresponding football jerseys."

"What's your number?" I asked, like what's fair is fair.

He gave me the number of the hotel and said they'd put me through if I called. I wrote the number on a piece of paper I had in my purse and then looked up at him.

"I remember numbers by writing them down," I said.

He laughed. I wanted him to know his subtle chastisement hadn't gone unnoticed. And hadn't wounded me in any way. I may have had a huge crush but that didn't mean I couldn't spar.

"You're smart, aren't you?" He was smiling.

"I was tested in kindergarten and apparently I had a high IQ."

"Tell me what it was." His voice was sexy and secret-requesting, as if he'd said, "Lift up your skirt."

"142," I said. "But I'm sure it's gone down since then," I demurred.

"Hmmm."

He helped me with my coat, we kissed, a long kiss like in the movies (which made it feel all the dreamier), and I left.

I took the elevator down and went outside into the cool air, my hand on my face. My skin warm and abraded from kissing and I could still feel him lying next to me. I thought about how he'd laughed when I wrote down the number he'd given me. What would happen next? Would I call him? Was he expecting me to call him?

But then I returned to my body and the breeze in the air. It was early morning, and the sun wasn't yet visible from behind the mountains. I knew I was supposed to do something other than stand in front of the hotel reliving the night: the exchange at the Old World, the bartender, the "Good evening," on the phone, the invitation. I worried he'd look out the window and see me standing frozen on the sidewalk, but I remembered his room faced the other direction. I felt giddy, replaying it all, and finally started walking.

There's an Emitt Rhodes lyric: "Love will stone you, but you'll come down." Not that this was love. Well, it wasn't for him. I didn't know what it was for me, but whatever this feeling was, I'd probably come down. For now, I was delighted and even laughed when I pictured myself as a mad scientist, rubbing my hands together and saying, "My plan is working."

I'd met him, and then some.

I didn't know what would come next. Maybe he'd disappear again, off making another movie, like the previous year and a half he hadn't come into the Old World. I had no control over the future, but I was also realistic enough to know I wasn't Natalie Wood or Julie Christie. I was a nineteen-year-old girl from Tarzana with no real career plan and a splint on my finger from a judo class at the YMCA.

But I was smart.

8

A View from the Bridge

My dad and I were sitting in the living room. I was on the big brown couch, and he was perched on the coffee table, holding his trombone mouthpiece, which not only kept his lip in shape but protected him from being caught empty-handed. Like someone might catch him relaxing. It was midday and the room was gloomy. The drapes were closed because Mom was in charge of the drapes, but she didn't get up until around 2 p.m.

Dad and I sat in the gloom.

"We think it's time you moved out."

My first thought: *But I'm only fifteen!* My second thought: *Oh, yeah—I'm twenty.*

I waited for him to say something more.

He continued. "We think it would be a good idea for you to be a little hungry."

Yeah, and I think it would be a good idea if Mom got up before two in the afternoon. I didn't say anything.

He blew into his mouthpiece—just a quick buzz to keep the embouchure tight. Or maybe to deflect any expectation that he should say more.

"Wow," I said, gathering my thoughts.

The phone rang and our mynah bird Charlie Parker chirped out: "Barbara Nash, Dick Nash's wife," which sounded more like

Barbaranashdicknashswife. Dad's service called often about studio work, so someone needed to answer the phone. This usually fell to my mother, who—with little patience for niceties—avoided the whole tedious process of unwanted conversation by answering *Barbaranashdicknashswife.*

Despite her politics and seemingly bold manner, deep down, she was still just Dick Nash's wife, which she'd learned when she once confronted him about some money thing.

He'd told her, "When you make the money you can have a say." No wonder she was depressed. Silenced by The Saint.

As Mom wasn't up yet, my dad had to take the call. Maybe that's why she stayed in bed so long, to avoid having to answer the phone. Dad got up from the coffee table, went into the kitchen, and picked up the receiver.

"Dick Nash," he answered.

I was still on the couch. I hadn't moved. Maybe he expected me to start packing. After hanging up the phone, he looked over at me.

"We don't mean today, but in the next six months. You know, something like that," he clarified.

"Okay," I said. I got up from the couch to signal we didn't need to discuss it further.

"Good talk," he said. Confirming we were done talking. He went back to the kitchen table, where he was watching the Dodgers game on a small TV while doing the Jumble puzzle, occasionally tooting into his mouthpiece.

I went up to my bedroom and sat on the cushioned window seat. I looked around the room, feeling lost and abandoned. I wasn't sure what to do next. I'd taken up painting—having inherited paints from a drunken family friend after a divorce—but it seemed pointless to continue with the still life of a wine bottle and a piece of rye toast because soon I'd have to "pack it up and move on."

I called Warren.

I'd known him less than a year by this time, and we talked every week or two and got together whenever he wanted. I had no hold over him, nor did I want one. I was in the take-what-you-can-get-without-asking-too-much phase. Maybe he liked that; maybe it set me apart from the other women. I may not have known how it was all going to unfold with him, even with my childhood vision of "in my life forever," but for now, I was happy that he always took my calls.

I told him about what my dad had said. That I felt unsettled.

"How old are you?" He asked as if he knew and was just confirming, but to me it felt both like a reprimand—like I should be out of the house by now—and a reminder that he didn't always remember much about the actual me, or the things in my life.

"Twenty," I said. "Jeez, my mom was married and pregnant at twenty."

"When I was twenty, I was still a virgin. I came from a religious family. I was a slow starter."

He'd told me this before, but I felt I should respond. "You've made up for lost time."

"I'll have to call you back."

"Okay."

Shampoo had just come out and he was an even bigger star. I wondered if he was still dating Julie Christie.

I went to my desk and pulled out a drawer with no idea how to start packing, let alone move out. I closed the drawer and thought about going downstairs for ice cream.

The phone rang.

"That was fast."

"Is this Nikki Nash?"

"This is she."

"This is Bart Lester returning your call."

"That's nice except I didn't call you."

"Nikki Nash?"

"Yes. But I still didn't call you, Mr. Bart Lester."

"Ahh. Service must have gotten their wires crossed. Sorry for the intrusion."

And my first thought was, *I wonder if he's cute.*

The next day, despite feeling a bit desperate about the prospect of moving out, I went to my acting class where the big claim to fame was Erica Hagen, who had been one of the Furniture Girls in *Soylent Green*. Otherwise, a bunch of nobodies. Including me.

That night, alone in my room with cereal and whipped cream, the phone rang.

"Hello?"

"It's Bart Lester."

"I swear I didn't—"

"I know it wasn't you. Let me explain."

"Explain away."

"It seems a friend of mine is trying to fix us up."

"Who?"

"I'm still getting more information. But now I'm curious about what it is we may have in common."

"Hold on a second, I'm in the middle of a painting." I wasn't—I was eating—but I wanted to sound interesting and busy. Not just a sloth who hung around in my bedroom waiting for possible wrong numbers.

"You're a painter?" He sounded impressed.

"Trying. You? Are you a doctor or musician or something? You have a service."

"No, I'm a lawyer. And a writer. I'm in town to meet with some people. I live up in San Francisco."

We chatted about writing and San Francisco, and he told me that his wife, a prima ballerina, had been murdered the year before by the Zebra Killer. We talked about a play he was writing, and I told him about the scene I was working on for class.

"You're an actress."

"I'm studying acting but I work at the Old World. It's a restaurant in Beverly Hills."

"I know it well. I'm part-owner of the Rangoon Racquet Club. Down the street. In fact, I'll be there tomorrow afternoon."

I was forming a joke about racquetball when he said, "We should meet. Someone seems to be fixing us up for a reason." We planned to meet the following afternoon before I had to show up at the restaurant for my evening shift.

Before work the next day, I felt anxious and excited walking down Beverly Drive to his restaurant. It was February and drizzling, but it was a short walk. I was a few minutes early to the Rangoon Racquet Club, so I went in and looked around the restaurant—not much going on—and went upstairs to the bar where we were meeting. The stairs delivered me to a landing with two payphones and a fake palm tree; I guess to give it that exotic Rangoon feel.

I continued up to the nearly empty bar and ordered tonic water. I was nervous enough for a drink but didn't drink before work. After about fifteen minutes of getting a stiff neck from all my casual glances at the doorway, I looked in the direction of the bartender until I caught his eye.

When he was in whispering distance, I said, "Excuse me. Do you know if Bart Lester has been in?"

"What's the name again?"

"Bart Lester. He's co-owner of this place."

"Maybe he's a silent partner or something. I don't know. I usually work nights."

I sat a bit longer, feeling embarrassed that I looked pathetic sitting alone waiting, which in turn meant at any minute, I'd be focusing on my thighs and how fat I thought they looked. I left money and departed. I went halfway down the stairs to the payphones and the fake palm tree, put money in the phone, and dialed the number Bart had given me. No answer. Not even the service picked up. With no apparent white knight on the horizon, I put more money into the Burmese pay phone and called Warren, who sounded both sexy and busy and said he'd call me back later. Which usually meant I wouldn't hear from him.

And I had to laugh. I was disappointed by a guy I had never met, and the fallback guy was *Warren Beatty*.

Maybe my dependence on him was getting in the way of my dating someone "real," i.e., not someone I'd been—and continued to be—obsessed with since I was fourteen.

The following day, I called my friend Ronna who worked at the Old World. Ronna was the new manager who had taken Mitch's place. She lived at the Fountain Lanai which sounded quite dreamy until I'd been invited to her apartment to play poker and realized it was just another Hollywood apartment building: a two-story U-shaped building with a pool in the middle of the U and subterranean parking.

"Busy?" I asked. She was a fast-talker and would either say yes or no. "What's up?"

"My dad says I should move out. If you could keep your ears open."

"I think 205 might be available. On Bozo's floor." It had become common Fountain Lanai lore that the "original" Bozo lived in 210. But how would anyone know? Without the red wig and big shoes, he could have been any middle-aged guy in a crappy apartment, living off the reputation of a clown.

A month later I moved into The Fountain Lanai.

Warren was single again and was one of my first visitors. My new place felt fun and colorful until he came over, and then it felt cheap and shoddy. But that didn't stop us from having sex against the narrow kitchen wall. Thank goodness it was daytime, and the cockroaches were napping. This may not have been the glorious Mary Tyler Moore apartment I'd imagined, but then again, I was having sex with Warren Beatty. Afterward, we sat on a denim couch I'd inherited from the previous owner. I congratulated him on his new movie.

"You know what the hardest part is?" He looked off into the distance.

"Tell me."

"It's the applause. After *Bonnie and Clyde,* I was anxious about how I would top that success, and then I did *Shampoo.* Even more applause. And now I feel the pressure to top it again. I don't know if I can. It's a lot of pressure."

He asked how I was, and I told him about acting class. I was working on a scene from *A View from the Bridge*.

He followed that up with: "Have you ever had a threesome?"

"No," I said. "Why? You want to?" We often slipped back and forth from real things to sex things, although sex was also real, I suppose.

"I do. With you."

And who else?

"Surprise me."

And I did. I invited Erica Hagen from class and a few weeks later, she and Warren and I had a threesome in my dumb little canopy bed I still had from childhood. No one seemed bothered by the bed. I was happy for any chance to be with Warren, but I also hoped my willingness to participate—even to go as far as to invite someone as gorgeous as Erica—would indicate to him how I was not like other girls. I was confident. Fun.

When Erica left, all tall and lithe with her long blonde hair and long legs, Warren and I went back to bed where he told me he loved me. That he loved that I would do that with him. That we could share that.

It was such an indirect way to feel special. To feel I mattered.

In May, I quit working at the Old World Restaurant—management started changing things around, plus my purpose for working there had been more than satisfied—and took the only job I could find, not that I'd done an extensive search. A friend from high school told me there was an opening at Walt Davis Enterprises, which sounded like a chance to work in entertainment. I showed up for the interview wearing a skirt and blouse.

Walt Davis was swarthy and wore red satin dolphin shorts and a black, sleeveless fisherman shirt. You could see his nipples poking through the netting. I kept my eyes on his face. I was hired. He had a four-story building and sold questionably available Sony televisions to a bunch of questionable characters. There was a showroom on the first floor with a lot of black leather couches and sample TVs, although he had no physical customers, all transactions were handled by the girls on the phones.

I discovered after about seven minutes of working there that the company consisted of Walt and six young women—all wannabe actresses. They told me he helped them with videos, and car payments, and I learned they were all sleeping with him. When his invitation for sex came my way, I politely declined, not realizing that this was a requirement and not a perk. The next week I was given the newly created Saturday morning shift, which was cleaning the "showroom." When I arrived for my shift, I found the black shag carpet was scattered with dried-up cheese slices, greasy and curling at the edges, empty Coke cans, wine bottles, glasses, and used condoms. A lot of used condoms. Showbiz!

Fortunately, I didn't depend on Walt Davis for a career in acting (or whatever porn might have been going on upstairs) but kept studying at the theater where I'd met Erica. After doing a scene from *A View from the Bridge,* a couple of the older students and I formed The Agape Players. Panos, an energetic Greek guy, was playing the lead and also directing; Edna, kind and matronly, was subsidizing the production with the help of her wealthy husband. And I, being young, played the young niece. Although I was busy most of the time with work and rehearsals, I occasionally thought of the phantom Bart Lester, mostly out of curiosity but also with a sense of unfinished business. He'd stood me up and I wanted to know why. Shed a tear and move on. Sometimes, it's not so easy.

Several weeks later I called Warren and told him about the play we were producing and that we were opening the following month. I told him about the scene in the play where my character is supposed to blush on cue and told him I used the memory of our first encounter at the Bob Altman party, and that I successfully blushed every time.

He laughed and said he'd like to come to the opening night.

"Warren, it's a crappy little theater. It's not going to be some snazzy opening."

"I still want to come. Put me on the list."

"Do you want to bring anyone?" I was hoping he wouldn't be bringing Julie Christie.

"No. I'm coming to see *you*."

A week before opening, I came home late from rehearsal, got into an oversized T-shirt, and poured a glass of wine. The phone rang, startling me.

"Hello?"

"Yes, this is Dr. Hillman. My service gave me this number."

"No, I'm sorry. I didn't call."

"That's fine," he said. "I'm a psychiatrist and sometimes people reach out and then change their minds. I always like to call back. In case."

"I didn't call."

"Sorry to bother you," he said.

But something was triggered, and I wasn't sure I should hang up yet.

"Wait. This happened to me a few months ago."

"What happened a few months ago?" He was sounding a little shrinky. I worried I was inadvertently signing up for therapy, but he hadn't mentioned money so I pressed on.

"I got a call from someone I didn't know."

"What happened?"

"It was weird. I was living with my parents at the time. I told the guy that I hadn't called and then he called me again, saying someone was trying to fix us up. We decided to meet but he never showed."

"Do you remember his name?"

"Bart Lester."

"And I'm sorry, what's your name?"

I told him. No response. "Why? Do you use the same service?"

"That's not it."

He was silent, maybe going through the names in a mental Rolodex for anything familiar. I lit a cigarette. Then he said, "Why didn't I put this together sooner? Before I say more, please—and slowly—tell me any details you may have about him. About Bart Lester."

I was getting my hopes up in a strange way. I told him the story.

"Did he tell you anything about his background?"

"He said he was an attorney or something and he was writing a book."

"Did he mention he'd lost his wife to the Zebra Killer?"

"Yes!" I felt a shiver at the back of my neck.

"One last question," he said.

I felt nervous like I was on a game show shooting for the Grand Prize.

"Go ahead."

"Are you a painter?"

"I dabble." Jeez, did I say dabble?

He took a deep breath and went on to explain that he worked at UCLA in the Acupuncture Department on a Guggenheim Grant. And he had been treating Bart Lester.

"For what?" I blurted this out; maybe he had tuberculosis or something. Although that could have been romantic, sitting on the deck chair tending to my love who was struggling to breathe. But wait, this guy was a psychiatrist. That was ominous.

He interrupted my reverie. "I can get into that later. But first, have you ever met him?"

I explained again how Bart and I were scheduled to meet but he never showed. I waited for Dr. Hillman to say something. Took another drag of the cigarette.

"Miss Nash. I'll have to call you back. If you don't mind."

"I don't mind." I was going to ask if he wanted my number but remembered he had called me.

I paced around, which felt like a big cliché. Even though I was expecting the phone to ring, I jumped when it did. I took a beat before answering: A girl can't look too eager. She might be busy "dabbling," for fuck's sake.

He explained that on his way to meet me, Bart Lester had had a car accident on Pacific Coast Highway in Malibu. He hadn't been seriously hurt in the accident, the police had shown up, checked out the car, found the brake cable had been cut, and asked Bart if he knew who was trying to kill him.

"You think I was trying to kill him? I didn't even know the guy." I worried it sounded like backpedaling, but in truth, I was going for the more distancing insouciance to mask my excitement.

"We don't think that at all," he said. "Bart's coming to Los Angeles. He may want to meet with you, if you approve, of course. But we'll need to do a background check on you as well."

"For what?" Shades of the FBI driving by my house when I was a kid.

"We'll talk in the morning. I promise. And Miss Nash—."

"Yes?"

"Lock your doors."

The next morning, I made coffee and waited to hear from Dr. Hillman. Or was I supposed to call him? I was up early with a low buzz of nervous anticipation. I had showered and dressed and was waiting, if not by the phone, then near it. I was startled by a knock at the door. Was it the Secret Service? Or the FBI? Or maybe a hitman?

I peeked out through the louvered windows and standing there was a pale man about my height with short frizzy hair, like a beige Afro.

"Who is it?"

"It's Bart Lester."

I opened the door. He was wearing khaki pants and a plaid button-down shirt. He had a dark leather briefcase in his right hand.

He said, "Do you know me?"

"We've never met."

He exhaled and his shoulders dropped. "Thank God. I had no idea who you were when they mentioned your name."

He said nothing further, so I invited him in. I offered him the couch. He smiled, staring at me, very *Stranger in a Strange Land,* as if he'd never seen a woman before.

"So," he said.

"So." We launched into the story of our phone calls and our plan to meet at the Rangoon Racquet Club. We laughed about it all, how crazy it was. I made coffee. He told me about the play he was producing with Buck Henry and then showed me some plans for the set, with fabric swatches stapled on the side. Like we'd been friends forever. Catching up.

"What do you think?"

"I have no idea. What's the play about?"

"I should let you read it. You'd be great in the part. I mean, if you can act."

I laughed, and we talked about things we had in common. I told him about my parents and their political stuff, and he talked about the Illuminati, and I nodded like I knew what he was referencing, even though I only had a vague idea about secret societies and the thing on the dollar bill. When it was time for him to go, he said he'd like to see me again.

"Shouldn't you check with Dr. Hillman?" I teased.

"I think you're safe to be with. You wouldn't kill me in my sleep, would you?"

"Oh, so now we're sleeping together?"

He laughed easily, and when it was time for him to go, he shook my hand and said he'd be in touch. I was both relieved and encouraged.

Rehearsal that night felt light-hearted and fun. I was surprised when there was a call for me at the box office. It was Bart. Just checking to make sure I was okay. I told him I was still alive. He said he was still alive as well.

Driving home that night, I thought I saw the headlights of a car tailing me; maybe I'd been spooked by Bart's call. I took a turn, and the car followed. I took another and the car continued to follow. I turned right onto Sweetzer and drove slowly, but no one was behind me. After parking in the garage at the Fountain Lanai, I walked slowly up the ramp to the sidewalk, using my peripheral vision to watch for strangers. Ronna's apartment was dark. I went up the stairs. Bozo's apartment was dark, but then again, his place was usually dark. Maybe he was dead.

I let myself into my dark apartment. It was quiet. I turned the light on in my tiny kitchen, waited for the cockroaches to scurry, and made a cup of hot chocolate.

There was a knock on the door. Was someone here to kill me?

"Who is it?" I said, staying in the kitchen.

"It's me."

I exhaled with relief and opened the door. Bart went right to the couch and said he found out who was trying to fix us up.

"Who?"

Bart told me I'd find out tomorrow.

"Why tomorrow?"

"We're having lunch with her at one o'clock. I have to go back up north in a couple of days, so it was the only time that worked."

I thought it presumptuous that he'd made plans without seeing if I was free, but I also liked that he was taking charge. He didn't seem the take-charge type.

We talked some more, laughed some more, he told me how long he'd be gone (like he already cared about me), and about the progress of his play, about his writing, and asked me about acting and how rehearsals were going, how I got into a role. As much as I enjoyed his company, I was glad he wouldn't be around for the opening of the play. I didn't want to be torn between giving attention to Warren Beatty and Bart Lester. In case Warren even showed up.

Plus, if Bart was going to be my new boyfriend, it meant I wouldn't contact Warren—the thought of which made me sad—but my moral compass for dating pointed toward monogamy, even if Warren wouldn't notice.

"I should go," he finally said. We were both tired and exhilarated. He put his hand on mine. I felt the heat of his palm. And the softness. It felt good. Intimate. Connected.

"Where are you staying?"

"Don't worry about me."

"I have been," I said, "It's late. You can stay here if you like."

He looked at me like I was an angel. "Are you sure?"

"Yes. But you know, just to sleep."

"Of course."

Which turned into not just sleeping. He was a gentle lover, and I wondered what a life with him would be like. The next morning was awkward, but we managed. I gave him the number at Walt Davis. He said he'd call with the lunch details. We kissed at the door and he left.

I went to work and waited to hear from him. One o'clock came and went, and then it was two, and I was running out of adrenaline, as well as any dopamine surge from falling in love and the anticipation of a future that didn't include condom duty at Walt Davis Enterprises.

I tried calling Bart but there was no answer. I felt a shiver of fear, wondering if something had happened to him. Again. Then my feeling turned to rejection rather than fear. I kept working; I kept waiting. By the afternoon, I figured something *had* happened. That night at the theater, I kept waiting to hear from Bart when I had a flash. I could call Dr. Hillman; I knew where he worked. The next morning at work, I called UCLA. I asked for the Guggenheim Grant Department. A woman answered the phone, and I asked if Dr. Hillman was available.

"Dr. Hillman?"

"Yes," I said, clarifying: "In the Acupuncture Department."

"What is your name?"

"Sorry. Nikki Nash. But I'm actually trying to reach Bart Lester. I spoke to Dr. Hillman a few days ago." I wanted to sound professional and not like a stalker.

"And where are you now?"

I said I was at work. I figured she was going to take the number and call me back, but instead, she asked if there were other people around me. I said yes, but this was getting weird. Maybe she was secretly in on the plan to hurt Bart. What if Dr. Hillman was in on it?

My face was heating up for no reason.

"You're in a safe environment?"

"Yes."

"I'm sorry to tell you but Bart Lester and Dr. Hillman are the same person. He's been approaching and sometimes attacking women in the L.A. area for the past several months. I would advise you to have nothing to do with him and hang up if he calls. I can give you the number for the police and our contact there, so you can report any calls you've gotten from him. Have you had any contact?"

Contact? I'd fucking *slept* with the guy. My heart felt like it had stopped and I tried to breathe. The woman asked me a few more questions but I don't remember what they were.

I got off the phone and felt sweaty. I was panicked and then surprised to find I was also disappointed. Disappointed at the loss of my potential romantic future when it all crashed in again that I was, in fact, mourning the loss of a psychopath. Which immediately flipped back into shame and panic.

And as they say, the play must go on. He never again called the theater. Or my apartment. I never saw him again. I never spoke to him again.

A few days later, we had our opening night of *A View from the Bridge*. Panos was anxious before we started and peeked at the audience from behind the curtain, happy to see a full house. But then again, we'd invited all our friends and family and acquaintances and anyone else we could think of.

"Oh, my god," he said.

And for a second I thought Bart Lester was in the audience. Although Panos would have no idea who he was.

"What?"

"Warren Beatty is in the audience!"

I was as surprised as Panos. I had put Warren on the comp list the night before, just in case he remembered, but I hadn't expected him to show up.

"He's a friend of mine," I said, playing it off, but inside I was excited and relieved and delighted to be tethered to something familiar. This not only allayed my opening night anxiety but felt like a new chapter after my near love affair with a psychopath.

"Don't tell anyone he's in the audience," I said. "I don't want them to be nervous."

The curtains parted and we began.

When the time came, I blushed on cue.

9

Ding!

There once was a family of crabs living in a land of abundance. With enough real estate for everyone, the family was able to move about freely. One day, the crab elder went off to explore and came upon a clearing. He put one little leg onto the unfamiliar territory, only to find it barren and slippery and seemingly uninhabitable. He returned to his family and announced his findings.

"Do not go west," he pronounced.

He ventured east, only to find the same barren landscape. He returned and made his pronouncement, "Do not go east."

Another crab said, "That is strange but makes sense. It has started to feel a bit crowded of late. Like we were on our own small rectangle of land."

And so it was for these crabs.

Once humans started shaving and waxing and manscaping, viable real estate diminished. This leads me to wonder, where do pubic lice now live with barely a landing strip to inhabit? Or worse, with nothing but smooth skin. Do they simply slide off?

This was not a problem back in 1975. It was a bushier time when I got crabs. I was twenty-one and seeing Warren when he was free and/or thought of me, but I was also dating Elliot, who was funny and employed, and I liked the way he kept a cigarette in his mouth when he talked.

Somehow, I'd compartmentalized my time spent with Warren, or more accurately, he was on a parallel path alongside my "non-Warren life," and it was easy for me to cross over and back. And oddly, it felt like we shared that ability. He dated co-stars and then came back to me when he wasn't seriously seeing anyone (although maybe to him I was merely interstitial), and it created a romantic kinship in my mind. I met new people, although Warren remained my secret other life.

I'd met Elliot when he came into Walt Davis Enterprises to buy a Sony TV for work; we got to talking and we got to dating. He was an associate director at Swanson/Bailin Productions and mentioned there was an opening. I immediately said goodbye to Walt Davis and condom cleanup and started at Swanson/Bailin as an assistant (i.e., glorified gofer). My first job was to go to forty-seven supermarkets throughout the Southland to buy all the Pillsbury biscuit dough that existed. The food prep person baked them—group after group—until she had the perfect twelve. Truth in advertising.

Elliot and I spent most of that summer working on commercials, doing cocaine, and going to clubs where we danced under silver disco balls: KC and the Sunshine Band. Donna Summer. Georgio Moroder. It was a glorious time. Unless you didn't like disco. Or didn't like cocaine. But then again, you could also get poppers and Quaaludes.

And crabs.

Elliot lived in the Hollywood Hills. I felt very grown-up living on my own, helping him with dinner parties, and occasionally spending the night at his place. I was also seeing Warren at the time but had somehow reconciled that he was grandfathered in, having been my obsession from such a young age. I was successfully living the duality of seeing Warren and Elliot.

Elliot apparently had the same skill for secrets, as, after a work trip to Dallas, he returned with crabs.

"It must have been the mattress," he said.

I'd never had crabs. It was the grossest discovery to itch and then scratch and realize these little beings were living in my pubic hair.

Elliot seemed familiar with this problem and was quick to get a prescription for Kwell, which sounded like something you get to tamp down a public (pubic) uprising.

We got the crab situation under control, but not before I'd passed them along to Warren. I thought: That's it. He'll never forgive me. He'll never see me again. But he also seemed to take it in stride, and I wondered, "Has everyone had crabs except me?"

I told my brother Ted about the crabs. Ted was five years younger than I was, and it was like I was reporting back from the field of adulthood. He asked all about the crabs, what they looked like, how did you get them, and did they go away. From a very young age, he was worried about earwigs crawling into his ear, then into his brain where they'd lay eggs. It seemed like an urban myth or an old *Twilight Zone* episode, but his fear must have carried over to this fascination with crabs and the fear he might get them. I felt bad for having said anything to him.

By Christmas, I'd broken up with Elliot, which had nothing to do with crabs or his possibly sleeping with someone else but was more about my immature vision of love, which didn't take into account the initial hormone buzz wearing off. When it did, I was confused and thought, *This isn't working.* Or maybe I just didn't like him that much.

But it was still working with Warren. He was the perfect lover for me: he wasn't always available, and I never speculated about a future. Hence, I could say and do almost anything with him in the present without the fear that my words or subtly veiled needs would push him away. He was like a starter-boyfriend. That I wanted in my life forever.

On Christmas Day our family gathered for the long ceremony of opening gifts. The room was festive, with fake holly running up the banisters to the second floor. Fake frost on the windows, every flat surface covered with nutcrackers, Santas, and candles, and by the large front window, a Douglas fir overloaded with lights, tinsel, and ornaments. Like most siblings, my brothers and I loved Christmas. I loved having everyone in one room at the same time. Dad played Santa and would deliver one gift to each member of the family for a round of opening. As we each opened a gift, one at a time, we expressed gratitude but also gave a little witty commentary. Gramma Ruth often exceeded what felt like the family-accepted limit for glib commentary, going on about some gift that was "exquisite." Or maybe she simply wasn't funny enough. But we had a hotel bell, and if someone got too boring, *ding!*

There was a lot of pressure to be clever and entertaining, and if you spent too much time or expressed too much sentimentality, *ding!*

Halfway through our day of unwrapping presents, Ted was handed a small box. When it was his turn, he read the card (the gift was from me), unwrapped it, opened the box, looked puzzled, looked at me, and the realization washed over his face. I'd saved one of the crabs from six months before, and there it was, dead and nestled on the cotton in the jewelry box, hardly anything more than a poppy seed with legs. Before anyone could ask what it was, I hit the bell. *Ding!,* and Ted laughed. Moving on.

The following year, when Warren was making *Heaven Can Wait* and needed to learn how to play the soprano sax for the movie, I mentioned that my brother was a child prodigy and could teach him. They got together and Ted taught him a few things: How to hold the instrument, some basics on fingering and breathing, and how to form the proper embouchure.

If crabs were discussed, it wasn't mentioned to me.

Here's the thing about pubic lice—*ding!*

10

Fetch Ben Stein and Other Odd Requests

I'd been fired from Swanson/Bailin after breaking up with Elliot, who had gotten me the job, and I was having no luck so far with acting. My agent was some fly-by-night woman who once put my picture in *Variety* along with about four million other young, hopeful nobodies whose tiny faces live on in anonymity for those who may have saved the issue, i.e., me. My mantra was apparently: If at first you don't succeed, give up.

I was twenty-two, living alone, and unemployed. I still hoped for acting magic, but it was time to get a real job—if working in TV was considered a real job—and my dream was to work on the popular 1976 show called *Mary Hartman, Mary Hartman*—an absurdist and satirical farce about a bored housewife.

My mom and I loved the show—it provided a vague, triangular bond for us. Although I could understand my mom's attraction to the show's themes of suburban discontent and ambivalence, what surprised me was discovering that she had a girlish crush on Bruce Solomon, who played Sgt. Dennis Foley, and it made her act silly. Dad remembered that a fellow trombone player named Bobby was married to Viva Knight—the producer on the show—but when he asked Bobby about my getting a job there, Bobby groaned.

"I can't. Viva made me swear to stop asking her to interview people's kids." My charming dad sang my praises and Bobby said he'd try. He reported back: Viva would meet with me, but only a five-minute hello to get her husband off her back.

I found the offices on the KTLA lot on Sunset Boulevard, checked in with a secretary, and was ushered into a large office. I handed my very slim resume to this imposing woman with short blonde hair who appeared critical and unsmiling before I'd even sat down.

My work experience in entertainment consisted of two things which I tried to dress up with titles while downplaying the actual jobs. First was Walt Davis Enterprises, where I handled "sales and distribution," making no mention of porn or condoms. Next on the list was Swanson/Bailin Productions, where I was a "production assistant," which meant I was a gofer, and the only skill I'd demonstrated was my ability to drive and my ability to buy biscuits. This made for a resume that was mostly air, so I filled it in with a couple of items.

I wrote: "Went to Charm School when I was fifteen, but I don't think it worked," because I thought it was funny. I had, in fact, gone to Charm School when I was fifteen because one of the teenage girls next door had gone and I thought it sounded fun.

I learned three things in Charm School: 1) Not to mix gold and silver jewelry, which my mom had already taught me. 2) How to walk a runway, pause, turn, and walk back. I would never be a high-fashion model, but even now, I can do the end-of-the-runway turn. Sometimes I do it when I'm alone in an elevator. And 3) How to correctly enter a room—either in the daytime or the evening. I'd had no idea I'd been doing it wrong.

Entering a room involved putting one's forearm on the door jamb and pausing before entering. The difference was that daytime was more casual as the hand was placed on the same linear plane as the head, and you paused for about two seconds, whereas in the evening, the hand went up further, and the pause was five seconds, creating more drama and giving more time for champagne-drinking aristocrats at the gala to appreciate your gown This skill did not come into play when I was fifteen, nor did I see any evidence of the effect of Charm School on the teenage girls next door, who sipped leftover beer in the backyard and lit small fires with a magnifying glass while their dad was passed out somewhere.

On my slim resume, below the Charm School thing, I typed: "I have a nun's habit." I mentioned it because humor is the way my family covered up for deficiencies, like education. Plus, most people like a good laugh. And it was true.

The clock had started ticking on my five minutes. Viva looked over the resume. She asked me about Charm School, and I admitted I didn't have a lot to put on my resume and so I'd thrown that in. She asked what it was. I explained with feigned earnestness how I'd learned to enter a room depending on the time of day. It was hard to tell if she was getting my humor, but I played along with a serious face like this was a normal job interview.

"Show me how you would enter a room."

"Day or night?"

"Night."

I walked outside her door. Her secretary looked up and seemed on the verge of giving me an apologetic smile, like *Don't feel bad, Viva doesn't like anyone*. But I turned back toward Viva's office, stepped into the doorway, and placed my arm above my head on the door jamb. Full vamp. I waited five seconds and then strolled in, all feigned nonchalance and glamor.

Viva indicated the chair, and I sat back down.

She didn't smile. She looked back at my resume.

"You have a nun's habit," she said.

"Yes."

She tapped the resume on her desk as if it contained twenty pages. Set it back down and looked up at me.

"You're hired."

I learned many things about television production from Viva, but only two have stayed with me on a conscious level: Never go anywhere without pen and paper (in case she gave me a note or a phone number or a list of things to buy or do), and never distribute revisions that haven't been three-hole-punched. I only made that mistake once.

The first time I'd stepped into her office to deliver her un-punched script revisions, she took them from my hand, glared at me, and pretended to force them into a three-ring binder, saying, "Do you see the problem I'm having?"

Even forty years later, I'd make sure the PAs at the Conan O'Brien show knew to three-hole punch everything, although the pen-and-paper rule has been rendered obsolete by the advent of the cell phone, and paper revisions were becoming obsolete, as production companies have been switching to email and tablets.

As a production assistant at *Mary Hartman*, one of my many job tasks was manning the copy machine for show rundowns, scripts, budgets, editing notes, and deal memos. I made an extra copy of everything, which I saved and read at night to get an idea of what was going on in television production. Information is power, although in my case it was more like *looking stupid is embarrassing*. And since I knew pretty much nothing and was too afraid to ask, I taught myself after hours when no one was around.

In my spare time, I created a bible of facts for the show because the writers were always asking me to research things like, "Did we ever mention where Mary and Tom were married?" Or "How old is Cathy Shumway?" I gathered all the scripts and went through them at night, made notes of anything factual, created a bible, made copies, and distributed them to the writers.

Another one of my jobs was wearing costumes, which I might have guessed based on Viva's interest in the nun's habit reference on my resume. She liked that she had a willing participant who could keep a straight face and used me whenever she wanted for her snarky little comedic errands.

Al Burton was a Norman Lear executive who worked across the street at KTTV, and he and Viva spoke on the phone daily about the show. Al was a sweet man, small and twinkly like an elf. He'd been to our offices many times and was kind to anyone he encountered. He remembered people's names. He was a good counterbalance to Viva's often abrupt and dismissive nature. There was, however, a time when Viva needed Al for a meeting, and he was late.

She had wardrobe dress me up as a cop, and my job was to go across the street to whatever meeting Al was in, "arrest" him, and bring him back to Viva. When I entered Norman Lear's office, I spotted Al, walked straight to his chair and arrested him. He acted surprised (although he knew who I was), and he didn't resist. I kept a straight face, marched him back across the street, and delivered him to Viva. These antics seemed to delight her.

A few weeks later, Viva called me into her office. I grabbed a pen and paper and went in.

"Nikki, Ben Stein is coming into town next week. LAX. I would like you to fetch him."

"What flight?"

She gave me the details and I wrote them down.

She added, "I want you to wear your nun's habit and hold a sign that says, 'BEN STEIN.'"

"Of course."

I had no idea who Ben Stein was. Maybe he wasn't anybody at that point. Other than, well, himself. Ten years later, he would gain recognition as the economics teacher in *Ferris Bueller's Day Off,* and go on to star in the game show, *Win Ben Stein's Money.*

I made a professional-looking placard that read 'BEN STEIN,' drove my crappy VW to LAX, and found the other drivers who were waiting for arriving passengers. They were all men, all wearing black suits, white shirts, black ties, and black limo hats. I was wearing black and white as well, but it was the nun's habit. I settled in alongside them, holding my 'BEN STEIN' placard, as we waited for our clients to deplane. I didn't look around. I didn't know who I was looking for and figured Mr. Stein could read the sign I was holding and know what to do. A man approached and stood in front of me. He nodded. I nodded, took his bag, and we walked to the parking structure. Neither of us spoke.

I drove us back to KTLA, dropped Ben off in front of our offices, and went to park in the employee lot. I thought for a moment I'd offended him but was more hoping that we'd both appreciated—in our shared silence—the ridiculousness of the situation and were simply playing our parts.

Al Burton, the object of my faux arrest weeks earlier, came by one afternoon to see Viva, and when he saw me, he gave me the thumbs up and said, "Ben Stein. That was a good one."

He and I became pals.

Delivering scripts, I also learned more tangible things about TV production, schedules, and editing by visiting all the departments and studying what went on. Another part of my job was running errands, which included driving to a house somewhere in Laurel Canyon to pick up "pharmaceuticals" for Louise Lasser, who played Mary Hartman. Sometimes she wouldn't come out of her dressing room until I returned with said "pharmaceuticals." She spent as little time with other human beings as possible.

I was in my own small world of wonder. I had a new best friend, Ellen, who was the associate director (I wanted to be her when I grew up), and a budding friendship with Mary Kay Place, who played Loretta Haggers on the show. I was so immersed in all I was learning and all the fun people I worked with, that I forgot this was a show a lot of people watched. Not just my mom. This became more obvious when I was hospitalized for a week with an infection, and Greg Mullavey, who played Mary Hartman's husband, came by to see how I was.

I was surprised after he left to hear all the nurses aflutter with whispers of, "Do you know who that was?"

It was at *Mary Hartman* that I became friends with—and then dated—Martin Mull, who eventually had his own show, *Fernwood Tonight*. I'm not sure I ever gave this relationship a chance because I was pulled more toward alcohol, Quaaludes, and binge-eating, which didn't leave a lot of spare time, although I never missed work. It was like I had multiple personalities: I was the professional girl at work, the drunken party girl with Ellen, and the solitary bulimic when I needed a break from everything. Maybe I was more like Louise Lasser than I wanted to see at the time. Although I really liked Martin, I never let him see all sides of me, and instead, I ended up canceling plans with him when my crappier side emerged, choosing isolation rather than risk being seen and possibly rejected.

The only time I didn't feel the pull of these addictions was when I was with Warren. It wasn't like I was on good behavior; if anything, I was invigorated by him and felt myself with him.

Maybe I'd been starved to be myself with another person, having calibrated my responses and tamped down my neediness for so many years, but I felt an unexpected freedom with Warren. If he had been available all the time, or if I had thought we really might end up together, I might have slipped into the old patterns and become cautious, rejecting him out of fear as I had with Martin. The fear of having to hold my breath, be perfect, temper my addictions. Maybe deep down, I figured it wouldn't last with Warren, and therefore I had the freedom to be myself. Sometimes giddy and delighted, sometimes serious. But rarely cautious. Maybe because I was the one who chose when we had contact, or perhaps I sensed he wasn't really listening, so there was nothing at risk.

Whatever the case, this intermittent and unlikely love affair had already outlasted my other relationships, although it may have been a stretch to call it a love affair. It was more like a sexual relationship with someone whose main contribution was answering the phone when I called.

But still.

11

Headshots

I'd been studying acting for ten years, and at twenty-three, I had a total of one review to put on my yet non-existent acting resume. The *Hollywood Reporter* had sent someone to our tiny production of *A View from the Bridge* who wrote: "As Eddie's niece Catherine, Nikki Nash is probably the standout performer in the troupe. Though still not a seasoned professional, she breathes believability into the shut-in near-adult."

I had no idea that this would be my last play or that I would never become a "seasoned professional," but at the time I thought: *Here we go.* I was worried that if I continued working in TV production, I'd never get out; that this job at *Mary Hartman* could lead to other production work and, if so, when was I going to give the acting a shot? It was now or never. But first, I'd need headshots.

About headshots. Let's say you're an alien and, to get an idea of what humans are all about, you've chosen Hollywood as your starting point. (Maybe your first mistake.) You'd see a lot of young attractive people walking around with 8x10, black-and-white photos of themselves. You'd see a young man walk confidently into a building on Sunset Boulevard, his photo in his hand, and not long after, you'd see him exit the building, no longer holding the photo and looking a bit dejected. He'd light up a cigarette. You'd wonder: Was this currency?

Did humans buy cigarettes with photos? Why was the man sad? Had he run out of headshots to buy things?

Or you'd see a pretty girl go into a dry cleaner and place a photo of herself on the counter. Was this a way for the clerk to identify her clothes? Is that why the wood-paneled wall was covered with 8x10 photos of attractive people who had hand-written their names on their pictures? Or were they photos of people who had forgotten their clothes? Is that why the old photos were signed?

Or if you stopped in at Mel's Diner at 3 a.m., you'd observe young attractive people sitting in the booths looking at sheets of photos, the pictures so small they needed a magnifying device to discern minor differences. Were these inspectors of some kind, in charge of headshot approval and distribution? These people didn't look particularly professional or in charge of anything but usually lingered, having more coffee and then looking again at the hundreds of small photos, focused on the arduous process of circling some and crossing out others.

However, if you were not an alien but lived in Southern California or New York, you'd know headshots were 8x10, black-and-white photos of an actor's head. On the bottom of the photo was printed the actor's name, and stapled to the back was pertinent information: where she'd studied, what she'd done, her agent's contacts if she had an agent, and miscellaneous information she hoped would give her a leg up in casting: Can throw a baton, Can ride a motorcycle, Can swordfight, Can speak with an Irish accent. I can do one of those things. I'd been to a bookstore on Sunset to buy an anthology of monologues for acting class and also—on a whim—bought a cassette: "How to Speak with an Irish Accent." You know, like everyone my age was doing.

I found a photographer and he convinced me I didn't need just the headshot, but I should have the whole deal—a folio of sorts—with my face and name on the front as usual, but more shots of me inside, which was supposed to represent my wide range of acting talents.

I said *sure*. One picture showed me walking down the stairs in my parents' house with my brown hair in a ponytail; another is a photo of me in a white evening gown I'd found in a thrift store, which I'd accessorized with my mom's sparkly necklace and earrings, proving I was ready to stand next to James Bond at a baccarat table or drink champagne with fancy foreign diplomats, looking both attractive and intelligent. In another, I'm wearing a Russian fur hat for no reason while smiling like the blue-eyed California girl I was in 75-degree California weather. In another, I'm wearing a dress and a straw hat, and in another, I'm wearing a perky blouse and, yes, another hat, a bowler of some sort.

Maybe in addition to my skill "Can speak with an Irish Accent," I could add "Can wear hats."

In the last photo on the back, I'm sitting in a wheat field wearing a white two-piece bathing suit, because, what—I'm a farmer? Not that any of those acting jobs came my way. But if someone needed me to walk downstairs, stand at a poker table, or sit in a field, I was ready.

Maybe I didn't need all these photos. Maybe the photographer was charging by the outfit. Or by the hat. Like many of my endeavors, I'm more about presentation than depth, and I spent a lot of time picking the right paper, layout, and font for my name.

My focus on the superficial ran deep.

And would remain so for years.

When I eventually ended up working in television production full-time, I was often in meetings with executives and, because I always felt something else was better than what I was actually doing, I figured I'd make a good executive. So I bought a suit. I hadn't read scripts, taken writing classes, met with pitch people, or learned any financial aspect of the production business, but I had the suit. A red suit. I never wore it, and eventually, I gave it to a local thrift store. Maybe some young hopeful would buy it for her headshots to show she could play a businesswoman.

I never became an actress—or an executive for that matter—but I can still speak with an Irish accent.

12

Jules et Jim

I was frustrated and wanted to end it with Warren. Which in past relationships meant I would disappear without explanation. But for some reason, with Warren, I felt safe enough to speak up.

We were on the phone, and I said, "Why don't you ever call me? I'm always the one who calls you."

This was a scary thing to say, as I'd learned at an early age to suppress my needs. I took a risk and was hoping for a response that would include something along the lines of, "You're right. I'll try to call you more often," or "I can see how that would bother you," or even "It works having you call me, and I appreciate hearing from you."

I got none of these responses.

Warren took a moment and then said, "You call me. Why is that? I talk to you because I like you. I sleep with you because I like you. But admit there is a payoff for you. You get something out of this, right? Or you wouldn't continue to call me."

I was stunned, then I felt embarrassed, and then I felt busted. Because I liked calling him. I liked slipping in slyly to get a jolt from him when I needed it without having to admit I needed anything. After hearing his comment, my tendency would have been to make nice, get off the phone, and never talk to him again. But not wanting to disconnect so quickly from the fantasy Warren, I had to consider what the real Warren had said, and I agreed he might be right. We were both operating from the rules of an unspoken deal: I called, and he responded.

He wasn't abandoning me but pointing out the truth I was ignoring. I was also intrigued by the change in his voice when he answered my question. He didn't verbally pat me on the head and say I'm adorable. (I knew he didn't see me that way.) He didn't ignore the question or try to return to the more seductive tones to keep it light. He'd thought about it and had responded with the truth: my veiled seeking masked my deeper needs. He wasn't Svengali and I wasn't whatever-her-name-was who was under his sway. The sway was my choice, my experience. He was being real—which I liked—and I was feeling rejected—which I didn't like.

"Okay," was about all I could say, which was better than hanging up.

"And Nikki," he added, "I call you back because I want to. Because I like you."

"I like you, too."

"Good."

This may have been our first conversation that held any vague sense of conflict, and I was glad I hadn't shed a tear and moved on. Maybe if he hadn't been a long-time obsession, I would have disappeared, as I had with any other relationship when even the smallest-seeming conflict arose.

Warren was still living at the Beverly Wilshire, and I often spent the night there. Some nights, Jack Nicholson would drop by and order caviar and the three of us would spend an evening talking about how post-production was going on *Heaven Can Wait*, or what silliness was going on at *Mary Hartman*.

When I was twenty-four, Warren took me to a party at Jack's house on Mulholland Drive, where famous people swanned around, and a waiter circulated with a cereal-sized bowl filled with cocaine. Although I'd done some cocaine with Elliot when I'd worked with him on commercials, I hadn't yet discovered its diet and list-making benefits, and Warren didn't even drink—let alone do drugs—so the bowl passed us by unmolested.

Yet the three of us became friends. It reminded me of a Hollywood version of *Jules et Jim*—a 1962 movie my mother had loved—in which Jules and (*et*) Jim were both in love with Catherine. The three of them palled around in black-and-white France: two men in love with one woman. Although with Warren and Jack, it always felt more like they were in love with one another, and the women they occasionally shared were placeholders while one or the other was busy making a movie, providing the connecting filament between them. Not that I was sleeping with Jack, but that's the idea.

Jack got busy with a movie, and Warren and I continued seeing one another. He took me to the Playboy Mansion and wanted to introduce me to Pat Caddell, who was a political pollster—whatever that was. He had something to do with Jimmy Carter.

Warren said, "You'll like him. He's smart like you."

He wandered off and I was left standing on the grass near the grotto with Pat, and we talked politics. To clarify, he talked politics, and I listened and nodded. And to prove I was interesting and not just someone who was sleeping with Warren, I trotted out an old Black Panther story so as not to be confused with the other women at the party, who were mostly naked and semi-immersed in the grotto a few feet away. Nothing like being fully clothed to stand out in a crowd.

Another time at the mansion, Warren and I ended up talking to some woman, and the three of us went back to the hotel. He kissed me while he had sex with her—which I found very romantic—and after she left, he told me he loved me. Maybe he needed someone to see and accept this part of him, just as he seemed to see and accept me. Maybe that *was* love.

When Jack was again free, Warren and I stayed at his house after another party, and the next morning the three of us watched football. I knew enough about the game to say relevant things here and there, but mostly I felt like the third wheel.

After seeing Warren for a couple of years, lots of talking on the phone, and a few trips to Hugh Hefner's for parties, I occasionally felt like this whole thing was a fluke, like I was ultimately interchangeable with any number of women. Maybe he was with me because I was easy to be with and didn't fawn, but deep down I would say yes to anything he offered.

And now I was here with Warren at Jack's. The three of us were watching the game, and the two of them were talking. About women. What women want. Why Angelica Huston was finicky, and then Jack showed Warren a scarf he'd gotten for someone named Helena—for her birthday—and I listened, thinking Warren has *no* idea when my birthday is.

I was privately pouting when I heard him say to Jack, "You know what I like about Nikki?"

I'm sorry, what? I tried not to perk up too quickly, but it was weird to hear Warren using my name in a sentence as I'd never heard him talk about me to anyone.

"What?" Jack asked, looking over at me and then back at his pal Warren.

"She doesn't take my shit. If I say I'm coming over at nine and I don't get there till 9:30, there's a note on the door saying something about rescheduling. To call her the next day. I find this delightful."

"She sounds smart."

"And she's sitting right here," I said.

I hadn't previously given much thought to how he saw me, but now something in me shifted as I witnessed myself through his eyes. I was strong. I was my own person. Maybe I'd chosen him not to fill in my missing parts, but to show me I was more than my missing parts.

This exchange got Jack's attention—or maybe he was picking up the slack when Warren started working—and the next month he invited me to a Lakers game. He picked me up in a Rolls-Royce that was idling by the dusty ivy in front of The Fountain Lanai. I figured it was a one-time thing, then several months later, Jack invited me over for dinner. He and I were alone in the sprawling Mulholland house, but then an exotic woman appeared and made us Greek food for dinner. She was his live-in something (chef?), and when he said, "Thank you, Helena," it occurred to me this was the Helena Jack and Warren had talked about. Who'd been given a scarf for her birthday.

After dinner, Jack and I slow-danced in the living room, which seemed strange but may have worked with other women. Other than it being one of those out-of-body experiences (I'm dancing with Jack Nicholson?), it wasn't memorable in terms of any authentic connection. Maybe he was waiting to discover what Warren found so delightful about me. Or maybe he missed Warren, and I was the stand-in until he was back from a movie, just as I missed Warren and accepted Jack as the stand-in. Before I left, Jack kissed me. Nothing. Warren kissed like you mattered the most. Jack kissed like *he* mattered the most, and I knew I would never sleep with him, which put him on a pretty short list.

Eventually, Warren, Jack, and I continued our weird, seemingly platonic threesome when we went to a party at Robert Towne's house. Robert Towne had written *Chinatown* and *Shampoo*, among other things, and what I remember most about this night was that Jack and Warren were now both between movies, which provided a culinary green light, and they let themselves eat whatever they wanted. It wasn't like we were in the living room among the fancy guests, uniformed waiters gliding around with silver trays of canapés and caviar. No.

The three of us were in the kitchen, where the waiters and caterers rushed around, ignoring us. Jack had the fridge wide open and was forking hunks of cheesecake into his mouth. Warren did the same, albeit not as ravenously. I don't remember any other guests in the kitchen with us. Just an occasional glance from a waiter passing through while I watched Jack and Warren eat cheesecake out of the fridge.

At one point, leaning on the refrigerator, Warren told Jack he'd had a weird dream his teeth were falling out, and Jack said that meant he was afraid of his declining sexuality. It was like being with two girls who were chatting away while snacking. Then came a lively lexicological discussion about word choice and usage. In this case, Jack asked Warren which he preferred: "cunt" or "pussy." Warren preferred "pussy" because it didn't sound so hostile. Jack disagreed. He thought "pussy" was too soft. I wasn't consulted. Although I interpreted being a witness to the conversation as an indicator of the comfort level they had with me. Or maybe they'd forgotten I was there. It was hard to tell with them.

A year and a half later, I was working as a script supervisor on *Roller Girls* (a sitcom about female roller derby and an excuse to feature five young girls either putting on or taking off short shorts in a locker room), and I started dating Brandon Tartikoff, who was the NBC executive on the show. Jack and Warren were working on *Reds*. Warren was dating Diane Keaton, and Jack had gone back to Anjelica Huston. It seemed we'd all gone our separate ways—the end of an era. Maybe my time palling around with luminaries had come to an end.

Then Brandon and I broke up—maybe I'd slept with him too quickly. But I took it gracefully, only doing one or two drunken drive-bys of his house in Westwood.

And now I was single. Again.

And then Jack called.

13

Jack Nicholson and the Skydiving Story

I was twenty-five when I almost died. It wasn't drugs, but skydiving. Many of my adventures were the result of saying yes to whatever was presented, without much consideration or expectation.

Wanna be in a Robert Altman movie? *Sure.*
You should try stand-up. *Okay.*
Wanna get a tattoo? *You bet.*
How about a three-way? *Why not?*
You should start painting. *I'll get some paints!*
Here's a Quaalude. *Thank you.*
Ever played poker? *I can learn.*
Let's go skydiving. *When?*

I knew close to nothing about most of these things, but that didn't stop me from saying yes to all of them at some point. It wasn't that I was a grand adventurer, but these activities bought me time to avoid the pressure of figuring out what I should do with my life. And adventures gave me something to talk about. I also found it easier to avoid embarrassing failure when the idea wasn't mine in the first place. I merely stumbled forward into whatever might happen, whatever was next offered. I was either stupid or fearless. Or maybe naive and fearless. Or maybe this was exactly how I wanted to live my life, and I didn't know it at the time. A life of *yes*. But was it the *yes* of action or an abdication of choice?

I'd first heard of skydiving—albeit in the abstract—when I was in high school. I was between classes when a tall, dynamic, blonde girl came down the hall and caused a stir. She had gone to Reseda High a few years before me and had been popular and I heard other girls in the hallway talking about her in mythic terms. What I remember most was the sotto voce wonderment when they said, "Did you know she goes skydiving?!"

I stored this away. Skydiving. Which may have been shorthand for: Do this and people will speak of you in mythic terms; you'll be popular in the abstract.

And then I forgot about it.

Until I was twenty-five.

I was working as a script supervisor (Wanna be a script supervisor? *Sure!*) on a sitcom called *A New Kind of Family,* starring Eileen Brennan and some fifteen-year-old kid named Rob Lowe who was playing a fifteen-year-old kid named Tony. Just another young wannabe trying for his shot in Hollywood, I thought, like I was some jaded, middle-aged woman whose life had passed her by, having myself failed at acting.

In addition to having a minor story about working with Rob Lowe, *A New Kind of Family* provided me with a couple of life's unexpected turning points.

1. I was invited to join the Directors Guild (I wasn't sure what that was, but *Okay!*), and
2. I became friends with Don, the lighting director. He had always wanted to try skydiving and asked if I wanted to go. (Sure! Skydiving!)

Don and I drove to Perris, California, a dusty rundown area where it all seemed like low buildings, dogs on chains, and cars on blocks when we came upon a hamlet of risk-takers easy to spot by their proximity to the planes—a DC-3 and a couple of smaller Cessnas. After parking, we walked past the parachute-folding tables in a large open-air structure, beyond which was the "drop zone," which was nothing more than a circle of dirt where you were supposed to land after jumping out of a plane. You'd choose your exit point from the plane based on a small orange windsock.

There was also a bar called the Bomb Shelter, which was nothing more than a hot, metal barracks-like building next to a small, chipped swimming pool. I was attracted to the friendliness of those around me, the sense of inclusion and camaraderie, as well as the secret language these people spoke. I loved knowing a secret language, learning new words, feeling initiated into an elite tribe. The first day, Don and I heard murmurings someone had "bounced," which was skydiver-speak for landing on the ground without having successfully opened one's chute, i.e., dying. It turns out the bounce happened in Lake Elsinore, which was a competing skydiving facility with its own bar called The Drop Zone.

I noticed that the instructors and the other students took this news in stride as if it wouldn't happen in Perris, so Don and I put on our jumpsuits and were given helmets and heavy army boots. The first test was to see if we could jump off a nearly nine-foot ledge, which involved looking at the horizon, keeping one's knees loose, and imagining yourself rolling the moment you feel your boots touch the earth. The drop-and-roll. They started us off with a jump from a bench, then from a table, then a six-foot ladder, and finally we jumped off the nine-foot wall. This was back before first-timers exited the plane in tandem with seasoned jumpmasters and when they still used round army surplus parachutes rather than the rectangular ones they later used. The old round chutes slowed the descent enough to avoid death, but the landing still needed to be handled to avoid injury. Drop and roll.

By the afternoon, the winds were calm, and we were directed to head over to the beat-up DC-3 that was sitting on the crappy little runway. Once inside the hollowed-out plane, Jumpmaster Jeff attached us to a static line that would open our chutes for us in case we froze or had a heart attack once we'd jumped out of the plane.

The DC-3, like a tired metal whale, rumbled across the runway and lifted off, and something felt absolutely wrong about going up into the sky with a wide-open maw at the back end. I hoped they'd close it up soon until I realized that was where I was headed in a few minutes. The waiting was deadly. Once connected to the static line, all we had to do was sit on the ledge on the back of the plane, take in the whole planet below us, and fall forward like a drunk into his soup while arching and stretching our arms.

When it was my turn, Jumpmaster Jeff gave me the signal to sit down at the edge of the plane. My feet dangled in the open air. He reminded each one of us, yelling over the roar of the engine and the wind, to arch. The arching was the most important thing, as without it, you'd tumble about and the parachute could wrap around your body. And you'd most likely bounce. More experienced jumpers carried a knife so they could "cut away" the tangled lines of a faulty or mis-packed parachute and open the reserve. We had enough to think about with "arch" and "drop and roll"—and general, overall panic—to worry about knives.

Jumpmaster Jeff gave me the signal to go, and I fell forward, arching my ass off.

My chute opened immediately—due to the static line—and now all I had to do was feel the adrenaline and the relief and rushing wind on my face, which also felt strangely like silence. I rolled successfully, experienced my heart beating in a new way, gathered up my chute, and walked back to the folding tables. I lived.

And then we went back up and did it again.

Don and I returned the following weekend for more of the same. And by that I mean terrifying and fantastic. I would later try stand-up comedy (*Sure, why not?*) and found that standing off-stage waiting for my name to be announced felt much like sitting on the edge of a plane waiting for the jumpmaster to say go. Both brought on feelings of "Why the fuck did I sign up for this? And is it too late to change my mind?" Followed by (if things went well) a feeling of euphoria and relief.

It wasn't until the third weekend in Perris—when we'd graduated from the DC-3 to the Cessna—that I almost died. My first thought was *I'm lucky to be alive*. My second thought was *This will make for a really good story*.

I hadn't seen Warren for a few months and wasn't sure if I'd see him again—but then I often felt like the last time would be the last time—so when Jack called out of nowhere and invited me to a dinner party at his house, it felt like an indirect connection to Warren. Plus, I was feeling blue after the break-up with Brandon. So *Sure, why not?*

I drove up to Jack's place, which was familiar to me after our strange dancing date the year before. I was wearing dark pants and a silk blouse. I was hoping Warren would make a surprise visit and then hoped he wouldn't because I didn't want to see him with Diane Keaton. Or have him see me with Jack. But it was just me and Jack standing around awkwardly until the doorbell rang.

In came the dinner guests. No Warren. I don't know what I was expecting but in walked Michael Douglas and his wife, kisses and hellos. And then Michael Caine and his wife, followed by Sean Connery and his wife. Great. *Hello. Nice to meet you.* What??!!

It was a beautiful spring evening in the Hollywood Hills. I was out of my element (if I had an element), and at twenty-four, I was younger than these luminaries and their luminous wives (and their starry names: Diandra, Micheline, and Shakira), and I wasn't the least bit famous. I mean, sure, I'd been in a Bob Altman movie. But still.

We gathered at the large table in the middle of the large room, and somehow, I was at one end of the table and Jack at the other. A waiter, or someone in a black and white outfit, had delivered our drinks. I was unusually quiet. Intimidated. There was a lull, and I wasn't good with lulls. But then again, this wasn't my party, and I didn't have to carry the ball of scintillating conversation. I could sit quietly, listening and smiling until dinner was over, and probably no one would notice that I hadn't spoken since hello.

Jack didn't see it that way. "Tell them the story, Nikki."

"Which one?"

"The one you told me on the phone." He commanded attention. His guests looked at me with expectation. "When you almost died."

"Really?" I asked.

A couple of the wives gave me a nod of encouragement.

"Okay," I said, looking at Jack as if to say, if this falls flat it's on you. (*Oh, that Jack and Nikki. Such a fun couple.*)

"So," I began, "I was skydiving last week. We were up in an old Cessna. It was my fifth time and Jumpmaster Jeff had explained how we'd exit the plane, and I trusted him with my life, quite literally, as he had also packed my parachute. I was up first."

I looked around the table to make sure no one was nodding off. All good. I continued.

"We were told to reach out of the plane and put our hands on the strut under the wing and then step out, putting our feet on the wheel. We were trained to keep mentally and visually connected to our jumpmaster, and the most important thing to remember, when it was time to step off the wheel, was to arch."

I demonstrated the arch, putting my arms out like Jesus on the cross, and explained the importance of arching. The whole tangling thing.

"I'm mentally preparing and I look at Jumpmaster Jeff. He shouts at me over the roar of wind and the plane, 'Okay, take your feet off the wheel.' I took my feet off the wheel, ready to hang by my hands on the strut until he said *go*, but I slipped off the plane. I couldn't hold on, so there I went head over heels, over and over, sky, ground, sky, ground. I didn't consciously think about what to do, but at maybe five hundred feet, something kicked in and I arched, got stable, and brought my left hand to my belly and my right hand to the handle and pulled, bringing both arms back out into Jesus position."

I made the motion but realized it probably looked more like a flasher opening his coat.

I looked around at the guests. Famous men and lovely wives were staring at me with wonderment. One or two looked over at Jack and then back at me.

"My chute opened, and I landed without much room to spare and seconds later, Jumpmaster Jeff landed next to me. He was more panicked than I was and said, 'Don't ever do that again to me!' Like it was a practical joke or something."

"Oh, my god," a couple of the women at the table said.

Jack looked at me—one eyebrow raised as I'd seen him do in the movies—and said in a low, conspiratorial voice, "But then you went back up and it happened again."

I nodded. Like we'd had this long relationship, and he knew all my stories.

"Yeah, I fell off the plane again. I'm an idiot. Or I have small hands. But after that, we figured out a different way of exiting the plane."

I'd come to the end of the story, and anything after this was a step into the boring "look-at-me" territory. Plus, dinner was served. Jack and I may have looked like a couple familiar with one another, but he felt more like a stranger to me, and I was simply playing the female lead in this little movie. Although not the part of silent arm candy but of a bold raconteur who had enthralled my fellow dinner guests with my tale of fearless—or foolish—adventure.

I left when the other guests left, maybe to avoid kissing Jack.

I never saw him again. Except in the movies.

14

The Oscars

The intended prey went to the mailbox and discovered a letter-sized white envelope with only a name—in block letters—written on the front. No address, no return name or address, no stamp. Meaning the stalker had been there and had slipped this into the mailbox. The night before? That morning? Just now? Inside the envelope was a single ticket for the *1812 Overture* at the Hollywood Bowl and a short note—also in block letters: "If you are up for an adventure, show up. I have the other ticket."

No signature. Only a phone number.

The prey called the number that afternoon.

PREY: I got your intriguing note in my mailbox. I'm flattered, but I'm not available.

STALKER: It was worth a try.

PREY: Yes. Thank you. (Awkward silence.) If you'd like to pick up the ticket, I can hold onto it for you. Or I can mail it back. Although I don't have your address.

STALKER: You're very kind. And I feel foolish. I'll stop by and pick it up. When is a good time?

PREY: I'll be home this evening. You obviously have the address.

The stalker, who had gotten the address from one of the talent bookers on the Academy Awards where the stalker and prey had crossed paths, drove up to the home in the Hollywood Hills. Knocked on the door.

The prey was with other people but invited the stalker in. There was a lot of drinking and laughing and telling of the *1812 Overture* tickets story, and the prey ended up inviting the stalker over the following night for a drink.

I'D CROSSED PATHS WITH ROBERT Hays a few months before when he'd been a presenter at the Academy Awards and around the time he made it big with *Airplane!* It was 1980, and Blondie's *Call Me* competed with Michael Jackson's *Rock With You* for the same thing: the satisfaction of lust. I was twenty-six, boy crazy, and working on the Oscars, the first of four Oscar shows I'd work on as a script supervisor.

I had developed the skill of being boy crazy right along with being a hard worker. I could somehow give my all to both, although perhaps the former fueled the latter. I worked hard on the show and although I was rarely star-struck, I loved seeing Robert Hays in person. He was tall with thick dark hair, a boyish face, and a welcoming smile. He reminded me of Warren, albeit a perkier and less complicated version.

Although this was my first time working on the Oscars, it wasn't my first time being *at* the Oscars. My first experience had been with my dad when I was five. He had played trombone in the orchestra for the show and would continue to do so for many years. But back then, it was before Reagan had been shot, before celebrities had personal security, before selfies, before TMZ, and before anyone cared who came and went. As a child, I wandered around the Shrine Auditorium by myself while the orchestra rehearsed. I loved the empty theater and ran up and down the aisles until the break, when I got to have lunch with my dad.

When I was a teenager, my mom and I had a ritual of watching the show together. She'd put out lox and bagels, we'd dress up in sparkly outfits, and when the show was over, we'd wait to hear the garage door open, and into the den came Dad, wearing his fake tux made from a suit and a bow-tie and a cummerbund my mom had sewn. Dad didn't know much about movie stars, but he knew about music, and it was fun learning, for example, that when the best movie was about to be announced, the musicians all had five different pieces of sheet music on their stands, one for each movie, and as soon as the winner was announced, they had to grab the right piece of music, look at the conductor for the downbeat and launch into the winning theme.

Three years before I'd actually started working on the show, I'd been invited to the Sunday rehearsal and the Monday broadcast by Tim Steele, a friendly network executive I'd met somewhere along the line. The Oscars had moved over to the Dorothy Chandler Pavilion, and it was exciting to see behind the literal curtain as people ran around on stage doing important things.

Watching the rehearsals, I was mesmerized by a dynamic woman with red hair—I'd later learn she was the script supervisor, Danette Herman—running the talent through their paces for the next night's live show. It was fun seeing the stars, but for me, it was all about watching Danette at work. I had once wanted to be an Oscar winner. Now I wanted to be Danette.

My dad was still down in the pit with the other musicians. I'd waved down at him when Tim and I came into the theater, and just as when I was five, I had lunch with Dad during the break.

Tim knew I wanted to work on the Oscars and, once the show was wrapped, recommended me to Danette. I went into the offices for an interview, but it felt more like she was doing it for Tim and had no sincere interest in me. *Thank you and goodbye.* I didn't even get to meet the director, the infamous Marty Pasetta.

Two years later, Danette was moving up to talent coordinator/booker and needed a script supervisor to take her place. I got a call to come in and meet Marty Pasetta. I mentioned the upcoming interview to an audio guy I was working with and he clued me in: Marty had a trick question he asked, and if you knew the answer you'd most likely get the job.

I went into Marty's office. He was a block of granite in a grey cardigan, and he had a pock-marked face, maybe from childhood acne, although it was nearly impossible to imagine him as a child. It looked like he'd been sitting in his worn leather chair for decades, never smiling.

I sat down. Handed him my slim resume, which he took from my hand without looking at me.

After a cursory read-through he asked, "Do you know what user bits are?"

There it was. The trick question. He wasn't looking at me, but I knew he was listening.

I said, "When pre-taping music numbers to a pre-recorded track, the audio guy will lay down one stream of info—user bits—on the recorded track. Since most takes are noted by the time of day timecode, it's easier in editing to connect each take to the user bits on the track, rather than trying to sync up each take to the frame manually."

Marty looked at me. Silence.

"Or something like that," I added.

"Okay, you're hired," he said, looking away. He busied himself with papers, which I took as my cue to leave his office.

The script department's job was stressful and non-stop, as we were in charge of creating the master script, which included: collecting information for the staff and crew list with all phone numbers and addresses, gathering all the presenters' names and slugging them into the correct categories, creating a phonetic breakdown of nominees' names and movie names (for example, in 1980 the French film *Mon Oncle D'Amerique* was nominated for a writing award, but an actor might not speak French, so phonetics were important.) We were in charge of breaking down the music with lyrics for the five nominated songs and overseeing the pre-recording of the music to confirm the breakdown matched what we'd put in the script, and I was finally grateful for the ten years of piano lessons as I knew meter and bar counts. We included the rehearsal schedule, seating assignments for nominees so the cameramen would know whom to shoot for each award and reaction shots, and countless other details that had to be right, or you'd be yelled at. Once it was all gathered, this massive hand-typed script was driven to a mimeo house for copying. But before the script left the building, it had to be reproduced on a slow copier in the office—one page at a time—in case the runner driving the original got into a fiery crash and all was lost. The mimeo house made hundreds of copies and early the next morning we would label and distribute the scripts to everyone.

And not to sound all five miles in the snow, but in 1980 there was no tapping a *send* button. No email, no cell phones, no texting, no answering machines, no computers, no printers. Fax machines were starting to arrive on the scene, but I don't remember us having one. What this meant was, if anything changed, forty or more people had to be called on the landline telephone (we were lucky we had push-button and not rotary phones—this saved us, well, minutes), and we'd give them the changes verbally. Revisions were then typed up, and runners were gathered to drive these paper revisions to offices and homes all over Los Angeles. We didn't even have Post-its. Or liquid Wite-Out. We had to use a small plastic rectangle of compressed white powder to type over mistakes. Most of us in the script department were supplied with IBM Selectrics, which were electric typewriters rather than manual typewriters, but we could never guarantee the font ball that came with the Selectric was what we needed for the script, so we all had our own Courier font balls we brought from show to show.

In addition to the nearly endless paperwork and revisions, there was navigating all the personalities. Howard W. Koch was the producer (also one of the executive producers of *Airplane!*), and his secretary—who would have been called a battleaxe if this had been the 1930s—was fiercely protective and made sure everyone knew that any correspondence directed to her boss *must* refer to him as Howard W. Koch. I respected her attention to detail and her demands as the gatekeeper, but I also had a friendly relationship with Howard.

Toward the end of production, I needed to send a memo over to his office and wrote:

TO: Howard W. Koch
FM: Nikki W. Nash
RE: The Academy W. Awards

No one seemed ruffled by this. Or maybe no one noticed.

Around this time, I'd been dating an actor from the sitcom *Barney Miller*, and by dating I mean I drove an hour at night to his house in Topanga Canyon to climb up a ladder and sit on the roof with him while he smoked pot. We were drifting apart—or maybe we couldn't see one another through the haze of pot—and Warren was busy making *Reds,* which is when I met Robert Hays.

I'd seen *Airplane!,* the movie that would make him a star as well as provide people with catchphrases, like "Does anyone speak jive?" Robert was handsome and tall and kind. He reminded me of Warren, although he had a self-deprecating style that I wouldn't see in Warren until he played Lyle Rogers in *Ishtar* (although he couldn't completely let go of being all Warren Beatty). But now I was showing Robert around the stage, rehearsing his entrance with him. I realized it was going to take more than just crossing paths at the Oscars for something to happen.

I had already bought two tickets for the *1812 Overture.* I had a habit of buying the tickets every spring, thinking surely I'd have a boyfriend by August. ("Don't call me Shirley.") The *1812 Overture* was so damn sexy with its slow build and eventual shooting of cannons. I mean, come on. It was like *Bolero* but with less foreplay. I had two tickets and no one to go with.

I got Robert's address from a friend in the talent department, put one of the tickets in an envelope with my short note: "If you are up for an adventure, show up. I have the other ticket," and I drove up to his house in the Hollywood Hills. I put the envelope in his mailbox.

And I waited.

After a few drunken evenings, we started dating, although for me there wasn't a big difference between a drunken evening and dating. But I tried to straighten up and he was sweet and gallant and a little more formal than I'd anticipated, based on both how silly he was in the movie, as well as how we'd first gotten together. I didn't feel completely myself with him as I kept trying to tamp down my wilder side, and all the tamping got in the way of the relationship, and although we stopped seeing each other romantically, we remained friends.

The following year, I was brought back to work on the Oscars, which was scheduled for Monday, March 30. Which was the day Reagan was shot in Washington, DC. John Hinckley Jr. was trying to impress Jodie Foster by attempting to assassinate the president. The assassination attempt threw a wrench into the Academy Awards telecast, and the decision to cancel or continue with the show that night was debated. Back and forth. Pros and cons, and the show ended up being rescheduled for the following night.

We experienced another near show-stopping wrench-in-the-works the following year when Marty's binder, which had maybe 300 pages of script and info and blocking and shots and special effects notes—the bible for directing the show—went missing the night before the big day. And so the script team, stage managers, and cameramen stayed up all night with Marty as we recreated his script from scratch. We were aided by amphetamines provided by someone's wife. The show must go on. A binder-minder was then hired whose sole purpose was to carry the binder (as if it were the nuclear football) wherever Marty went—a tradition that carried on for years.

Although I would go on to work with Marty the following year on the Oscars, and on several other shows, for some reason this show took it out of me. Maybe it was the amphetamines. I don't remember the particulars, but I do remember the feeling of working day and night for six weeks and then our job was done once the show was on the air. We'd been indispensable one moment and obsolete the next. Above-the-line people, i.e., not the staff and crew, went to a party afterward to congratulate one another for the well-deserved recognition of a show well done.

I went home and crashed.

I never doubted the quality of my work, but when I went into the offices to collect my Selectric typewriter Courier ball (take my ball and go home) and to file any paperwork I needed to keep for the following year, I thought: Where's the 'thank you' to the script department? Or the crew, for that matter? I was paid, which, admittedly, was all I was guaranteed, but still.

I went into the supply room at Marty's offices, pulled a sheet of Pasetta Productions stationery and an envelope, addressed both to myself, and typed myself a thank you note for all the hard work our department had put in. A lot of kind words about the "solid team," the "success of the production," and ended with: "As you know, there is hardly a minute to say thank you after the chaos of the show, so I am taking that opportunity now. Thank you."

And I typed, "Sincerely, Marty Pasetta," with a space for his signature.

I brought the letter and the envelope into Suzy's office, Marty's secretary, and put it in the inbox for Marty to sign.

A week later I got a phone call from Suzy, who told me she'd put the letter in front of Marty, who'd read it, and then looked at her. Confused. Suzy explained to Marty the letter had come from me. That I had written it. More befuddlement as he thought this over. She said she was anxious standing there. But then, she said, not only had Marty signed the letter to me, but he then had Suzy send individual letters to everyone on the staff and crew thanking them for their hard work.

MY DAD CONTINUED TO PLAY in the orchestra every year, and I still, from time to time, saw Bob Hays as a placeholder of sorts for Warren, who was a placeholder for an imaginary love that might solve everything. Just as I may have been Bob's placeholder for a more god-fearing, less complicated girlfriend.

But Mr. Hays lives on. Nearly forty years later I was the associate director on *Conan*, where we—the crew—occasionally played a game that was standard fare on most shows I'd worked on, usually to let off steam after a difficult rehearsal. On this particular day, we were in the calm after the storm of a tense afternoon, and a cameraman started things off. We were all on headset, so it was an intimate exchange among the crew only. A shared private riff featuring all the one-liners from *Airplane!*

Cameraman: "I picked the wrong day to stop sniffing glue."
Stage Manager: "A hospital? What is it?"
SFX Guy: "A place where sick people go."
Graphics: "Jim never vomits at home."
Tape Playback: "Do you like Gladiator movies?"
Director: "Ever seen a grown man naked?"

At which point I always wanted to say, not only had I seen a grown man naked, but I'd seen Robert Hays naked. A bunch of times. But I never said this. It wasn't "look at me" time; you don't break up a square dance with a solo. It was family time, and these guys were my family; I was beyond delighted to be living this moment with them. In all our silliness and shared references.

Instead, I said, "Surely you can't be serious."
The Lighting Guy said, "Don't call me Shirley."
And then it was back to work.

15

How Lovely to Be a Woman

I got engaged to Karl when I was twenty-seven and I blame Ann-Margret. Karl lived in Las Vegas and was Ann-Margret's lighting and sound guy, and maybe by extension, I thought I'd get some of her stardust and have a fabulous, glamorous life. And maybe red hair.

When I was nine, I saw *Bye Bye Birdie*, and I wanted to *be* Ann-Margret. Dad had the movie soundtrack, and although Ann-Margret may not have been the best singer in the world—as my mom pointed out—I didn't care. I wanted to be her when I grew up. She could sing and dance and entice, as well as entertain herself alone in her room for hours. What more could a girl want? Attention *and* solitude.

She sang "How Lovely to Be A Woman," which would be decried now as anti-feminist, but to me, Ann-Margret *was* a feminist role model. Ann-Margret did whatever the hell she wanted; she wasn't embarrassed to be sexy while remaining kind. When I hear Ann-Margret as Kim singing "How Lovely to Be A Woman," it's from the point of view of the girl/woman looking outward. She is in charge of her own presentation and recognizes her effect with lightness and humor—a young woman enjoying makeup and still calling the shots. Why choose Eleanor Roosevelt as a role model when you could be Ann-Margret?

Parents in the '60s were quite aware of Ann-Margret because she aroused the dads and made the moms nervous, but despite this, when

I was eleven, my mom showed up at Tarzana Elementary and told the teacher she needed to take me out of school for personal reasons. I didn't know what was going on and Mom wouldn't tell me. We drove to RCA Studios in Hollywood where my dad was on a record date. With Ann-Margret! There she was, with her thick red hair and twinkly eyes. My dad introduced me to her, and then I listened to her sing for a while. During a break, it was picture time. Dad had his camera in his trombone case, which wasn't out of the ordinary because he was always taking pictures, his face behind a camera for most of our childhood.

Dad pulled out the silver comb he kept in his wallet, and I thought maybe my hair was messy—my pixie cut was growing out—but he handed the comb to Ann-Margret, who'd indicated to him that she looked disheveled in some way. She was wearing a white sleeveless dress with tassels at the bottom. She knew how to stand for a photo.

> *How lovely to have a figure*
> *That's round instead of flat,*
> *Whenever you hear boys whistle,*
> *You're what they're whistling at!*

I was wearing a dress my mom had made with fabric imprinted with really sexy Revolutionary War memorabilia, and I posed next to Ann-Margret, one of us embarrassingly flat-chested. I still made a vague attempt at attitude with one hand on my hip. Early documentation of the popular teapot pose.

Not only did I love movie soundtracks, but movie soundtracks also brought my family together.

My dad played trombone on a lot of them, and my brothers and I liked dancing around the living room to songs like "The Baby Elephant Walk," from the movie *Hatari!* We'd put a cheek to a shoulder and pretend one arm was a trunk and swing it around to the music. My parents had a lot of albums from the movies my dad had worked on, from *Breakfast at Tiffany's* to *Planet of the Apes*, and a lot of our family entertainment came in audible form, sitting around the living room listening to a sound effects record, playing fun games like "raise your hand if you can still hear the tone," and "name that sound" (it was bacon frying). This was back before video games. Back before Pong even, where the player bounced an electronic ball back and forth across the screen. Hours of fun, like watching a metronome in slow motion.

We also did radio shows. Dad set up the music stands with microphones and copies of a script—usually detective stories—and we'd each play a role, one of us enacting footsteps on the large board Dad had brought in from the garage. I loved these times together.

Soundtracks also bridged the gap between accepted music and "that crap,"—which is how my dad described rock music—allowing "One Last Kiss"—an obvious rock and roll song from *Bye Bye Birdie*—to fall into the acceptable category of soundtrack, rather than the dumpster that was "that crap." I could feign an interest in the soundtrack when it was the rock and roll I was craving. I thank my brother Bill for defiantly introducing the family to other kinds of music. He'd inherited a bunch of albums from an older cousin who'd passed through town, records like Quicksilver Messenger Service, Cream, Jimi Hendrix, and Big Brother & the Holding Company.

As a teenager, I loved "Piece of My Heart" for the wild and raw nature of Janis Joplin, although, unlike Ann-Margret's confident anthem, the song is plaintive and pleading, a woman begging for love to the degree that she'd give everything to a man, including internal organs. I sang both Janis Joplin and Ann-Margret songs with great fervor in front of the living room mirror, although it is Ann-Margret who stayed with me. Her lyrics would provide an unexpected soundtrack while I went through my life—sometimes encouraging me and sometimes mocking me.

AFTER WORKING ON THE OSCARS, I could almost keep it together with the alcohol and the cocaine, but it was the underlying depression that got me. Or maybe it was the depression—perhaps inherited from my mom and Gramma Ruth—that led to the need for alcohol and cocaine. I had a harder time keeping my public and private selves separate, and I spiraled downward. I could rise above briefly with the burst of energy and charm that came from a new love affair, and give the appearance of enthusiasm and connection to someone, the falseness of which left me further in the hole. I had no business being in a relationship; I could barely stand to be in the same room with myself.

> *How lovely to be so grown-up and free!*
> *Life's lovely when you're a woman—like me!*

And then I met Karl, who not only worked for Ann-Margret but for Frank Sinatra. I was the script coordinator for the Reagan Inaugural in Washington, D.C., where Sinatra was the headliner. I was a mess, and any appearance of confident independence was beginning to slip. I couldn't see my way through the depression, which further contributed to the slavery of drugs and alcohol. I didn't know how much longer I could fake it. Fine, but really dying.

I needed a solution, and in this case, it was—unfortunately for him—Karl.

Karl was older than I was, had a great smile, and he lived in Las Vegas. His quiet confidence seemed to me like another sign of comforting maturity. He never rushed around and that calmed me. Our flirtations were sweet as we were the go-betweens for production and Sinatra, and after a few days, we were off and running. My parents loved him, and my brother Bill thought he was great. Karl steadied me. But in addition to my seeing him as an anchor, the cokehead in me also saw him as someone who could more easily afford cocaine than I could. When I introduced him to the insidious white powder, it embarrassed me to see him go along with it, if only because he loved me and wanted to make me happy. I didn't need someone to go along with me. I needed someone to stop me. But how would he have known that.

> *How lovely to be a woman,*
> *And have one job to do:*

To pick out a boy and train him,
And then when you are through,
You've made him the man you want him to be

The only thing to keep my head above water was a work ethic that pulled me through the darker times. I always showed up for work. I always worked hard and did a good job, and I felt a boost when I started working as an associate director, a job I'd seen depicted in *Diner*. One of the characters was a girl who worked for a sports show. She had a stopwatch and counted backward from ten. She was an associate director! And I realized that becoming an associate director was, in fact, the perfect job for me. She looked happy. I'd be happy.

And hey! I could count backward from ten, so now all I needed was a stopwatch. I was practically there.

However, drugs and alcohol have a way of muddling one's thoughts, and the consideration of a life with Karl—who drank as much as I did—provided one possibility of escape from making any real changes in myself: I could move to Las Vegas. The concept, "Wherever you go, there you are," was not yet part of the lexicon, although it wouldn't have resonated with me at the time. It didn't occur to me that my unhappiness would remain, but now I'd be in Las Vegas. As I continued to fall apart, my only options were: a) break up with Karl, b) kill myself, or c) go on a diet. Stopping all the alcohol and pharmaceuticals was not on the list. A life without alcohol wasn't worth living, and really, what was the point of having to be on the planet with other people if not for the reward of a cocktail or five at the end of the day?

But instead of getting sober or maybe even getting therapy, I got engaged.

Maybe Karl had his own demons, but I wouldn't know because my self-involvement and self-loathing were all-consuming, and left little room for really seeing others. I wouldn't learn till years later how to be considerate, how to make amends to those I'd hurt. That there were actually other people on the planet, which had never occurred to me.

But now, in Las Vegas, this kind man who remembered my love of Ann-Margret took me backstage for her show, and afterward we went up to her room at Caesars Palace.

> *How lovely to be a woman,*
> *And change from boys to men,*
> *And go to a fancy night club,*
> *And stay out after ten!*

I was excited to again see my childhood idol, but it was bittersweet; I felt so very far from the innocent girl I was when I had first met her at RCA. Ann-Margret said lovely things about Karl and was gracious to me, but I was losing the ability to sustain good feelings and sank back into despair, which I buried with false enthusiasm. Which made me feel more lonely.

When Karl and I first started dating, we talked about birth control, and I told him about a time on *Mary Hartman* when I'd gotten an infection that had left me scarred and unable to have children, and so of course, the next month I was pregnant. This was a week before a trip to South Africa with Karl to look at a new venue for a Sinatra concert. Neither of us wanted kids. In my case, I'd learned indirectly from my mother that having kids was the end of one's freedom and joy. I had an abortion in Hollywood, and Karl was kind enough to go with me.

I was lying on the hospital gurney in a private room with my legs in the stirrups, wearing only a thin hospital gown and socks. I had forgotten to shave my legs. Karl and I didn't say much to one another.

> *How marvelous to wait*
> *For a date*
> *In simply beautiful clothes*

I wasn't anxious, but I had to laugh at one point when the doctor, a middle-aged man with hair dyed black, was busy with the procedure and Karl was sitting on my right, absently holding my hand, while they engaged in small talk. Karl mentioned Frank Sinatra. The doctor looked up and launched into a screenplay idea he had about a famous singer, and they went back and forth talking about his idea and how to go about getting it out there.

Had this been more recent, I would have used the current, semi-snarky vernacular and, indicating my crotch area, said, "Hey. Eyes down here, buddy." But instead, I counted the tiles on the ceiling.

Two days later, Karl and I were flying to South Africa for the start of the Sinatra tour.

South Africa was hot, and there was a lot of vodka and a lot of lying by the pool in Sun City, Bophuthatswana, which was promoted as the first non-apartheid resort. At night, I was running the lighting board with Karl for the Sinatra shows. Well, he did all the real work, but let me bring the house lights to half with a pull of a lever. Night after night we did the show, while the days were a blur with a combination of drinking, overeating, self-loathing, and then another new diet that would fix everything.

Two weeks later, we were packing to leave for the second leg of our trip to Sao Paulo, Brazil. Karl and I had our suitcases on the bed and were starting to pack. I blacked out, and when I came to I was on the floor with Karl kneeling above me. He looked panicked and then people came in—hotel personnel—and when I was finally sitting up, leaning against the bed, Karl explained that we'd been packing and then I fell to the floor and started shaking, and he didn't know if he should put something in my mouth.

The doctor explained I'd had a grand mal seizure. I liked his South African accent, although I was foggy and not sure what he was saying. I think there was drool on my face.

> *How lovely to wear mascara,*
> *And smile a woman's smile.*

The seizure had been severe, and Karl scheduled an EKG for Brazil, where we were heading next. The EKG was normal, and when I finally got home, I saw my childhood doctor who put me on anti-seizure drugs. I later learned that seizures were a side effect of the increase in antidepressants he had recommended *before* the trip, as he'd assumed I'd be depressed after the abortion. The same doctor who prescribed me Valium for years. He was also the doctor who had prescribed amphetamines when I was a teenager and felt chubby. Dr. Feel-Something-Else. After the abortion, when he'd upped the antidepressant dosage, he told me not to drink, but when I asked, "Even wine?" he said, well, maybe an occasional glass, which I took to mean all the vodka I wanted. Hello grand mal seizure.

My depression continued to pull me down. I figured the problem was Karl. I had a limited concept of others or my effect on them, and rather than break up with Karl directly, I merely saw him less and less, with excuses of work in Hollywood, and hoped my distancing would lead to his eventually forgetting me, as if I'd never existed in his life at all. Long-form ghosting. Any sadness I might have felt, I masked with the adrenaline surge of an unexpected affair with Alan Thicke, a Canadian talk-show host whom I'd met on an Ann Murray special in Nova Scotia.

Karl, of course, noticed my increasing absences and my inconsistent giddiness and called me on it. I admitted to the affair (one way to get out of something), and things ended with anger and tears on his part and numbness and silence on mine; I wouldn't make sense of my behavior until I stopped drinking and took a cold, hard look at how I hurt people.

However, before it all came crashing down, before I'd slept with Alan, before it was over for Karl and me, before I'd finally stop drinking, there was Monday Night Football.

I'd been traveling for months with Karl and Frank Sinatra, who became a friend and was to be the best man at our wedding. That winter (six months before I'd started my slow disappearance), Karl and I were both again in D.C. I was working on *The Kennedy Center Honors,* and Karl was with Frank, who had a concert nearby. When we were both free, I usually went to the Madison where Karl was staying, to spend the night.

We usually wore nightshirts and socks in the evening, and we drank martinis and ate a lot of Triscuits with mustard. We were classy.

It gives you such a glow,
Just to know,
You're wearing lipstick and heels.

There was a knock at the door.

We looked at one another. We hadn't ordered room service.

Karl looked through the peephole and then opened the door. Jilly Rizzo, Frank's buddy who may or may not have been in the mafia, was standing there, all wiry energy and hyper talk. (Nine years later, Jilly was convicted of fraud for something that may or may not have been mafia-related.) He and Frank were staying in the suite next to Karl's.

Karl looked at me.

"We're in our pajamas," I said to Karl.

"Come as you are!" Jilly said. He sounded determined, like this was Frank's request, and Jilly wasn't going to take no for an answer. It wasn't exactly a horse's-head-in-bed threat, but we knew we had only one option.

"Don't make me look bad. It's next door, for fuck's sake."

He left, and I brushed my teeth. Karl grabbed the key, and, in our nightshirts and socks, we padded ten feet down the hall to the suite next door.

They'd ordered room service. A square cart with a white tablecloth was set up in the middle of the living room area. Snacks and beer. I sat next to Frank and knew enough about football to hold my own, to the point where he and I were speculating on who would win and why. He'd contest my opinion by backhanding me lightly on the arm. Playful. Like a brother.

I briefly left my body and saw a twenty-six-year-old girl in a hotel room in D.C. with Karl, a mob guy named Jilly, and Frank Sinatra.

Watching Monday Night Football.

I wasn't wearing lipstick and heels, but how lovely to be a woman.

16

God Died and Left Me Boss

I was always searching. When I was barely a teenager, I spent a lot of time alone in my room reading Edgar Cayce books, in which he claimed to access other dimensions while in a trance. Other dimensions sounded good but I would have settled for only the trance part, which I more easily accessed at night with a big bowl of ice cream. I also spent time reading about crystal ball gazing. Any connection sounded good, even if it was with an oversized marble. I saved up my allowance and bought a crystal ball and followed the directions, which included wrapping the ball in silk and not letting anyone else hold it. I sat cross-legged on the floor and stared into the glass orb I reverently held in my hands. Hours of this. I may have once seen something shadowy but that's about it. It may have been a dead relative, or maybe a bird had flown past the window.

In my twenties, I found another trance-like state in the form of alcohol where I could say things I didn't remember and see things that weren't there. Like a mystic. A mystic who avoided people and threw up and had hangovers.

My religious and/or spiritual quest would grow stronger when—at nearly thirty—I quit drinking, and despite surrendering to a community of people who were struggling along as well, I felt utterly bereft. I was in meetings with people who had committed to a "higher power."

It was a toss-up as to which was more uncomfortable, being surrounded by people, or having to consider some ridiculous and possibly mythic higher power.

I read a story about a young guy who heard a voice (*oh, jeez*) that said, "Who are you to say there is no God?"

Something in me cracked—just a tiny opening—and I thought, "Yes, who am I to say there is no God?" I decided to give God a whirl. Maybe *this* was the connection I'd been missing. I started praying. Simple prayers: "Please watch over my parents as they have suffered," or "Thank you for waiting." I let myself feel carried by God and the tribe of the sober.

I remember only two things people said to me during the God period, and they both seemed more palliative than scientific. But for a brief time, I loved embracing these comforting concepts; I loved using them to make sense of the world. I was told:

1) *If you are driving and take a wrong turn and you're all pissed off, remember: It is God's way of keeping you off a road where you might have had an accident and died.* Which, although comforting, seems an ineffective way to learn about frustration and the management thereof. But handy in the short term.

2) *God is making you ready and making him/her ready, and when you're both ready he'll have you meet.* This was for single people who were sad about being single. Hope was a big thing in those days. Hope seemed a way of immersing oneself in the possibility of something better in the future, which again, offered little in the way of learning acceptance. I was probably single for any number of reasons, but I don't think it was because God hadn't yet gotten around to making me and my potential mate "ready" for one another.

During this time, I went to a Congregational church. The Congregationalists claimed they could commune directly with God—or in this case Jesus—without going through the time-consuming channels of priests or confessors or bishops or whoever all those people were wearing expensive, sparkly outfits and tall hats who had all the answers, but just not in English. Sounded good; I like being on the inside with access to secret information. I even got baptized and have the document to prove it. So far not one person has asked me for proof of baptism, but I stand at the ready.

And yet.

It was an ephemeral commitment on my part. It felt like many of my relationships, in which I was enthusiastically in and then disappointedly out. I tried. I went to a weekend retreat in the mountains with the flock, or pride, or whatever you call them. I wanted to feel part of something and maybe it would happen at the retreat. There was communal cooking and communal get-togethers and communal worship and talk of communal good works. I ended up making out with one of the younger guys, sitting on a big rock overlooking a valley. Nothing stuck. Nothing penetrated my defensive self-lamination. Not the good-natured communal amateur talent shows, or the guy on the rock.

I didn't go back.

Then I hung out at The Bodhi Tree, which was a bookstore in West Hollywood for all things metaphysical. I sat on one of the little stools, drinking tea and trying to read something about Buddhism because I wanted to look spiritual, but I ended up looking around at the other people reading. I was torn between embracing and mocking, which was my liminal comfort zone. It was exhausting.

Years later, I'd work these observations into a standup routine: "I saw a guy at The Bodhi Tree and he was reading a book about prosperity. It's three in the afternoon on a Wednesday. You want prosperity? How about you start with a job?"

Or I saw a girl reading about attracting a mate with crystals. "You want a boyfriend? Maybe get the rocks out of your bed and someone would sleep with you." I sounded like a grumpy old man. I kept going back to The Bodhi Tree, reading pamphlets from the front desk and I thought: Wicca! Now there's a fun community. Drapey costumes and candles at night. Romantic! I bought a book and went home excited to have found my spiritual people. But sitting in my crappy apartment reading a manual about rites and rituals, I was disappointed to discover I didn't have enough room to accommodate the outline of a five-foot pentagram.

I'm a big reader and became interested in quantum physics, or the idea of it, even if I didn't understand. I found something magical about Schrödinger's Cat. And the particle-wave theory. Granted, I got my information from *The Dancing Wu Li Masters,* which was a mystical soup of information from Buddhism, Taoism, and quantum physics but it was esoteric enough to make me feel special. Like I was in a secret society. I could drop little hints of my vast knowledge, which went no further than the little hints. But maybe someone smart would think I was smart.

Then there was neurobiology which was a slippery slope, sliding me away from blind faith and into science. My reading led to more investigation about brain chemistry, and I wondered if we're wired for God as a survival tactic, or simply a device for those in power to control the masses, or if it was a vestigial story-making device for making sense of the world. Egyptians believed the scarab beetle pushed the sun across the sky, as an example of resurrection. With one foot still in the world of magical thinking, I was reading Carl Jung. His story about mentioning a scarab and one flying through the window was enough to keep me believing in mystical possibility. Maybe scarabs were the answer! Not that I believed these beetles literally pushed the sun anywhere, but the resurrection aspect seemed fun. So I got a tattoo of a scarab beetle on my upper arm, which I thought was really special until someone pointed out it looked like a *Journey* album cover.

My slide away from faith continued when I watched *Battlestar Galactica*. I went along for the whole journey—which portrayed people of different faiths, and different searches for religious icons from the past. I felt connected happily believing in my own God, and then *bam*, in the last episode, it was revealed that we're all simply making stuff up. People made stuff up; people in the past made stuff up, people in the future would make stuff up; the producers of the show made stuff up. I understood this was just a television show, but it was subversive, and I was ripe for unbelieving.

And that was the end of God. Like the flip of a switch. Or the snap of a finger. It was that quick, leaving me once again bereft.

I have no regrets about my faith-dabbling because believing softened me. It was difficult to remain judgmental—to think I have all the answers—when my own answers could be so quickly discarded and replaced by new-and-improved answers. I'd gone from atheist to believer to atheist. Maybe it's simply a matter of where on the timeline you found me.

In my smarty-pants phase, I summed it up. Question: If you were at a table with an Atheist, a Buddhist, a Hindu, a Jew, and a Catholic, who would you be drawn to? Answer: The one who was kindest to the waiter. The best I can do is be kind, I suppose. But even my kindness can be suspect as my best intentions go out the window if I'm tired or constipated.

However, a tiny flame of longing still burns somewhere inside me; I can feel tears well up when I think of the old Motel 6 commercial, with its irresistible tagline: "We'll leave the light on for you."

Which was the genius of advertising at work, although I've read the line was ad-libbed by Tom Bodett, who was the Motel 6 spokesman. Either way, genius.

Here's how I break it down:

WE'LL: Implying there is a group of people somewhere inviting you to join them.

LEAVE: And this group is willing to sacrifice something for you. You are worth the sacrifice.

THE LIGHT ON: And they want to guide you to them where it is warm and cozy and you will be welcomed. You can come in from the cold.

FOR YOU: They are talking to ME. I AM special, dammit!

At least to Motel 6.

I told my brother Bill about this commercial and how it always affects me.

He said, "Do you remember when Mom and Dad would go out for a special dinner? Just the two of them?"

"I remember Mom taking forever to get ready. And her perfume. And Dad's army hat to keep his wavy hair smooth until they were ready to leave."

Bill said, "Do you remember how before they left, Mom went around and turned off all the lights in the house? Like if they weren't home, why would they leave the lights on? *Hello!* We're still here! How about you leave a goddam light on for *us!*"

Now when I think of the Motel 6 commercial, it makes me laugh. Which isn't so bad.

Maybe after all is said and done, there really is just laughing with my brother Bill. Laughing with a friend. A simple life.

But wait. I haven't tried Scientology.

17

Snap Her Little Neck

I'd broken up with Karl. I'd stopped drinking. I found God. I lost God. I limped along, went to meetings, took commitments, did an inventory, and felt grateful. My life was better, but I didn't use that as a reason to stay sober. If I allowed myself to drink if things seemed worse, I'd find a way to make things worse. Where there is no option there is a strange freedom: freedom from insanity, freedom from choice.

However, I was still secretly bulimic. Warren and I still talked and saw one another occasionally—when we weren't dating other people—but I would never tell him this secret. Or tell anyone. I figured once a problem was brought into the open, a solution naturally appeared. Best to leave it a secret as long as I could. I was managing it. It was no one's business.

But at thirty-three—after five years of being sober—I felt completely out of control. I could barely drive by a 7-11 without stopping for several plastic-wrapped carrot cakes and donuts if they had them, maybe a bag of chips and some chocolate. Then throwing up and doing it again when I passed another 7-11 later in the day. I wanted to blame 7-11.

When the eating disorder was at its worst, I found a therapist.

I'd been to a couple of therapists when I was younger. One had written a book on teen suicide, and I usually took an amphetamine before going into his office to make it easier to talk about something, like how weird it was to see flamingos standing on one leg. Important stuff. We never got past my frenetic chit-chat.

Next.

Another therapist had no boundaries, and I invited him to a Halloween Costume Party and he came, probably a Psych 101 No-No. He was dressed as Freud. Bob Stoller, a family friend and paranoid schizophrenic, borrowed a Styrofoam wig holder from my mom and attached it to his shoulder and came as someone with multiple personalities. Bob and the shrink found one another and ended up on the couch talking for hours.

Next.

But now I was sitting across from an older, female therapist who seemed, well, delicate. She had stiffly curled mousy beige hair as if she got it "done" once a week, and then sat upright until her next salon appointment. She wore a cameo at the collar of her prim, lacy blouse and she kept her hands folded nicely on her lap. There may even have been an antimacassar on the back of her chair; the room felt stiff and cloying like dust was accumulating on everything from lack of activity. I was in crisis and felt I'd explode at any moment.

She wanted to talk about my early childhood, and I wanted to snap her little neck. She didn't seem to understand the urgency of my inability to go a day without bingeing and vomiting. She sat quietly asking her tiny family questions in her boring passive voice. It was like going to the hospital after slicing your wrists and having the doctor sit down and ask you questions about the type of knife and where it was purchased, while you bled onto the floor. I finally told her she seemed very nice but I needed someone who could deal with the immediate problem that was completely paralyzing me. She smiled beatifically and gave me the number of a therapist who worked primarily with eating disorders.

Next!

My love/hate history with food and my body began in my teens.

In a way to guarantee I could stick to a diet, I made a bet with my dad that I could go from 145 down to 116 pounds by my sixteenth birthday. I'd been on a diet all year, putting myself on a rigid routine of scrambled eggs and hamburger patties, and combined with fasting and my mom's diuretics, I reached my goal. I forget now what the reward was from my father other than his approval and a thumbs up, but I very clearly remember the reward I gave myself: a day of eating whatever I wanted, which on my birthday was a cream cheese and olive sandwich on Wonder bread, and all the birthday cake I wanted. (I've never been a sophisticated eater.)

The next day I saw no reason to immediately go back to my rigid diet plan—enjoy a few days off, I figured—and in a matter of months, I was back up to 145 pounds.

It was time to try something different.

Which is when I discovered Ipecac. Ipecac was used to induce vomiting in cases of accidental poisoning. One online entry states: "Ipecac root itself is a poison, but in this diluted form, its ability to induce immediate vomiting means that the syrup is seldom fatal." The viscous fluid came in a small glass vial and sat in the medicine cabinets of many households like ours, recommended by the parenting manuals to keep on hand, in case your child ingested lighter fluid or something. Manuals that also said you either hold a crying baby or let a crying baby cry. I guess it depends on what decade you were born. I was apparently born in the Yes-To-Ipecac and No-To-Holding era.

I found the vial in our medicine cabinet alongside the familiar Band-Aids, iodine, Ace bandages, amphetamines (Mom's), and No-Doz (Dad's). When I'd asked my mom what Ipecac was for, she explained its function, adding, "Thank God, none of you kids ever needed it."

I didn't tell her I needed it now.

When the family gathered in the kitchen for dinner, I happily announced I had ingested two teaspoons of this magic elixir, the expected result being that in about an hour, I'd start throwing up. The taste of the Ipecac was still on my tongue and in my throat. It was like hazelnut motor oil. My parents didn't say anything about my plan—I'm sure they were tired of dealing with a teenager who was obsessed with her weight.

My brother Ted took it in stride—he was probably thinking about something else—but my brother Bill exclaimed, "Don't let her sit next to me."

Everyone laughed. Yeah, that Bill was a crack-up.

This became a regular thing, although I no longer announced it to everyone. My mother was kind enough to buy more when the liquid in the small bottle was getting low, maybe so I'd stop stealing her amphetamines.

I discovered that the efficacy of Ipecac as an emetic wasn't guaranteed, when I'd been asked to babysit for the Cavalarises next door. They were a Greek family with two young kids—Sparky and Athena—and I thought I'd make the most of what would probably be a boring evening by helping myself to any new and interesting dessert items I could find in their refrigerator. All I found was baklava and some sticky buns that looked like donut holes. It would have to do.

I took the Ipecac, put the kids to bed, and ate as much as I could while leaving some in the fridge to hide my gluttony. I topped it off with some foreign-looking crackers and tap water.

And waited.

Waited for something to happen.

Nothing happened.

The waiting turned to panic and then resignation.

I went to school the next day having ingested probably 8,000 calories of Greek food, feeling bloated and gassy and depressed and I felt abandoned by my dietary helpmate. Fortunately, Ipecac never again let me down (maybe the Greek food was the problem), although fifteen years later I'd need a mouthful of fillings and crowns as the result of all the acid that washed back up into my mouth.

For a while, I tried to use Ipecac responsibly, limiting it to the weekends: my reward for having worked hard all week. For having to be friendly to people. But it became a more frequent occurrence and served not only the purpose of providing a break from my constant self-vigilance, but eliminated any need to say yes to evening invitations. I'd claim I had to be up early for work, but my secret evening plans involved going to the drugstore, buying Ipecac, and then a stop at the bakery where I bought whatever looked delicious.

I once tried Starch Blockers. They were on the market for about five minutes in the early '80s. The label said something like, "For every Starch Blocker capsule, you can enjoy two pieces of bread Guilt-Free!" Extrapolating, I swallowed ten capsules and ate twenty pieces of toast. Another time I bought a jar of soy nuts. I read how many portions were in the jar, poured all the nuts onto the table, and divided them into sixteen piles. I wrapped each pile in aluminum foil and pleased with my work, I enjoyed one portion of soy nuts. I logically figured I could have initiated this little plan the day before and I ate *those* soy nuts. And the nuts from the day before *that*. Until, of course, no little packets of soy nuts remained. Only a pile of wasted aluminum foil. I also used to camouflage all the cake I was buying at the market, by throwing in some candles and balloons.

One cashier said, "Looks like someone's having a party," to which I said, "Yes. My daughter."

"That's a lot of sugar for a child." I was offended someone was questioning my parenting abilities, even though I had no children.

I employed other workarounds to keep my weight under control. I knew a glass of wine had ninety calories, but Valium had *no* calories, and I'm a smart girl. So instead of a glass of wine I'd take a Valium. Having just saved ninety calories, I had a glass of wine. It's obvious where this went.

Light beer had 100 calories. On a camping trip with my boyfriend Cliff—a keyboardist in Bill's rock band—I brought a supply of light beer and allowed myself exactly two a day. One afternoon I was sipping the first of the two while we drove to a campsite. He asked for a sip. This would throw my entire calorie-counting scheme into chaos as I would have to open another can but not drink all of it, then I'd be one short for the trip. I was insane with panic. I wanted to kill him.

I looked at him and said, "Sure."

Cocaine was another diet aid that worked for a while. I was very thin. And crazy. If I was still speedy and grinding my jaw when the sun came up, I would feel weary, depressed, and disoriented. Out of sync with the world and its happy sunrises.

Or as my friend Lorna explains it, "Those fucking birds."

Now I was thirty-three. And crazy. Instead of snapping the little neck of the passive beige therapist, I took the number of the doctor she'd recommended, made an appointment, and found myself in the waiting room in Beverly Hills of Dr. Kastner. I was nervous but also had an unfamiliar peaceful feeling like maybe I'd finally get some help while concurrently thinking everything was hopeless.

I was early—it's important to make a good impression—and after judging the small, framed photos of pastoral settings on the pale blue walls, and with little else to do but feel anxious, I absent-mindedly did a subtle nose pick. I found a small nugget and then looked around and discovered there was nowhere to put it. No trash bin, no tissues.

So I put it back. Which made me laugh. I hadn't laughed in a long time.

Dr. Kastner was in her late thirties, had long dark hair, and wore snazzy, chic outfits. (It took me a year to realize she'd bought every outfit at Harare's which was on the ground floor of her building.) In comparison, my shoulder-length hair was thinning and I'd dyed it nearly black. I didn't know how Dr. Kastner could help me—she was thin and beautiful—but I told her what was going on, which took a brief forty-five minutes of fits and starts to push out a few relevant sentences.

After a couple of questions, she said she would like to see me again the following week. I figured, why not, half-worried I hadn't adequately conveyed the dire straits I was in; that she'd bought my fucked-up-but-I'll-be-fine persona.

At our next session, after the basic hellos, and after I sat down, I didn't know what to say. Did I *want* her to think I was fine?

"So what do you think?" I asked.

"I think you belong in the hospital."

What?

She explained that I needed a lot of therapy (excuse me?) and rather than the slow process of weekly visits when I was in crisis, and the slow process of discovering old wounds, she recommended I check in to Midway Hospital—not far from my apartment—where I would benefit from daily therapy, group therapy, and family therapy, and have my food monitored.

Both horrified and relieved, I said yes. I didn't know what else to do.

I entered Midway Hospital as an inpatient in the eating disorder unit. Ipecac had continued to work for the most part, but I'd also developed pretty good control of my peristaltic system and was able to bring stuff up on command. Like a magic trick. That nobody saw. Or would want to. Sadly, I had no control over the other end of the peristaltic system which had frozen up, and I relied on Ex-Lax and suppositories to get things moving in that direction.

I was working in post-production on *Not Necessary the News*. I went to my bosses with proverbial hat in hand to explain that I needed some time off; that I had an eating disorder that I had to deal with. I had never taken time off and was anticipating an ultimatum: "job or hospital." Or possibly even a confused: "Not you, you seem fine."

But they were quick to say, "Take all the time you need." They were supportive and said my job was safe and they only wanted me to get better.

I was dating Jon, the tape operator on the show, and when I told him I had to go into an eating disorder hospital, he was confused. What eating disorder? On my last night of freedom, Jon sat by as I ate maybe ten peanut butter and jelly sandwiches. The next morning he drove me to the hospital and was allowed to come up and help me get settled. I heard the sounds around me of loving and concerned parents helping their daughters find their rooms and get settled. It was all very first-dorm-at-college with girls and parents and loved ones and bunny slippers and stuffed animals on beds.

I turned to Jon.

"Swear you won't get me anything soft and cuddly for my bed."

The following weekend we were allowed visitors and Jon brought a cheap, plastic, bright green fish, about a foot long, which adorned my bed for the rest of my stay. I still have the green plastic fish in a box in the closet.

The eating disorder unit housed maybe fourteen patients, all female, all suffering from one form of disorder or other. It was a three-week program but I figured I'm smarter than most people so I should be out in a few days; grab the basics and get out—my usual MO in life. The first night in the hospital I was surprised that any of the basic hospital ground rules applied to me. I understood why I had to sit with the others at mealtime—which was a challenge in itself as I had grown accustomed to eating alone, eating in secret—but the bulimics needed to be monitored and had to stay an hour in the group room to ensure we wouldn't sneak off to the bathroom to throw up. Which meant I had to hold my breath for another hour and hope no one would talk to me until I could go back to my room.

We also had communal walks every morning which were hideous. I didn't mind being with people on my terms, but feeling raw and vulnerable and constipated and then having to chat with all these losers was torture. Also, Midway Hospital was only a few blocks from where I lived in Park La Brea, and it was surreal to walk the neighborhood, knowing I could break away and be home in five minutes.

The next activity—from which I felt I should be excused—was the family group therapy coming up Wednesday night and would continue every Wednesday night once we were outpatients. My therapist Dr. Kastner, as well as Jodi, the intake supervisor, kept asking if my parents were coming. I dodged with excuses like they wouldn't want to come; it's not necessary; maybe next week; they're hard to reach. I got the feeling the therapists conferred behind my back, and Jodi was elected the spokesman and confronted me.

"We need you to call your parents." Oh, so now it was all about them and their needs.

"Why?"

"I'll help you."

"I don't need help."

But Jodi was patient. She gave me the words to say. I balked once again, explaining that my parents wouldn't answer, or I'd get the phone machine, and she said, "That's okay, you can leave a message."

It took me two hours of suppressed and then gulpy crying and sitting by the payphone with her words on a piece of paper before I could make the call.

And got the machine.

I said the words. "It would mean the world to me for you to come Wednesday night."

My parents showed up. My dad was friendly and supportive and even emotional at one point, and my mom was scared to death and hostile and gripped her purse, which was on her lap like a fortress wall.

At one point the therapist mentioned my previously expressed desire to have an uninterrupted conversation with just my father. My mom interjected that I could have a conversation with my father whenever I wanted, and the therapist pointed out she had just stopped that from happening. Mom never said much more in therapy, after having been—as what must have seemed to her—shamed and silenced.

But even now, I appreciate that she showed up week after week despite her obvious fear and discomfort.

We had a medical doctor on staff, as well as the family group therapist, and individual therapists, and I enjoyed my brief chats with him when I went in to be weighed twice a week. Although we engaged in nothing deeper than superficial chit-chat while he took my blood pressure, it was nice to talk to someone who wasn't judging me.

After a couple of weeks of this, he said, "You know, Nikki, some people don't make it and I'm afraid you might be one of them."

What the hell? I usually accomplished whatever I set out to do, how could I not make it? Who was he to judge me? He didn't even know me. Protecting myself with my own metaphoric purse, I left his office offended and frightened and planned to never speak to him again.

Another day, I was at the nurse's desk to pick up my towel for the shower. (I'm not sure why we couldn't have towels in our rooms. Maybe they thought we'd eat them?) She had the patient notebook open in front of her. I read the upside-down words and saw my name and the nurse's entry: "Patient continues to be defensive and angry." Fuck that.

I spent the next two weeks avoiding the nurse's desk to the degree that instead of being forced to go there and ask for a towel every morning, I re-used the same towel for weeks and went down the stairs at the far end of the hallway and then came up the other side. All to avoid seeing her.

After three weeks, some of the others who had come in around the same time as I had, were getting out, packing up, and having muted conversations together in other rooms like they were leaving a lovely hotel after a conference.

Jodi came into my room.

"Nikki—" She had such a soft and sweet voice, and I was expecting her to say something like "It's been delightful to have you here."

"Jodi," I said, interrupting her before she said anything more. "I'm not ready."

"Oh, we know that," she said, her voice caring and calm and full of love, and something let loose inside me, a feeling of safety, of having been seen for the fucked-up, angry, and frightened person I was; that they realized I needed more time.

I wasn't fooling anyone, which led to endless talk in therapy about "needs," which I had a hard time relating to. When my therapist asked me about my needs, all I could think of was when I was ten, my mom had the new Barbra Streisand album and one of the songs was "People Who Need People," which my mother summed up with contempt,

"Needing people seems more pathetic than lucky."

I'd therefore surmised that neediness and being loved were mutually exclusive and I'd therefore learned to suppress my needs in hopes of being loved. It never worked.

Since it was a three-week program and I'm so smart, I finally left the hospital after six weeks. I said goodbye to "Dr. Scared-Straight" who didn't think I'd make it. I'd eventually stopped taking the long way around to the showers and had started saying hello to the Scary Nurse. We understood one another when I hugged her and thanked her.

I cried the most saying goodbye to Jodi, maybe the kindest person I've ever known.

AFTER LEAVING THE HOSPITAL I continued with private therapy to understand the underlying issues that had led to the eating disorder. I'd intellectualized the concept of needs, but the concept hadn't tangibly manifested in my brain in any emotional way until something came up with Dr. Kastner. My weekly therapy appointment was on Monday, but one Sunday night I came down with the flu. I left Dr. Kastner a message that I wouldn't be in the next day. The following week she handed me her monthly invoice which I opened at the start of our session. I had been charged for the previous Monday and I felt a surge of superiority in finally catching her in a mistake, making us equals in my mind. I pointed out the error. Yes, I'd canceled but I had the flu. Why was I being charged?

"You're aware of my cancellation policy."

"Well, yes?"

"That I need twenty-four hours' notice."

"It was the night before. I got sick. I couldn't help it."

"But you understand my cancellation policy."

"Yes, I know! It's not like I planned it. I was sick."

She didn't say anything, and I thought, finally she sees the logic in my argument.

"So," she finally said, "what you're saying is I should put my needs aside for yours?"

I went into what felt like mental paralysis, unable to think or process, with no obvious or logical way out of this conundrum. I either understood her policy or I didn't. I did. Which meant therefore that—*Oh, crap.* The weight of this came crashing through my psyche, my face was burning and I felt sweaty. I realized: Yes, I'd been living since childhood looking for someone to put their needs aside for mine. What I'd wished my mother had been able to do when I was a child.

"Yes." But I couldn't look at her.

She waited.

"What do I do?"

She explained that some needs will never be met.

"Then why the fuck am I in therapy? Am I supposed to just live with this?"

"Yes. But it will get easier."

"How?"

"We'll keep talking."

And in time, I was able to put all those sadnesses into an imaginary velvet purse that would have a home near my appendix. I would keep the pain with me, not with revulsion, but with safety and gentle care. In time I would see the brilliance of Dr. Kastner's ability to keep her boundaries in the face of my pain, which led to this devastating and illuminating breakthrough. I would eventually have empathy for my mother who lived a life she hadn't bargained for. None of her needs had been met; how could she have had any time left for me? I'd have to stop blaming her for every little thing.

But that would take time.

Not that I was immediately freed from self-obsession, which was gently pointed out to me by my friend Eve Babitz, an acquaintance I'd made through mutual friends. I didn't know much about her (for example, I had no idea she was a writer), as I was usually more interested in how I came off to other people. I was always complaining to her about my weight, or were my bangs too short, or whatever. She listened. As always. So kind. But one evening I'd started in on something and after I'd laid out the big problem—like did these earrings make me look fat—she interrupted me. Gently.

"Nikki. People don't care what you look like. They just want you to be nice to them."

Wow. Other people. Who knew? This was a whole new world.

I've lived for more than thirty years free from bulimia, grateful to those who have helped me. I continue to carry the metaphoric little pink velvet pouch where the pains of the past have a home. Safe. With me.

But I will say this: A couple of years ago I got the stomach flu. I could feel it coming, that horrible wave and sudden salivation and rushing to the toilet. And then I was on my knees vomiting.

I was on the cool bathroom floor in the calm before the next storm, when I thought, "Damn, if I knew this was going to happen, I would have eaten a German chocolate cake."

18

Stand Up, Sit Down

Now that I was no longer throwing up, I had a lot of time on my hands. There was no acting career—headshots had long been buried in a box in the closet. Warren came and went, but I was tired of initiating contact. I felt adrift. I was thirty-three and it was time to get serious, which meant I'd try stand-up comedy. Not that it had been a dream of mine, but when I was editing a playback reel for the Emmys, my friend Anna was on the same floor editing an Ellen DeGeneres special, and when I popped in to say hi, she said, "She reminds me of you. You should try stand-up."

Okay. I'd take a stand-up class.

But first, I'd need *comedy headshots* (Hello horse, hello cart.) I found a photographer who specialized in: Comedy Headshots. She did my makeup and curled my shoulder-length hair; we chose some quirky '50s sweater my mom had passed down to me (which was too itchy to wear in real life), and I ended up with two versions of the 8x10 headshots. In one, I'm smiling like a normal person, which was much different from my earlier *acting* headshot in which I had big eyes and slightly parted lips and looked like a waif hoping to be rescued or adopted. In the other, I'm making a quirky face like, "Life—can you believe it?" A face I pretty much never make. And a question I never ask.

With a stack of headshots in the trunk of my car, I showed up for my first stand-up class. Our instructor, Greg Dean, took us through an exercise where one person had to sit on a stool in front of the rest of the group. I took my turn on the stool, and as instructed earlier, I was told to do nothing. No faces, no smiles, no sexual posturing, no funny body movements to indicate anything that might look like I was trying to get a laugh or attention. I had to sit and look at the faces of my classmates who, for their part, had been instructed to do nothing but look back at me. No obvious reactions were allowed, but it was suggested they send love and acceptance my way.

It was unbearable. I was overwhelmed, and even though I didn't move, I couldn't control the tears rolling down my face. It was foreign to receive love like this, without earning it or giving something in exchange. It was painful and frightening. And retroactively revelatory. How my brothers and I developed workaround needs: My brother Ted's need to avoid conflict, my brother Bill's need to keep things funny, and my need to appear needless. All to ensure in a roundabout way we'd be loved. The exercise left me with a hard question: Am I lovable doing nothing? I hadn't yet learned the other part of the equation, that an interest in others can be very satisfying as well.

The following week, Greg explained the framework for script jumps—a set-up with an unexpected punchline—and how to contrast seemingly disparate things. (For example, if I picked old people and gangbangers, I'd make a list of qualities for both and combine or conflate them. "The gangbanger knew he was getting too old for drive-bys when he realized his left turn blinker had been on for the last ten miles.")

I understood, I took notes, and I thought, "This should be a breeze."

My motto came from JFK: "We do these things because they are easy, not because they are hard." Or something like that.

However, in week three, Greg had us make a list of the ten most painful things we'd never talked about. When we showed up for class with our lists, he said to put them in the order of least to most painful. We did. Then he said, take the most painful thing from the bottom of the list, and do a routine about *that*. Jeez.

I dove in and talked about promiscuity and loneliness, with a smattering of dating stuff and drugs and found it healing to verbalize these secrets and get laughs—albeit from other empathetic students who would soon be anxiously exposing their own darkest secrets—as if the people laughing were taking on some of the pain indirectly. Diluting it.

For our final class, we performed in a bowling alley to an audience of friends and loved ones. My parents were always supportive of anything we did. When Bill joined a rock band and played around town in crappy dive bars like Madame Wong's, my parents were in the audience. When Ted played at Donte's—a jazz club in North Hollywood—they were there. Even for my little stand-up gig in a bowling alley, they showed up, my mom applauding and my dad behind his camera flashing away.

After one performance and some supportive laughs, I was on the road to a stand-up career. I investigated open mic nights in various clubs around the Valley. Often, I'd be the last to perform, which meant all the other comics and their friends had gone home, as well as any actual bar patrons, and I was left with a waiter or a bartender and maybe someone cleaning up. But I soldiered on. I performed a total of thirty-six times over several months and the biggest lesson was that to make the jokes funny, I had to re-experience the pain behind them. The more pain behind the words, the better the laugh.

And here is why my comedy headshots were premature: After those thirty-six open mic nights around town, I found I had exorcised whatever demons had led me to make jokes in the first place. I was done with those painful, humiliating memories, and I wasn't industrious enough to mine for any new material. Friends of mine who were working comics told me about the hours, the endless travel, the rejection, the constant writing, revising, and updating, and the dumpy dorm rooms they doubled up in on the road. It sounded too hard. I could be funny "in real life" if the mood struck but I wasn't driven to make a career of it. And frankly, who wants to dredge up painful stuff over and over?

I thought I was done with my stand-up career, but then I was asked by a producer I knew to do a warm-up for *Get Out the Vote*, a TV special that was being taped at Royce Hall, i.e., an audience of 1,500 college students. With my habit of saying yes to anything offered or suggested, I said sure. I was told I just had to "fill a little time" while Cheap Trick got set up behind the curtain. I had about five minutes of material, no skills at crowd work—the "Where are you from?" banter— and Cheap Trick took forty-five minutes to get their shit together. During an awkward pause when I'd run out of things to say, and while pondering self-immolation, someone in the audience yelled, "Sing something."

I figured this was my last hope of keeping them from throwing things. It was make or break time and I knew I'd lose them if I didn't comply. As this was an opportunity to connect with a roomful of restless and sexually charged college students, it could have been fun to have an older woman alone on stage singing, "(Let's Get) Physical" or "Hungry Like The Wolf."

Unfortunately, the only song that came to mind was a tune my dad taught me when I was nine years old. "Ten Cents A Dance"—a plaintive ditty about a depression-era poor woman in a rundown ballroom who gets a dime for every sad and desperate man she dances with—a song that was about as fun as the movie *They Shoot Horses, Don't They?*

About halfway through my shaky—albeit soulful—rendition, some of the guys started throwing dimes up on the stage. It was mortifying, but I finished the song.

Finally, Cheap Trick was ready, and I went home with about $1.60.

19

The Mastery and The Groundlings

I needed help. I wasn't ready to give up on comedy, but I didn't know where to turn. Or what to do next.

I learned about The Mastery from Jackson, a waiter I'd once flirted with. He was a struggling actor and we started hanging out. I didn't drink and he was a big pot smoker, which wouldn't have bothered me except he sort of disappeared when he was high. Although I have to admit, this was also attractive because I didn't have to give him a lot of attention and could settle into my own thoughts. Like dating somebody and nobody at the same time.

Jackson and I didn't talk about a lot of things, but one time he told me he'd done The Mastery and swore by it. He said it might help unblock me. I was so startled by his actually saying something to me—about me—that I said, *Sure, I'll give it a try.*

The Mastery was a weekend growth experience like EST (Erhard Seminar Training), which had been a controversial six-day self-help seminar that pushed people to their physical and emotional limits. The Mastery, however, was softer and gentler in that you could go to the bathroom and go home at night. And it was only three days. Why do something long and hard when I could do something short and easy? It was tailored to people in the entertainment industry to uncover and discard whatever was keeping you from your true essence and creativity. The idea being you couldn't repress selectively. If you blocked *some* things, you blocked *all* things. You block anger, you block joy.

I signed up and showed up, along with maybe twenty or so Hollywood hopefuls: comedians, actors, and writers. On the first day, we had to recite or perform a piece of material we'd chosen to give the "back row" an idea of what we had going on. The back row was made up of three people. I only remember Paula, who was dynamic and insightful and knew enough about human nature to call us on our crap. We all did our little monologues—although I can't remember mine—and then we had to walk alone around the stage, I guess to show Paula what our walking style indicated. Were we shy, defensive, over-confident? Then there was some chit-chat with the back row about why we were there and what our goals were. After assessing the participants, it was time for Paula to give us her feedback before we'd head into the weekend of unblocking and growth.

She called up Mina, a young woman who was wearing a lot of flowing things like a kimono over a long blouse over a long skirt. She was pretty and had long black hair, which blended in with her outfit, and the whole effect may have been hiding the fact that she was slightly overweight.

"Mina."

"Yes?" She apologized.

"You are very uncomfortable in your body."

Silence.

"For the rest of the weekend, you are not allowed to wear anything like what you've got on now. I want you to dress like a dominatrix. Short skirt. Fishnets. Heels. Cleavage. You get the picture?"

Mina looked horrified, but this was not some pervy man telling her to do this. This was Paula, an older woman with acne scars, giving her this direction. Mina looked like she wanted to flee but instead forced a vague nod and slunk back to her seat.

The next person up, Jesse, was a tough little guy about five-eight, muscled, with short spiky hair like a drill sergeant.

"Jesse."

"Yeah."

"You're pretty tough, aren't you?"

"As tough as I need to be. Why?"

Back and forth like this. Tough-guy banter. We knew something was coming.

"Jesse, for the rest of the weekend, you are not to go anywhere alone. You have to have someone hold your hand and you have to bring a blanket and toys and sit on the ground as often as possible. You ask others to walk you to the bathroom. You understand?"

Jesse was frozen in place.

After several more people got ripped apart (and I admit Paula was perceptive and spot-on with her observations—I loved listening to her give assignments), it was my turn. I couldn't imagine what Paula could say because I was pretty normal and well-adjusted. I was friendly with the others and supportive when they came off stage.

The back row, however, was a rough crowd.

Paula looked up from her paperwork. "Nikki."

"Hi."

"You seem very nice."

"Thank you." I smiled in a way I hoped conveyed both humility and confidence. Maybe kinship.

Paula stared at me. "That's not a compliment."

Nervous laugh from me. And it began.

"Nikki, we've watched you interact, and you never expose yourself. Instead, you are armed with a smile and a 'nice' quality that doesn't threaten anyone. It also doesn't let anyone see the real you."

Silence from me.

"I'm guessing," Paula continued, "you learned to be nice as a way of manipulating others and not risking disappointment."

My face got hot but I said, "I appreciate your insights."

"Bullshit."

I didn't want to make eye contact with anyone. I was ashamed and embarrassed and wanted to leave. But I remembered Mina's courage, that she had stayed.

Paula said, "Here's your assignment for the weekend. You are not allowed to be nice. No 'please and thank-yous.' You can't use 'if you don't mind,' or 'you go first,' or 'excuse me.' For the rest of the weekend, you declare what you want, take what you want, and you don't consider others' feelings. In other words, you have to be a bitch."

Panic overwhelmed me as I felt my only survival tool being stripped away.

But Paula wasn't done. "And this carries through when you all go out for meals at the Denny's across the street."

She described all the ways I had to get my needs met, and they all seemed rude. Not nice at all. Like: "I want more coffee." "Give me your napkin." "I want my check." The thought of doing this nearly destroyed me, which was the idea. My fear of being disliked or abandoned was so big that I'd do anything to avoid those feelings, including bending over backward to make it easy for people to be with me.

It helped to see the panicked faces of the others in the workshop. It helped to know there'd be an asterisk to my rude behavior in class; the others would understand this was an exercise. But Denny's? Maybe I wouldn't go. I could bring my own lunch. Or I'd disappear into the bathroom for a while or—anything but be rude to a stranger without explanation.

My "nice" tactics were so deeply ingrained that the first time I made a demand, I did so in barely a whisper, or nervously laughed after stating what I wanted. It got easier. With help from Paula saying, "Louder!" if she noticed my gentle demeanor. Eventually, I was a bitch left and right. Full voice. Not a care in the world.

"Give me your brush," to a girl in the bathroom with me during a break.

"Don't talk to me," to a guy who asked me where I was from.

"Get me water," to anyone within hearing distance.

The overwhelming panic I'd felt dissipated with each demand. I discovered that no one died, including myself. It was delightful! I gave Paula credit for so specifically fucking with me. For pointing out the ways I quietly manipulated others to get my unspoken needs met. I learned to speak up, and as the pendulum swung back to neutral, I didn't have to be bossy. I could just be me.

I also felt incredibly moved to participate in the transformations of those around me. Jesse and his blanket. Mina walking around like she owned the place. We had other exercises in trust and yelling and mirroring, and by the time the weekend was nearing the end, we each had to get onstage and repeat our opening monologues. Whether it was the relief we were feeling from having survived the weekend or the softer hearts we'd uncovered in trusting one another through the process, everyone seemed to have opened up, and the final speeches were rich and strong, and authentic. There were a lot of tears. I felt I was connecting with people through vulnerability, maybe for the first time.

We were instructed to find a small handful of people from class and set up a study group of sorts. We were to meet weekly to talk and share progress and offer support. Which led to my renewed feeling of optimism about life and a new energy for creative expression.

I was now drawn to activities of a more communal nature, as if I was creating the syllabus for my own personal growth as I went along. Making up for all the lessons I'd missed growing up. In standup class, I'd healed something by baring my most shameful secrets. The Mastery cracked the laminated shell in which I'd encased myself. I began interacting honestly with other human beings. But I still felt restless, incomplete, unmoored. Maybe I wasn't yet comfortable just sitting still with myself. Maybe I had more to learn.

It was the '80s, and it seemed everyone was hopping on the improvisation bandwagon, although at thirty-four I was maybe a little old for the bandwagon. But why not give it a whirl.

The most well-known improv group in Los Angeles was The Groundlings. They had a performance theater on Melrose with shows every night and offered classes in sketch comedy during the day. Many comedians got their training in The Groundlings, developing improvisation skills and comedic characters; some even going on to careers on *Saturday Night Live* and beyond. I'd been to Groundlings shows and the performers made it look so easy, so I signed up for the Beginners/Level I class.

Where I failed miserably.

This was my first exchange:

"Here's the file you ordered, Dr. Nash."

"I didn't order a file."

Two things can be learned from this exchange:

1. How NOT to respond in an improv class.
2. The degree to which my avoidance of community manifested.

After my scene-killing line, my teacher, Mindy Sterling, stood up. She was a petite and quirky fireball and would go on to play Frau Farbissina in the Austin Powers movies.

"Let's stop right there," she said.

I could almost hear the sigh in her voice. I was so used to doing things well and learning things quickly, that I didn't know what I'd done wrong, or why I was being interrupted. Didn't she know how delightful I was? How adorable I was?

Mindy said, "Nikki. 'Yes, and—' is Improv 101. You build on the premise. And you've just denied. There's nowhere for your partner to go with this."

I was confused.

She continued. "What can your partner do other than take the file and leave? End of scene."

I guess she didn't know that I preferred to think things through alone, and despite my growth in The Mastery, I still fell back into depending on only myself. In a later review, Mindy had written, "Areas For Improvement: You're thinking too much. You're too low-key. Relax and have more *fun*!" Her review went on like this. I got the gist.

When I first signed up, I'd been given all the appropriate paperwork about the class levels, schedules, and costs, with the unspoken (or perhaps inferred by the students) promise of *fame*. And although fame itself was never mentioned directly, they dangled the names of those who had gone before us who had achieved success and recognition. As usual, I was tempted to jump to the future where I was famous. Separate. Exalted. A future where my archivists—when doing research on my life—would appreciate that I'd saved all my report cards, electric bills, and letters for posterity. Not to mention the illuminating notes from Mindy, which would seem quaint after I'd "hit it big."

There was a progression to success, according to The Groundlings: Proficiency in Level I. After that, you could go on to Intermediate and then Lab, and after presenting the characters you'd developed to the Groundling committee, you might get to perform in the Sunday Night Troupe. After that, a possible spot in the regular troupe where you might get noticed by agents and swept away to bigger things, like *Saturday Night Live*. I liked having a roadmap and I was game to see where it would all take me. I'd be noticed. I'd be part of a family.

And I couldn't even get through my first exchange.

We were also given a sheet outlining the rules of improvisation, which I didn't think applied to me; I figured I could say funny things from time to time and that would be enough. Mindy had also written in my review: "Stop *being* funny and be part of the scene! It's better you contribute and let someone else get a laugh organically from the situation."

The rules I found impossible to follow were:

1. Love The Premise (why, if it wasn't my idea?)
2. Add Information (like what?)
3. Don't Deny (why should I believe something before I investigate more fully?)
4. The Answer Is In Your Partner's Eyes (I have a partner? I should look at them for answers? What if I have all the answers?)

5. Bring Something To The Party (I would prefer to simply get in and get out. Like, I don't really exist. In fact, not only did I rarely bring things to any party, but I tended to implement the French Exit when it was time for me to leave, scouting a side door and slipping out unnoticed as if I'd never been there. Which was similar to how I broke up with boyfriends.)

Of these five basic rules, I broke all five of them in my first scene. What a party pooper!

I continued with Level I, embarrassed every week by my inability to be part of a group and my inability to contribute. One memorable exercise had us pick a person we knew from real life and play the scene as that person, highlighting their main character trait. The others in my class picked dynamic people they knew, like a pushy car salesman, a know-it-all professor, or an over-emotional construction worker. Things were off to a rollicking start until it came time for my character to "add something" to the scene.

The person I'd chosen was Manuela, a lovely Swedish girl I'd met in the eating disorder hospital, and the character trait I chose to embody was the fact that she was bulimic and kept leaving to go the bathroom. It seems I'd picked a character who couldn't even stay in the same room with others.

Mindy busted me for this as well. "You picked someone who is always in the bathroom? Who isn't even on stage?"

This was not going well. We were paired off to work on "add information" exercises, and I was paired with a guy named Adam Carolla. Our scenes weren't good—apparently due to my inability to be generous—but we ended up dating and oddly enough, seventeen years later, I worked on his show, *Too Late with Adam Carolla*. Although Adam was fun, our dating experience and his show were both equally short-lived.

Aside from Adam Carolla and Mindy Sterling, Bryan Cranston was the only one to go on to an actual career in front of the camera. But then again, his career was already moving along when he'd popped in for a few brush-up classes.

The Level I class was twelve weeks, and I was asked to repeat it. I had made progress and was beginning to trust others, help *others* be funny, and I'd taken the rules to heart. And yet I saw no reason to repeat Level I. Once I began letting real people in, I no longer needed the possibility of future fame or attention to indirectly fill the lonely parts of myself. I also realized my general nature was not suited to improv as I was more of an observer and quiet sideline commentator in life. Maybe I should have considered a career in golf announcing.

However, The Mastery and the Groundlings changed me. The two-step process of my humanization came first with The Mastery, where my tendency to "act nice" was shattered. Then on to the Groundlings, where my defensive self-protection was replaced with actual skills for participating in the world around me—to develop empathy. I went from *acting* nice to *being* kind. They may look similar, but the former is false posturing, and the latter is an organic result of my involvement with others, of being human.

Maybe we're drawn to hard lessons, as if our subconscious has a better instinct for what will provide the healing and growth necessary to thrive and contribute to others' thriving. Maybe I had a sixth sense about the lessons that would introduce me to the world, show me how to be, how to receive, and how to give. Although I was still not entirely sure why I'd chosen Warren at such a young age to be a part of my life, maybe I'd learned things from him that weren't yet apparent. Maybe I needed him as the standard by which I charted my growth. Or maybe the reason was yet to reveal itself. That might take time.

But I found that after completing only Level I of The Groundlings, the rules had embedded themselves in my psyche and stayed with me like strange, unasked-for mantras for living: Love the Premise, Add Information, Don't Deny, The Answer is in Your Partner's Eyes, and Bring Something to the Party.

I remember exactly where I was when I noticed something in me was changing. I was in the edit bay working on an episode of *Not Necessarily the News*. I was seeing others around me for what seemed like the first time. Mark, the editor, was tapping away at the keyboard as he assembled the segments for that week's show. Amy, the other associate director, had just had a baby and was on the floor near the playpen she'd set up. We'd been working all morning, figuring out the timings and edits and shot fixes, and during a lull while Mark implemented the changes, it was a good time to get coffee.

Usually, I would have said, "I'll be right back," and slipped out. My usual invisible exit.

This time I stood up, walked as far as the door and stopped. I turned and said, "Can I get anyone anything?"

20

An Affair to Remember

I never wanted to get married.
Which, by extension, meant I never wanted to marry Warren Beatty. Or at least I never allowed myself that fantasy. He'd dated a billion women or something. Many of them were his famous co-stars, like Natalie Wood, Julie Christie, Faye Dunaway, Goldie Hawn, and Diane Keaton, and if he hadn't married any of them, I knew I didn't stand a chance. But I still counted on Warren being available when one of my affairs ended. It was like there were three parallel lives: His with other women, mine with other men, and ours with one another.

I'd often bored my girlfriends with stories of my failed love affairs, and they'd give me the usual answer (maybe so I'd stop complaining): "You just haven't met the right one," or an occasional "Maybe you sleep with them too quickly," which stung but I tried to ignore.

My friend Kelly—one of the few who knew about Warren—said maybe I didn't give these other relationships a chance, knowing Warren was the fallback guy, that I didn't make room for anyone else. That could have been true. Maybe deep down I didn't think anyone would love me and I'd avoided testing that theory, employing instead my usual cut-and-run-and-call-Warren routine. He was always there for me on the phone, and if we were both free, we'd see each other, have sex, and enjoy pillow-talky chit-chat, which was usually him talking and me listening. We had become so familiar with one another—albeit in a casual way—that it was easier to return to him when all else failed.

And I'd gotten used to his dating his costars. The affairs didn't usually last long; maybe he and I were similar in that way. And even if we were both with others, I'd never tested if we were actual friends in between being lovers. Could I call on him if I needed something other than simple contact? Granted I still wasn't great at needing anything from others, but maybe it was time to give it a try. Warren was safe in that way as half the time it seemed like he wasn't paying attention so I could slip a need in there, and if there was no response, it would give the illusion of having my needs met.

After talking to Warren the week before about the movie he was working on—*Ishtar* with Dustin Hoffman and French actress Isabelle Adjani—I knew he'd be in New York. I was also in New York and had unexpectedly broken up with some guy I'd been dating long-distance. I found myself alone in the city, at night, cold, and with nowhere to sleep.

Maybe I could stay with Warren.

I called his hotel, gave my name, and they put me through.

"Good evening." You could almost hear the sly smile in his sexy voice.

This was his common greeting whenever I—and I presume any woman—called him. The promise of further seduction. Even if it led to nothing other than a phone chat, it fueled me. After a little back and forth about his new movie, I explained I was stranded nearby and asked if I could come and stay with him overnight. Over the years, we'd spent many nights together at the Beverly Wilshire Hotel when he lived there, or occasionally at Jack's place, not to mention his staying many times at my place at the Fountain Lanai and Park La Brea, and to me this seemed no different. We'd be spending the night together somewhere, and in this case, it was New York.

"Nikki, how are you?"

"Fine." Did he not hear the question?

"I'm sorry. Isabelle Adjani is coming in tomorrow." Which to me implied he had a new leading lady/lover, and there'd be no room at the inn.

I wanted to say, *But this is one night. I'll be gone in the morning*, but I didn't. First, that was whiny. Second, asked and answered. I said some generic niceties and got off the phone.

Even though I found someplace else to stay, I was both disappointed and encouraged. I was disappointed that he couldn't help me or didn't want to see me, but I talked myself into feeling encouraged that I didn't get the bland, "I'll be working. Let's talk later this week." Like maybe this was a new and deeper dimension to our relationship, that he'd actually explained about Isabelle Adjani. Like she'd be passing through and we'd talk about it when it ended; he may have been sleeping with her, but he was telling *me* about it. Women came and went, but we still talked. Which, to my way of thinking, meant I mattered. I was exhausted by my endless parsing.

When it ended with Isabelle Adjani, and we were both back in Los Angeles, he came over to my place at Park La Brea, although he said it made him anxious because he had to be cleared at the gate, not like the guy at the gate was going to alert the press or anything. We saw each other off and on. I went by myself to see *Ishtar* and appreciated his attempt at portraying a goofier, looser character, although he didn't seem capable of entirely letting go of the "Warren Beatty" part of himself. Or maybe he didn't have a goofier, looser side. The movie wasn't a big hit, but I liked it. Then again, I'm not entirely objective.

I didn't talk to him much when he was in pre-production for *Dick Tracy*. I'd been dating Arsenio Hall—whom I met before he was "Arsenio Hall"—when we'd both worked on a Smokey Robinson special. I generally wasn't a good girlfriend, i.e., straight man with comics, because I, too, liked to banter and ended up feeling that—to them— the relationship was more competitive than romantic. And I wasn't the type to play the girly sidekick. Warren wasn't particularly funny, so my being goofier than he was went unnoticed or wasn't a big deal. If anything, he probably found it refreshing, considering I was less careful about choosing my words than he was.

While Warren was making *Dick Tracy*, I started dating a guy named Ian. I was working on *Love Connection,* and part of my job was building the playback reels of the three contestants in the running for a date. Ian was the guy who'd been picked for the date. He was smart and funny, which I discerned from the forty-five-second clip we used. When he was on the show and revealed his date hadn't ended well, I called him, explained who I was, and we started dating. I'm sure the HR department would have had something to say about that, if there had been any HR department.

When it ended with Ian, I called Warren. Who was now dating Madonna, which I didn't take seriously. I mean, I saw *Truth or Dare* and couldn't imagine Warren sitting in the background with someone who needed so much attention. There wasn't space in the room for both of them; Warren wasn't going to hide his light under her bushel—so to speak. Of course he'd sleep with her as he did with most of his female costars, but it seemed he was jumping the shark with this one. And as I'd expected, it didn't last long.

Back to the drawing board for both of us, I guess. Neither of us seemed like the marrying kind, and maybe because of that, we suited one another.

In 1992 that all changed. Warren married Annette Bening.

I'd talked to him while he'd been in pre-production on *Bugsy.* I'd gone to see the movie when it came out, and my usual thought when I saw him with a co-star was they'd hook up, date, promote the movie, and move on—but that didn't happen. This felt like an entirely different match-up and it made sense for him to marry her. They were on the same plane. She was beautiful, smart, and looked like she could hold her own.

But I was still surprised when I heard he'd actually gotten married. Maybe because I thought he'd be single forever.

And what was I doing? What did I really want? Was I holding out for him to marry me? No. Even if I *could* imagine his marrying out of his own universe, it wasn't what I wanted. Although I'd had some practice in thinking, *it's over with Warren*—mostly when *I* was seriously dating someone—I never expected it would be because he was no longer available to *me*.

Whatever it was, I realized we might be done.

A couple of years after Annette and Warren got married, the happy couple made *An Affair to Remember*—a mushy remake of the 1957 movie that starred Cary Grant and Deborah Kerr. I went alone to the theater, and I was bereft. I finally had to admit that it was over.

I'd given up alcohol, addressed my eating disorder, and was healthier than I'd ever been, but maybe I had to give up this final crutch, this fallback drug that excited me with its reliable hit of dopamine; this obsession that had started in childhood and had grown into something more, about which I felt protective and even sentimental. I had to give up Warren, but it seemed too soon. Like there was still something we needed to learn from one another. I wasn't ready to give him up or give up on him. But I knew I had to stop calling him.

I stopped calling him.

I was quietly brokenhearted. I couldn't talk to anyone about why I was so sad, except my friend Kelly. I felt foolish and alone—bereft from the ending of Warren in my life. I fell into a depression. I thought it was time to revisit therapy. Address why I had used him as a crutch all these years. Figure out why I always pulled a cut-and-run with the other men in my life. I had been in therapy before—when dealing with the eating disorder and its underlying causes—but that was before Warren had gotten married.

Maybe it was time to call Dr. Kastner and do some deeper work. Find out why it was so hard to accept Warren was gone from my life and I was alone, why he'd mattered to me all these years.

But I was tired of therapy. It was hard work. It was expensive.

So instead, I got married.

21

Husbands and Wives

"Can I talk to you about something?"

Tommy Lee's voice was low, almost conspiratorial, although we were alone in the booth of a studio in Hollywood where he was recording a new album. He was standing near the mixing console, which took up half the dark room, leaving just enough space for a ratty couch against a wood-paneled wall where I was standing. He was dark and tattooed and sexy and a musician, not unlike my newish husband, who was on the other side of the big glass wall, joking around with the other musicians.

"Sure," I said. A kind of goofy, laissez-faire "sure" to cover the fact that he'd taken me by surprise with this question. Maybe he needed to talk about my husband, or maybe this was his way of flirting, which seemed dangerous, and also premature, as I didn't sense any connection between us. We'd known each other a total of two minutes, not long enough to know if there was something there. I need at least five minutes.

It was 1993 and my husband was laying down some harmonica tracks for Mötley Crüe's studio album, and he'd brought me along, dumping me in the recording booth to hang out with Tommy Lee while the other musicians were setting up. Tommy was married as well, to Heather Locklear, which I knew because I'd read the covers of the tabloids when I stood in line at the supermarket. I like to stay informed if it doesn't take too much effort.

He picked up his cigarettes and a cheap lighter.

"Want one?"

I declined, as I no longer smoked, or drank, or slept with strangers. Although my husband was nearly a stranger when I married him only five weeks after meeting him. He still felt like a stranger.

Tommy put the cigarettes down and said, "Yeah. I'm not supposed to be smoking. The band made a pact."

He fumbled with the lighter as I thought about my marriage. I was thirty-eight, and I'd never wanted kids. Nor had I felt pushed by societal demands that I should marry. But I was confused by the dimming of the electricity one experiences with someone after the highly charged beginning, and I wanted to test a new theory: If you marry someone during the mad-love stage of the first few weeks, would that keep it from fading? I wanted to cement the feeling during this early phase, "phase' being the key word I was trying to ignore. Not to mention the word "cement," which doesn't lend itself to any kind of fluidity required between human beings.

Tommy put the cigarettes on the console and strutted back to the sofa where I was still standing. My hair was now long and blonde. I looked a little like Faye Dunaway, which was funny considering the Warren thing, but also funny because my husband had lived with Faye Dunaway just before moving in with me. I was wearing black leggings and an oversized blue blouse with shoulder pads. I realized it was the same outfit I'd worn weeks before that had prompted my husband to say, "You should dress sexier."

"Have a seat," Tommy said. I sat at one end of the couch, and he plopped down several feet away from me, in what felt like an almost Victorian distance of propriety, and I wondered if to him I was some new breed, more prim than porn. He'd said he wanted to talk to me about something and I waited for him to start using his words. I put on my listening face.

"I don't know why my wife is giving me such a hard time."

"About what?"

I tried to stay focused and push down my unexamined feelings about my own relationship. My husband had been fun and attentive for the first few weeks but then became sullen and inattentive. Our relationship quickly devolved into his blaming me for anything wrong between us and my not speaking up, so I was starved to have a heart-to-heart with someone about anything, even relationships. Tommy had barely said anything and already it felt more honest. More engaging than when I was with my own husband.

"She thinks I'm cheating on her. Fuck. I'm working my ass off here and sometimes I don't want to go home at night, I mean we live up north and it's a long drive. Does she want me to crash on the freeway? Like, fall asleep at the wheel? So I get a fucking hotel. What's the big deal?"

"That sounds frustrating." I felt like a therapist who was trying to stay focused, but my mind wandered off to my own last intimate conversation with my husband, which was something like, "Give me five bucks for cigarettes."

"I mean we've been through this before and like I put her in this great house in Ventura and she could be grateful, you know? I'm there most of the fucking time with her."

"That seems fair," I said while I wondered what it would feel like to have someone "put me in a great house." Not that I wanted to be caged, but I'd ended up at the other end of the spectrum, marrying someone who had no home, no job, and no dental coverage. It was more like an adoption than a marriage. But I never said this out loud to anyone. Except for my friend Kelly, who knew I cried on the floor of my office at least once a week.

I was married and had no distraction for my sadness; calling Warren often led to sleeping with him, and that wasn't something I was willing to do while married. But then I remembered he, too, was married. And I'd probably never see him again. I was suffocating with no outlet and saw no solution.

"And I tell her before when I'm going to stay in town, so it's not like I just don't fucking show up at the house. I don't want her to worry, you know."

"That sounds really considerate."

"I mean what the fuck am I supposed to do? I give her everything and she's not happy."

This felt like an out-of-body experience as I watched myself sitting on the couch having a heart-to-heart with Tommy Lee, as he complained about his wife and unburdened himself about the confusing aspects of his marriage. It seemed like I should be taking notes—maybe I'd learn something—but I nodded as if I understood. I was at a loss as to what to say. I'd only just met him, and I didn't know his wife so how could I give any marital advice? Plus, what marital advice could I possibly offer?

He seemed distraught and intent on unloading all this in the short time before he was needed in the studio with the other musicians. So maybe better if I didn't say much; let *him* have the time.

"I mean *you* guys seem happy." He indicated my husband on the other side of the glass, who was now warming up with the other guys. Although I don't know what it takes to "warm up" a harmonica.

"I don't know what more I can do. Fuck." He was nearly in tears with frustration. And I wanted to help.

But I was also distracted as just over his shoulder was a picture taped to the wood paneling. It was a full-color close-up of a vagina. A full, legs spread close-up. I listened to him with my wistful understanding face, but also looked around as if I was thinking about his words. Now that I looked more closely, I realized all the photos taped on the glass and wood paneling were close-ups of vaginas. Not like veiled photos of women in sexy poses who happen to be spreading their legs; no innocent wheat stalks in glossy mouths or playful cans of motor oil. There *were* no faces. No bodies whatsoever. They were photos of just vaginas. Almost gynecological, but without the romance.

I appreciated that as Tommy talked to me, he didn't seem to give a second thought to these photos. I liked the lack of artifice or even slight embarrassment. Just the vaginas, why buy the cow? Like it was part of the usual setup when they rented the studio.

I imagined the owner of the recording company: "It's Mötley Crüe, put up the vagina pictures." My mind wandered, and I pictured a string quartet somewhere, with pictures of demure décolletage taped to their music stands, a little cleavage to get their motors running. I thought of Gustave Courbet's *The Origin of the World*, a beautifully rendered painting of a woman's nether regions, from her lower torso to her thighs, but the big feature was her crotch area. I thought—as the title suggested—maybe Courbet was showing respect by giving credit to women for giving birth to everything. Or maybe he just liked pussy. Maybe both. Maybe he was the Larry Flynt of oil painting.

Later, I learned the original painting had included more of the woman herself, her head, her face—she was a person—and the painting had only later been cut down to "just the facts" when purchased by a Turkish collector of erotica before it ended up at the Musée d'Orsay in Paris. I also thought of the European Gentleman's Clubs of a bygone era, oil paintings above the bar of nearly life-sized naked women lying down. Men drinking and admiring the art, i.e., breasts featured prominently with a hint of more flesh under a well-placed hand or a fold of fabric.

I don't fault men for reacting to their own testosterone-fueled arousal need—it's biology—but then call it what it is. Or maybe that's the fun part, calling it art. But it smacks of typing *boobies* on an upside-down calculator—if you were a teenage boy in the '70s. In contrast, I liked the no-bullshit approach of the pictures taped around me in the recording studio.

I turned back to hear what Tommy was saying.

"Things were so great in the beginning," he said, looking at the lighter he still held in his hand. A remembrance of things past—when he used to smoke?

I nodded as if I understood. Which I did. I didn't tell him about my "cementing" theory, as clearly it hadn't worked for me. He'd been married for years, and I'd been married for months, so what did I know? On my first and only date with my husband, he'd borrowed someone's car to take me to a friend's restaurant for a couple of free meals. I thought it was adorable. He was charming and I was easily charmed in those days—"those days" being a few months before. Maybe just as my mother had been charmed by a musician she barely knew and married without much thought. And possibly later regretted.

He went on. "It's not like the fucking isn't still good. I mean she's hot as hell, right?"

"She's gorgeous." What was I supposed to say? That my husband thought I didn't dress sexy enough? That he barely noticed me when I came home from work, as he was busy smoking and talking to someone in Texas?

At this point, Tommy, in his sweet and baffled admission of confusion, was more authentic about his marriage than I was about the true nature of things with my husband. It felt like Tommy and I were both stuck, but he was the only one talking about it, while I pretended I was a mature and knowing woman, listening to this man lay out his frustrations. He was not being sexy or hot or dynamic or all "Tommy Lee." He was trying to figure something out, trying to understand why things weren't working. He was suffering. Whereas I was sitting there pretending to be happy, and my husband was in the studio pretending to be cool.

Several months later, my marriage ended when I got the cable bill in the mail.

I'd opened the bill, checked the items, and found something I hadn't previously seen listed: the soft porn channel Spice, $4.99. I asked my husband about this and he said, yeah, it was one night and he couldn't sleep, blah blah. I said, "I don't mean to be prudish (God forbid), but this makes me feel bad. I mean we could go to the video store and get something and do this together."

I'd gone out on an unfamiliar limb and had told him how I felt.

He started tickling me, saying, "Oooh, look who feels bad." I guess we were done discussing this.

A month later, we were going to drive to Las Vegas where he had a gig that almost paid for a pack of cigarettes, and before we left, I got the mail and there it was. Another charge for the Spice Channel.

Now I was mad. As mad as I ever let myself become, which meant I was polite.

"What is this?"

"What?" he grumped like I was interrupting him.

"The Spice Channel."

"Again? What the fuck am I supposed to do at night? I mean, you're asleep because you have to get up *for work.*" He said "for work" as if this was my failing and I almost laughed.

"Okay."

"Okay, what?" he demanded. Maybe he wanted a fight. But I was done.

"I can't go to Las Vegas."

He took off on his own, gas card in hand. I knew it was over. A lawyer friend told me I should cancel any credit cards I'd given him which I thought was unnecessary, as only a child would still feel entitled to credit cards after the relationship ended.

When he returned, I told him it was over, and after a lot of his angry complaining, followed by angry bargaining, he left. I consoled myself with the fact that I could now restore my apartment to its original glory, once he retrieved the rest of his stuff: a Don Drysdale poster thumb-tacked onto the wall, Mexican blankets on the couch, clothes on the floor, half-eaten chips on any nearby surface, record albums strewn about, plastic slip-on sandals anywhere he'd left them, cigarettes, his guitar, the harmonicas. My apartment looked like a dorm room, which I was willing to overlook if the other things had been half-good. At least that's what I tell myself.

The next day I was at work, and the intern said, "Nikki, your husband's on the phone."

I was steeling myself for apologies and I'll-try-harders. Kelly had reminded me he was very persuasive and also a little desperate, and I should stand firm if he tried to convince me it wasn't over. I took a deep breath and answered the phone.

"Hello."

"What the fuck's wrong with the gas card?"

I explained I had canceled the gas card, and the long-distance phone card as well.

"How the fuck am I supposed to put gas in my car?"

"I don't know." I fought back the instinct to solve this for him.

In his defense, he had never consciously misrepresented himself. He was doing the best he could—with his street-urchin drug-addict history—to find people who would take care of him. Maybe I was simply next in line, plus I wouldn't have to test if I was lovable as I was paying for everything. It was easier to focus on what a mess *he* was than to look at where I was lacking. I probably knew a week after we were married that I'd made a mistake, but I'd fabricated some spiritual overlay that I was in this to learn how to be generous, how to be accepting. I'd committed to this, and therefore I thought I should stick around to see why. Although if actual love was coming my way, I wouldn't have recognized it. As I'd conflated sex and love, it seemed that whenever I was involved in a relationship that may have had both, I only recognized the sex part, and so it always seemed the relationship was missing something. Like I was color-blind to the love part. I was unable to comprehend "green" no matter how much someone greened me. Love-blind. I see now how many of my boyfriends had perhaps loved me, and I admit that if they had, I simply couldn't tell.

Instead, I kept leaving and trying again with someone else. The fault was in me, not in them. As my therapist had told me, these unmet needs from childhood will never be met. And with no clear option for self-repair, I wounded others with my confusing behavior. I'd be all-in until the first hormonal phase passed. I didn't see that I was as immature as my husband, but in a different way.

But for now, I was "happily" married, and Tommy was frustrated about his marriage to Heather Locklear, and I listened as he confided in me.

"This shit is hard," he said. More honest than I'd ever been.

I felt closer to him than I'd felt to my husband. I didn't try to offer solutions. I simply sat with him as he fought back tears. A strange and unexpected moment of intimacy, as I played the role of a therapist whose own life is beyond fucked up. I'd have some thinking to do.

We were quiet for several moments as his admission of confusion settled into the warm and safe space between us.

Just the two of us.

Alone in this small, wood-paneled room.

Only one of us being honest.

And pictures of vaginas taped everywhere.

22

Mrs. Sonny Barger

My long run of successfully getting along with difficult people would come to an end in 2004 when I worked with Dennis Miller, but I was beginning to push the boundaries in 2000 when I was hired to work on the *Dr. Laura* talk show. Due to her inconsistent emotional behavior, her recent staunch position on homosexuality, and harsh judgment of anyone unlike herself, most of the crew steered clear of her to avoid her wrath. Or her tears, depending on the day.

It was easy for us in the control truck to avoid contact with her, as she never visited. It was her show, so we all, of course, did our jobs and tried to satisfy her expectations. Our days were long and tedious. To let off steam and lighten things up in the truck, we made a wall of names—using white gaffer's tape and a felt pen—of everyone's real name and porn name. Anyone who came in got his or her name on the wall. There were about twenty-five pieces of tape on display when we had an unexpected visitor.

It wasn't Dr. Laura.

It was Dr. Laura's husband.

Maybe he'd wandered into the truck to get away from the drama in the studio. Maybe he was curious about who we were and what we all did. Maybe he was lost. Whatever the reason, there he was.

He looked at the wall, read some names, and looked confused.

"What is this?"

Oh, God.

I spoke up (as I was primarily responsible) and explained they were the porn names of the crew and how they had been derived.

He looked at me.

"Porn names?" His eyes had tightened as he looked at me. "First pet and first street?"

"Exactly," I said.

He nodded and said, "Where's the tape?"

And up went his porn name. Sox Twisted Oak. Or something. We never saw him again, although we were proud to have his name on our wall.

The show was canceled not long after it premiered. Everyone above the line folded up their tents and departed, which left me, Nancy (the post AD), and Jules (the editor) to make fixes, add graphics, and deliver the final week of shows. No longer did we get notes from the producers or the network. No longer did anyone oversee our work. We were alone. Plugging through shows no one cared about and few would see.

By the last show we said, "Fuck it," and we had the graphics person re-type all the credits using everyone's porn names. After delivering the shows, we left the control truck for the last time. We heard nothing back from any higher-ups. Cables were coiled; cameras were stowed; the truck drove away to the next gig.

I made a point to watch the last show as it aired—well, the end of the last show—and when the credits rolled, it was nothing but porn names. Nancy was credited as Fred Dolphin. Jules was Scott Sierra. And I was delighted to see:

Associate Director
Sylvia Quakertown

After *Dr. Laura* was canceled, I worked on a few other short-lived shows and finally got a job on a Dennis Miller talk show. This wasn't Dennis Miller's fun HBO show, but his political rant and bad behavior show. I'd heard from people who had worked with him: don't look him in the eye, don't engage him in conversation, but these stories were often apocryphal, and I didn't pay them much attention. I liked the challenge of getting along with people whom others seemed to fear.

Like Eric Lieber, the producer of *Love Connection*. He had been condescending, punitive, and hostile, and was feared by most. It was the holidays, and Debbie, our director, got the nerve to ask him why there wasn't going to be a Christmas party that year.

Eric asked, "Was there a party last year?"

"Yes."

"Did people take pictures?"

"Yes," Debbie said with a smile, thinking she was getting her point across.

Eric said, "Then get those fucking pictures out and look at *them* and leave me out of all your merry-making bullshit."

Eric was merciless. He was like a bully who wanted to be loved and who, deep down, wanted to be a part of something. Being the holidays and all, I'd worn a battery-operated flashing Santa pin to work, which he seemed to notice for the first time during the hostile Christmas party discussion.

"You want Christmas, look at her stupid Santa. What the fuck is that anyway?" he blasted, looking straight at me.

"Merry-making bullshit," I said.

"Hah!"

"Do you want to wear it?"

"I'm not wearing a fucking Christmas pin. One that blinks?" He was not only seemingly hostile, but he was Jewish, so the odds weren't good he'd take me up on it.

"Wear it for an hour and I'll never mention Christmas again."

"Fine. One hour."

He put the pin on his old, dark sweater—it was blinking away with good-natured holiday merriment—and I started a one-hour countdown on my timing device and held it up for him to see that the clock had started ticking. He could have easily gone to his office to sit out the hour, but he kept coming into the booth to ask how much time was left. Like he wanted everyone to see him with the flashing Santa. Or have an excuse to be with us. When the hour was up, Eric returned the pin with a grumpy sound like he had wanted no part of this and left the booth. Which, to me, meant he'd been delighted to wear it.

Debbie turned to me.

"How do you do that? With Eric."

I said, "It's both simple and hard. The simple part is all I need to do is like him. The hard part is liking him."

The same with Don Cornelius, the original host and executive producer on *Soul Train*, where I worked one weekend a month for almost a decade. When I was hired, I'd gotten the same advice from those who had worked with him: avoid eye contact and don't engage him in conversation. I had been introduced to him when I'd first started, and he nodded. Dismissive. That was about it. When he left the booth, everyone seemed to exhale, like phew, that went okay. But I'd never seen Don mistreat anyone. I'd always smiled at him when he came in the booth, although I didn't go out of my way to have a conversation if it wasn't necessary. One day he came in wearing a particularly nice suit.

Without thinking, I blurted out, "Don. You look so snazzy."

He lit up. Like no one had ever noticed. Or talked to him. I wasn't a sycophant; I was smart enough not to wear out my verbal welcome, and after that, we always had nice (brief) exchanges.

I was hired on *Dennis Miller* by the director, Clay Jacobsen, who, although not difficult in the least, was extremely religious. I'd first worked with Clay on *Leeza*—a talk show in the '90s—and we'd developed a quirky friendship. He was an evangelical Christian and had longish hair and a short beard which could have been an homage to either Jesus or Kenny Loggins. Clay probably viewed me as a pagan of sorts. He seemed concerned that I was on a wayward path without guidance from a God who could only be found in the church or scripture. I asked how he would describe a wayward path, considering I didn't smoke or drink. I showed up for work and worked hard. If there was a God, was it possible this God operated *outside* the church as well? He'd written a book (Clay, not God), which I read, and in turn, he asked to see some of my paintings.

He was confused by something in a '50s vacuuming painting, and I explained to him about butt plugs. He didn't blanch, asked a few more questions, and when someone else looked over our shoulder and asked about the painting, Clay was quick to say, "Oh, those are butt plugs."

I figured it would be no different with Dennis Miller. He was human and I was human. I was good at finding the intersection. What could go wrong?

On our first rehearsal day, Dennis fired the stage manager for no reason other than not liking how the stage manager looked at him. Dennis was a fear-seeking missile and could obliterate people with a comment or by firing them. The stage manager had a frightened obsequiousness, so he was the first to go. Dennis didn't suffer ass-kissers well, but as the prompter guy pointed out, maybe Dennis was simply afraid of people. From that day onward, the crew steered clear, except the audio guy who had to mic him.

Clay and I stayed in the control room, which shared a wall with the stage—only a closed door separated us from the "danger zone." Watching Dennis day after day on the monitor, I saw that he loved to complain, he loved to insult, he loved to rant, and whether his complaints were justified or not, everyone was afraid to respond to him. It was often hard to discern if he was blathering on just to be snarky or if he had a legitimate complaint. His hourly complaint was that it was too cold. He physically shivered sitting at his on-stage desk.

Part of my job was solving problems, and the first time Dennis complained of the cold, it sounded like a problem to solve. I turned to the producers in the back row. No one was picking up the phone to call maintenance. And each day, Dennis would complain to the new stage manager about the cold, then complain to whoever heard his mic, which was all of us in the control room. No one moved. No one responded.

After a week of no one doing anything, Dennis showed up at his desk on a new day and launched, yet again, into his usual rant.

"What the fuck is up with this polar ice cap? Did someone build this set on a fucking glacier? Does it have to be fourteen below zero in here? Anyone? What the fuck? How long am I supposed to take this?" Tapping his mic he fumed, "No one does a thing around here!"

No one did a thing.

And Dennis continued to rant.

I had a coat on the back of my chair that was big for me, but it was waterproof, so I kept it there for emergencies. I stood, pulled the coat off my chair, and opened the door to the stage. It was silent on stage except for Dennis's voice. It was quite cold. The stage manager looked my way; hardly anyone ever came through this door. He froze and said nothing as I crossed the stage to the desk.

When Dennis noticed me, he had a "Who the fuck are you" look on his face. I walked behind him, put the coat over his shoulders, patted him a couple of times, and walked back to the control room. I sat down and could feel eyes on me, from the back row, from Clay. Like—what did you just do? I picked up my pencil as if nothing had happened, ready for rehearsal.

Dennis looked stunned. Maybe he was too stunned to notice he felt warmer?

"What the fuck?" he said. "Who sent Mrs. Sonny Barger out here?" Sonny Barger was the founder of the Oakland Hell's Angels, and I have tattoos down my forearms and on my hands, so there you go.

It was impossible to determine whether he was giving me an affectionate nickname or was so enraged by my allowing myself access to him he hadn't yet come up with a more brutal counterattack to my attack-by-coat because if I'm honest, this *was* a subtle attack on my part. I was shining my sarcastic light on him and his babyish behavior, as well as on those in the control room who were afraid of him, people who tiptoed around, afraid to say anything. Afraid to do anything.

It was his show, but this was my own—albeit quiet, humor-veiled—tantrum. In this case, *I* was the bully. At the time, I thought I was simply being playful, finding a way in with Dennis. And if so, for what purpose? I didn't want to be friends with him. In my frustration, I was trying to show the passive people around me how to speak up. Or maybe I just wanted a laugh, although putting the coat on his shoulders was met more with horror than amusement.

I wasn't fired.

Probably because Dennis didn't know who I was, where I'd come from, who had hired me, or what I did on the show. However, he continued to threaten the crew with vague "Mrs. Sonny Barger" comments when something went wrong in rehearsal.

"Fix the fucking lighting (insert any number of daily complaints), or I'll send Mrs. Sonny Barger after you."

Although there was nervous laughter in the booth, I realized I'd crossed the line, and I'd put Mrs. Sonny Barger to rest, even if Dennis hadn't. I was no longer a cute twenty-three-year-old girl with a nun's habit, but a tattooed nearly fifty-year-old woman with a big coat, and at this point, I was probably pushing my luck.

Toward the end of the run, I saw the name Ben Stein on the rundown and felt a wistful nostalgia pass over me, of my early days on *Mary Hartman, Mary Hartman*, when I'd picked him up at the airport while wearing the nun's habit. Back when my irreverence was welcome, and I didn't know any better. I'd learned over the years that the guests' dressing rooms were the domain of the stage manager, so I asked our stage manager to let me know when Ben had arrived, mentioning that I knew him from the past and wanted to say hello.

Having gotten the okay, I went down the hall to the dressing rooms and knocked on Ben's door.

"Yes?"

I cracked the door and said, "Hi. I'm Nikki Nash. I'm not sure if you remember—-"

"Nikki Nash," he said in his best Ferris Bueller tone, low and droll, which I took to mean he was happy to see me. He waved me in. "I've got to tell Al." I knew he meant Al Burton, whom I'd pretended to arrest around the same time thirty years ago when I'd picked Ben up at the airport. He flipped open his phone, made the call, and waited for Al to answer.

"Al. Guess who's here? Nikki Nash. Yes, the nun's habit."

Al said something.

"No, she's *not* currently wearing it." Al said a few more things, and Ben ended the call.

"Al says hello. So good to see you." We chatted about the good old days, about Viva and Al, and we talked about jobs past, about silliness, about still being alive. We stepped into the hall when it was time for me to get back to the control room.

"Great to see you, Nikki." We hugged and broke apart just as Dennis was coming down the hall from his dressing room.

"Dennis," Ben said. "You get to work with this fantastic woman."

Dennis looked baffled, and while he was trying to put this all together, I turned away and went back down the hall to the booth. I was happy to have had such a warm exchange toward the end of an otherwise strange and uncomfortable talk show experience. Happy to find I could still connect with people. That I wasn't evil. That Dennis would see I had friends. That I wasn't Mrs. Sonny Barger. But, who knows, maybe Mrs. Sonny Barger was, in fact, very nice. I hadn't been.

Two years later, I would see Dennis Miller for the last time. I was working on *The Megan Mullally Show*, at KTLA—the same lot where I'd first worked on *Mary Hartman, Mary Hartman*—and saw Dennis Miller's name as a guest on the rundown. My impulse to say hi to him was a way of clearing the air, or righting my old wrong, or ending on a good note, or pretending we had more of a relationship than we did or laughing off the time I may have seemed like a bully. If this story had a theme song, it would be Don McLean's "Everybody Loves Me, Baby, What's the Matter with You?" Or maybe I was simply picking at a scab that would have been better left alone. Boredom or curiosity or wise-assiness got the better of me, and in the afternoon, I asked our stage manager to take me upstairs to the dressing rooms, where he knocked on Dennis's door.

"What?!" came the voice behind the door.

"Mr. Miller?" the stage manager said through the door.

"Open the door, for fuck's sake," he called out.

He did, and sitting on a bland little couch was Dennis Miller. His manager was standing near the snack table. They both looked over at us. I smiled.

"Hi," I said. "I'm not sure if you remember me from your talk show—" I stopped talking.

Dennis's eyes were wide and he looked panicked. He jumped up, gurgled something like, "No, no," his hands up to guard himself, ran into the bathroom, and slammed the door.

I didn't know if this was a bit—like he was making a goofy joke—so the stage manager and I stood in the doorway for several seconds, expecting Dennis to come out laughing. He didn't come out laughing. He didn't come out at all. Time froze, and I wondered if he had actually been afraid of me back when he'd called me Mrs. Sonny Barger. Maybe he hadn't been joking. His manager looked at the closed bathroom door, shrugged, and went back to snacking.

I looked at the stage manager, feeling embarrassed. I had no idea how to explain this odd situation to him without launching into a story we didn't have time for, but I was also afraid Dennis might back out of doing the show entirely, and it would be my fault. Fortunately, either I was quickly forgotten, or his manager had soothed his frightened client's tender feelings, a client who had run nearly screaming when he'd seen me. And the show, as shows must, went on.

The Megan Mullally Show was canceled not long after. For reasons that had nothing to do with Dennis Miller.

I don't know what Ben Stein or Dennis Miller are doing these days, but I would love to see one of them again.

23

Watching 24

It had been four years since Warren had gotten married, and our contact had stopped. Four years of not hearing his voice. Four years of forgetting about him and then remembering him. And forgetting again.

And then, in the fall of 1996, he called out of nowhere and invited me to a movie studio in Culver City where he was making *Bulworth*. As if no time had passed. I respected that he was married, and as I had now abandoned any hope of being "grandfathered in," I kept things light on the phone and was happy for the invitation.

At the sound stage, I was met by an assistant who escorted me in and invited me to sit in a director's chair in the crew area. A while later, Warren came out and greeted me. We had a quick chat in our small circle of intimacy—like we were just two old friends—and he went back to the scene he was doing with Jack Warden. The set was behind a wall, so there wasn't much to look at, although I entertained myself by pretending I was a mystery woman when people occasionally glanced over.

My mind wandered, and I thought back to when I went to the *Lost in Space* set when I was twelve. Nick Persoff—a family friend who was appearing on the show—had invited me and my brothers to come play with the fake rocks and look at the fake stars on the fake horizon. I loved it. Ted held a boulder up as if he were really strong, and Bill picked up a boulder and threw it at Ted. I was more excited by the interior of the ship than the rocks. Nick showed me the elevator that led down to the family's sleeping quarters. First, we stepped into the elevator. When the doors closed, I was expecting the spacey "whoosh," but nothing. Then I pressed a button to go down, and nothing happened. We went nowhere. Nick explained to me that the whoosh sound would be added later and that the sleeping quarters were actually on another sound stage. It was like Santa had died. But on the *Bulworth* set, there wasn't much to see.

I sat nearly motionless for several hours, feeling colder and colder. I stayed in the chair because I didn't know what else to do; I didn't want to make noise, and I didn't want to miss seeing Warren when he finished the scene. We were no longer lovers, but I still felt strangely tethered to him, if only for what he'd meant to me all these years.

When Warren emerged, he came over and asked me to join him in a production meeting. We walked to a blissfully warm office, where the designer showed him a three-dimensional version of another set. Warren introduced me to people with no explanation as to who I was. Just my name, which I liked. I stood in the small room with them, just listening, like I was either a guardian angel, or an auditor. I felt a small remnant of stardust mixed in with a cozy blanket of nostalgia. Or maybe it was simply that the room was warm, and I had stopped shivering.

When the day was done, he walked me to the exit where we had a chaste goodbye. The whole thing was odd.

When *Bulworth* came out in 1998, I called Warren to tell him how much I loved the movie. That he had allowed himself to be truly goofy. I didn't say the movie succeeded where *Ishtar* had failed; I simply told him how much I loved it. That it was funny and political, and I was so happy for him. I thanked him for inviting me to the set that day. He seemed sincerely flattered, maybe a little sentimental himself.

He began calling me more than he had in the past, and our relationship—albeit now platonic—picked up again. While I was working on *Leeza* at the Paramount Studios, he called, telling the intern his name was Stanley. I took the call and started calling him Stanley for a while.

"Where are you?" He asked, which sounded more like filler than actual interest.

"Not far from where you did *Heaven Can Wait*."

"You're at Paramount?"

"Yep."

"Hmmm." Which could have meant he was interested in coming by, or he was distracted, or he was thinking about how long ago we'd met.

"How long have I known you?"

I did the quick math. "Around twenty years."

"Hmmm." And then I had to get back to work.

We chatted on the phone from time to time, and then he invited me to dinner, which was memorable as we'd never actually been out for a meal in the whole time I'd known him. I think Annette was busy making *American Beauty,* so maybe he was at loose ends. We met at a place on Beverly Boulevard called Reds (which seemed sort of funny, considering his movie of the same name), and again, it was two old friends simply getting together for a meal. The waiters were solicitous, and I felt like minor royalty, which made me realize how infrequently we'd been out in public together.

I asked him how it was to have kids.

"I love having kids. I never knew how much I would."

"That's lovely."

I smiled. And wondered if I was supposed to keep talking about his kids.

"You know, Barry Levinson always asks me to see his movies."

"He directed *Bugsy*, right? You have *him* to thank for your marriage."

"I suppose I do." Then, "He has a new movie out, and as he and I are both directors, he likes my feedback."

"Isn't it a little late once the movie comes out?"

"Good point, he said. "Anyway, would you like to go with me? It's called *Liberty Heights*."

"Love to. Happy to fill in as your Plus One."

We met at the theater, sat in the back, and after the movie, he walked me to my car and said, "I can't hug you because of the paparazzi." I appreciated the concept of self-protection, but there were hardly any people on the street, let alone anyone with a camera.

A YEAR LATER, WE MET at a restaurant in Beverly Hills when we both had dermatology appointments blocks from one another. Two old friends getting chemical peels and talking about skin tags. Both our lives were busy, and talking to him occasionally was enough to keep some invisible thread intact. At least for me. The adrenaline rush he provided by simply answering the phone seemed to have lessened with time, but I still reacted to the subtle—if not feigned—sexual innuendo implied in his familiar greeting of "Good evening," which I'd missed hearing. It was more a reminder of times past than a promise of anything in the future.

In 2001, something in me had changed. It had nothing to do with the terrorist attacks on the World Trade Center and the Pentagon—which would change everyone's lives—but instead, it was the TV show *24*, a much-promoted new series starring Kiefer Sutherland that ran from 2001 to 2010. I'd called Warren earlier in the day—for no reason, except maybe boredom—and as usual he'd answered and said he'd call me back later. Which usually meant he wouldn't. This was a familiar old story by now, and not feeling particularly adored by this man I'd used as a placeholder—as a growth barometer—it didn't surprise me or bother me all that much. We were occasional friends, and I was no longer the adrenaline junkie seeking a hit from the sound of his voice. I didn't expect a callback and knew we probably wouldn't talk until the next time I called him.

At 8:59 p.m., I was in my pajamas, had put bread in the toaster, and was ready to settle in for a fun night of TV and toast when the phone rang.

"Good evening." And there it was. That voice.

"Hi," I said. "You called back."

"I always do." Well, I wasn't about to argue the point.

In the past, this was often a prelude to sexy talk, which was usually a prelude to, at this point, nothing. Since he'd gotten married, all our sexy talk went nowhere. But old habits and all. I could have continued with this conversation as I always had, saying something like I'd done in past phone calls, which usually went something like this:

"What are you thinking?"

"I'm thinking about you," I said.

"What are you thinking?" he'd say, with a smile in his low voice.

Which was my prompt to say something sexy about him. And off we'd go.

Except this time when he said, "What are you thinking?" I said, "Not much."

"Not much?" he asked as if I was implying more than what I'd said.

I knew what he wanted to hear. That I was missing him or felt sexual or had a dream about him or whatever. Maybe it was a small window of opportunity for him to experience a taste of his past life. Like he still "had it." What he had was a wife and kids, and we both knew—after all these years—there would be no crossing that line, and any flirtatious banter was just that. Banter.

Maybe *because* we knew it would go nowhere, there was no fear of any follow-through. We could pretend it might go either way, but it never would. We both knew it never would. But it was my job to play the game a bit longer. Give him attention. Get attention. In the past, before he was married, this might have led to getting together at his hotel or my place.

But this time was different. I was ready to call his bluff. Or maybe I was tired of all the flirty crap.

"Warren?"

"Yes," he said in a sexy prelude to nothing.

"Is this going anywhere? Because *24* is about to start."

I didn't have a VCR, so it was now or never for the episode I was about to watch. In the past, I would have dropped everything for another few minutes on the phone with Warren—or the possibility of getting together—but our talks were tired and well-worn, and this was a real TV show. I had better things to do.

At that moment, all the sexy talk was dropped.

"Oh," he said, audibly shifting gears. "*24*. I've heard of that. Is it good?"

I didn't pretend I was about to watch some erudite PBS special that might make me sound more interesting. I just said what I said. Like a normal person. Like he was talking to a friend about a new show.

"Yeah, I'm liking it. It's fun."

"Okay." He said. "We'll talk tomorrow?"

"Great."

My toast popped up.

Our exchange may have sounded mundane, but it was a turning point for me. Like I'd finally pulled my remaining foot out of fantasy and into reality. I was on solid ground. The spell was broken. Not sure whose spell, but I didn't give it much thought as I settled in on the couch.

When I told my brother Bill how I'd chosen TV over Warren, he said, "It's like the Tom Snyder story."

"I don't remember that one."

I knew Mom had liked *Tomorrow with Tom Snyder*. He smoked a lot and spoke his mind. She smoked a lot, but other than with sarcasm, she didn't express herself and was therefore drawn to outspoken people.

Bill explained. "Remember how Bob Stoller was always suicidal, and Mom was always talking to him late at night?" Bob Stoller was the paranoid schizophrenic artist who was a fixture in our house for many years.

I said, "She talked to him like every night. What was the Tom Snyder story? Or maybe I was gone by then."

"I think you'd moved out. This one night he was threatening to kill himself, again, and Mom listened for a minute or two and then said, 'Can you wait an hour? Tom Snyder is on.'"

Bill and I often fell into a usual riff when talking about our mom. Like cheery newscaster banter with forced segues into darker stories:

Mary: It sure is windy out there, Vince.
Vince: Oh, it is blowing, Mary.
Mary: I had to shellac my hair down with a ton of hairspray.
Vince: Speaking of shellac, seventeen children died when exposed to a shellacking agent found in common cereals.

Talking to Bill about the Bob Stoller suicide call led to a riff on Mom's smoking.

"Remember the chipped orange metal ashtray?" I said.

"With the silver lighter. And the brandy."

"They traveled everywhere with her like satellites."

"And a water back," Bill said. "No wonder she couldn't hug us. She was always holding a bunch of stuff."

"Pall Malls *and* Salems. Why did she smoke both?"

"If one won't kill you, maybe the other will? Along with the brandy. Or the vodka. 'For Christ's sake. Won't something please kill me?'"

"Speaking of suicide," I said.

"Always."

"Remember that nice lady at suicide prevention? When I thought dying sounded better than sobriety?"

"Yeah, who would ever want to get sober?" (We were both sober.)

I did the well-worn routine:

Hi, what is your name?

Hi. Yes. If I take about two hundred milligrams of Valium with some sleeping pills and vodka, you think that will do it?

(Concerned but still sweet) Where are you calling from?

I'm just looking for information.

And what is your name, dear?

"I thanked her but hung up. I didn't want to be rude, but I wanted information, not this tender handholding. I called the UCLA emergency room and eventually got some male intern on the line."

Question?

Hi. If I take about two hundred milligrams of valium with some sleeping pills and vodka, you think that will do it?

Yeah, that should do it. (Click.)

"Clearly it didn't. I took all that stuff, and I woke up *so* not dead."

"Big poopy liar."

"Stupid doctors."

We were both quiet.

Then Bill said, "I'm glad you're alive."

"I'm glad *you're* alive."

24

The Ring

In 2008, I needed physical therapy.

After my divorce, I'd taken up swing dancing. It was all fun and games until I tore my rotator cuff, and rather than have surgery, I'd opted for a year of physical therapy, which was longer than my insurance would have covered. Having inherited my dad's frugality, I wanted to find a little extra money somewhere; it was time to sell some jewelry.

I went through my jewelry box and found Gramma Ruth's old silver wedding ring, its two bands of square-cut diamonds fused long ago to form one double band. My grandmother had outlived three husbands, and this was the ring from her first—my mother's father—who had died in a car accident when my mom was fourteen. Gramma Ruth had given me the ring when her knuckles had grown gnarled, and even if I'd liked this retro-nostalgia ring that hadn't seen daylight in decades, and although it may have been considered a pretty ring in the 1930s, it felt sad on my hand, so I never wore it. Gramma Ruth was long gone, and my mother wasn't sentimental, so the ring sat in my jewelry box for almost forty years.

I found an appraiser in Culver City. Patrick was a five-foot-two-inch punk rocker who appraised jewelry to keep his band afloat. He had a banana in his drawer (not a euphemism), and I had a banana in my purse. I believed, of course, it was kismet when we both got hungry, and we both pulled out our matching fruit. We laughed and toasted with our bananas.

We joked around and I tried on the idea of him. His spiked hair gave him a couple more inches, but would he mind if I wore heels? Not that I wore heels often, but these were things to consider. Plus, he was another musician. Gramma Ruth hadn't had much luck with musicians (her first two husbands), and my family was filled with musicians. My father was a musician. His mother was a singer. My uncle was a musician. My brothers are musicians. My mother had been a singer. I'd already married and divorced a musician. Maybe it was time for a scientist or something.

But I thought, keep an open mind with this short, funny, musician/appraiser.

Patrick and I flirted.

I learned about the 4 Cs—cut, color, clarity, and carat, and that Gramma's ring was not all that great, even though what I thought was silver was, in fact, platinum. Patrick gave me the appraisal documents with photos and measurements and special seals of authenticity. We laughed some more, shook hands, and I never saw him again.

Saddened by the end of this not-happening love affair, I cheered myself up with thoughts of cash. Two grand? $1,500?

I tried jewelry stores but was told it was "not a good time." I tried consignment shops, but again, "not a good time."

Equally frustrated by the unfinished business of an unsold ring and the promises of lucre, I decided to unload it on Craigslist. I posted the photos, with the pertinent stats lifted from the appraisal documents, and would have been happy with $1,500. Even $1,200. But nothing. I heard from a few scammers, some of whom I responded to just to mess with them. I had used an email address that didn't include any personal information, and I knew enough not to meet someone at night in an alley, so I figured why not kill time with scammers if they pulled the whole cashier's check thing.

"Ooh, are you getting engaged?" I wrote, after getting an email from someone asking about the ring.

"Yes."

"How did you guys meet?"

"Friends." Like chatting with a Russian spy. After not much meaningful back and forth, and then the Western Union ploy, I stopped responding.

Months before, I'd gotten an email from the ubiquitous Nigerian prince who needed someone to do his U.S. banking for him, and could I possibly help him? I said it was possible but feigned an interruption from a kitty and then responded, "By the way, do you have any pets?"

"No."

"I love cats. Do you like cats?"

"Yes."

"May I send you some pictures of my cat?"

"Are you sending bank information?"

"Oh, yes. I want to help you but look at Mr. Riggles." I didn't have a cat, so I pulled pictures from the internet.

This went on for about a month. I'd send him cat pictures and he'd request my bank information, until I asked him to send me a picture of his cat. I guess he/she grew weary of the lack of funding, or didn't have a cat, and stopped contacting me.

Without even a goodbye.

And now, with much less patience for the whole online process, and feeling vaguely lonely after these electronic exchanges with people I had pretended to care about, I got an email from a man named Dan.

"I'm interested in the ring. Can you tell me more about it?"

I was annoyed at first. Weren't the photos and documents enough? My instincts told me he wasn't a scammer, so I explained I'd posted most of the salient facts but that I had appraisal documents if he was sincerely interested and needed additional information. It felt like a delicate balance between seeming too eager and simply presenting the goods and letting the buyer decide. Like cleavage. How much is too much? I didn't mean to come off as distant, but he needed to know I wasn't a pushover. Until I am, of course.

I got an immediate response from Dan, who explained he was getting engaged, and all hope of a "meet-cute" with him went out the window. I had had a vision of his wanting the ring for his mother or a sister or maybe simply for the diamonds. Like he was an entrepreneur. A hard worker. A go-getter. He was probably handsome, and we could tell people we'd met through an engagement ring. However, now I felt disappointed, and sorry for his fiancée, if this was the sad ring she was going to get.

I asked if he'd like to see more of the paperwork, and he said he was fine with the photos and stats and asked if we could meet. Any whiff of an alley at midnight and I would have said no. But I was open to a cafe or a diner. A walk on the beach. Then came another email:

"There's a Ben Bridge in Torrance. It's a jewelry store."

I felt oddly excited to have such a strong and decisive man tell me where we should meet. Like Petruchio taking hold of Kate's wrist. Yes. Take me. Yes. Ben Bridge. Yes. I reminded myself the man was soon to be engaged, but that didn't stop my mind from wandering into the world of romantic fantasy. Not that I'm desperate—I prefer to think of myself as a good planner—but I once wore my diaphragm to the supermarket in case I struck up a conversation with a nice man and we hit it off and decided to fly to Prague that evening.

"Ben Bridge. That sounds fine," I wrote.

Then I added, "You'll bring cash?" I didn't want to be forced to reject him if he showed up with a check, which is one con away from a Western Union request. I knew some things. I wanted him to think I was bold and savvy and I was asking my *own* questions.

He said he'd bring cash, and we picked a time for the next day.

"How will I know you?" I asked.

"I'll be wearing a red Members Only jacket."

Okay, a Members Only jacket. I mean, that jacket was sort of uncool back when it was popular in the '80s, let alone now, over twenty years later. Well, at least he admitted to it without irony. Maybe he was a simple and sincere type of guy. This would be a good challenge for me in acceptance. I was looking at my preconceptions and judgments and wondered: Could I love a man who wore a Members Only jacket? Ignoring, of course, the fact that he was getting engaged might impede our potential love affair. But then I figured the guy was probably sixty. Old jacket, old ring. Oh, well. But he didn't seem old in his email. Based on what? I re-read our exchange for more clues but found nothing to indicate we were meant for one another.

I looked up Ben Bridge to confirm it existed (savvy me). This was simply a transaction for which I would be grateful, and so there was no need to dress up or put on makeup. I did both. If this did indeed turn out to be some kind of "meet-cute," I wanted to look my best. I chose a light blue cotton dress that was belted at the waist and a cute pair of platform shoes. Then subtle perfume. Pink gloss.

I took about seven freeways. At least it seemed that way, but it was only six. The 101 to the 10 to the 110 to the 105 to the 405 to the 107 to left on Fashion Way to right on Hawthorne Boulevard. You can't miss it.

I felt a surge of adrenaline when I spotted the Ben Bridge sign. I found my way to the parking lot, drove around, and found a space in the back where I felt less exposed. I checked my purse to confirm the ring and paperwork were still in place, put on a refresher of pink lip gloss, fluffed my hair, took a deep breath, and opened the car door.

It was hot out. A breeze pulled at my skirt and blew my hair into my lip gloss. I pulled the hair away, getting gunk on my finger which I rubbed into the palm of my other hand. I locked up my car and walked to the front of the building, casually looking around like it was simply a nice day in Torrance, and I was going to a jewelry store. Both of which were true.

The front entrance was imposing. Marble tile on the exterior wall and large glass doors which led to a grand foyer. I didn't see Dan anywhere out front, so I pulled open one of the big glass doors and was hit in the face with cold air. The first person I saw was a young blonde woman sitting at a lectern. Like a hostess. I smiled at her but then looked past her and saw a red jacket. On a man. Whose back was to me. I looked back at the young woman.

"I'm meeting someone," I told her, indicating the man in the red jacket. Like this was a fancy restaurant and I'd found my date.

I took a few steps closer to the man so I wouldn't have to raise my voice. "Dan?"

He turned around. He *was* handsome, clean-shaven, and had dark brown hair with a little silver at the temples. He looked older than I'd expected and wasn't too forthcoming with a smile or anything.

"You have the ring with you?" Like a drug deal. Or like I was a prostitute and there wasn't going to be a lot of chatting, just getting down to the business at hand.

"Yes, I have the ring." I felt hurt by his lack of chattiness.

Pluses: Handsome; has money to buy ring.

Minuses: Doesn't think I'm smart enough to remember ring; is getting engaged.

Unknown: Sense of humor?

"Can you show me?" he said, with not an ounce of flirty playfulness.

I pulled a scuffed leather ring box out of my purse and opened it to reveal the ring. It was like I was proposing to him.

He took a step toward me and was close enough to touch the ring. But instead of touching it, he grabbed the box out of my hand, snapped it shut, and put it in his pocket. Then, in one swift move, he grabbed the wrist of my right hand, and using his other hand, he turned me around, bringing my right arm up behind my back. I wanted to scream.

In a panic, I looked at the blonde hostess.

"Help!!" I sort of yelled, torn between saving my life and making a scene in a fancy jewelry store. My eyes were all over the place and I looked back at her, pleading. "Call the police. Help me! Do something." I probably sounded more like a kitten caught up in a tree, but I was terrified.

I tried again, looking right at the blonde girl, "Stop him! Help!"

She was impassive, like this kind of abduction was a common occurrence at Ben Bridge, just another day in Torrance.

Meanwhile, Dan was roughly trotting me toward the front door, and I made yet another panicked turn to anyone who might be in the store who would help me. I tried to dig in my heels, which was hard while wearing platform shoes, and Dan was stronger than I was, by a lot. He pushed the door open with his foot, and he kept pushing me until we were outside.

I looked for somewhere to run. I tried to pull away, but he held me firmly in place. Two men wearing black rushed toward me from both directions on the sidewalk, and Dan passed me off to one of them, who grabbed my arm with force.

I panicked: This was some well-planned theft. First, the whole Ben Bridge ruse, and then I'd be dragged into some back alley I'd failed to notice. I wondered if they were going to kill me.

I was resistant to being taken anywhere and yelled at them to stop. I was louder this time as we were now outside.

"What are you doing?" I yelled at Dan.

I looked back one last time at the blonde inside the store. I was pleading for help with my eyes, but she looked as concerned as if she were thumbing through a new Sephora Catalog.

A third man in black approached.

I thought: *This is where they throw me into the trunk of some car.* I was struggling but they weren't actually taking me anywhere. Did they *want* this theft/abduction to happen on the sidewalk in daylight? In front of everyone? "Everyone" consisted of maybe two random people in the parking lot.

The third man said, "Her vehicle is clear. It appears she came alone."

The men, I realized upon closer inspection, were cops. Or FBI or SWAT or something. My adrenaline was surging. I could feel I was being held firmly in place, but I no longer feared for my actual life. Something very weird was happening and I didn't like it. Dan accepted I'd come alone and turned to me.

"You have the paperwork?"

"Can I reach into my purse?" It was a small purse, but I didn't want him to think I had a gun tucked away, wrapped in a hankie. I'd seen TV shows.

He nodded yes.

I pulled out the folded paperwork I'd gotten from Patrick the gem guy, and handed the pages to Dan.

"Where did you get this ring?" His voice was low but firm.

"It was my Gramma Ruth's. I told you in the email."

"Can you confirm that?"

"No. She's dead. But you can call my mom." I realized with a strange relief that it was after 2 p.m., so she'd probably be awake. "Why?" I said. "What do you want? What's going on?"

"Ma'am." That's how it starts with law enforcement, with a 'ma'am.' "We believe you are in possession of stolen goods."

"What? No! Call my mom." Which sounded pathetic—I was a grown woman. He nodded in Number Three's direction, who got my mom's number from me. He turned away and made the call on a big black mobile phone.

Dan waved to another SWAT guy type who was lingering near the parking area and who then led a tall woman with stringy hair past us and into Ben Bridge. Dan followed, taking the ring and paperwork with him.

Number One had let go of my arm because at this point, I was triangulated by guys in black and wasn't going anywhere. Number Three turned and said to Number Two. "No answer at the number of the residence given by the suspect." As if this was being documented for some legal case in the future.

Wait. Suspect?

"Call her again," I said. "Sometimes she doesn't like to answer the phone." Well, that sounded pretty stupid. Probably not the time to go into the whole late-night bourbon and Velveeta grilled cheese routine.

"Did you leave a message? Sometimes she screens her calls." I was worried about being too bossy with these guys. They ignored me.

Then came the anxious standing around while the SWAT guys, or whatever they were, looked anywhere but actually at me. I expected them to talk into their wrists at any moment. My adrenaline was still surging, and I felt damp in my armpits and wondered if the blue dress showed sweat, and then I remembered Dan was a cop and probably wouldn't care about my blue dress. Or my armpits. I felt embarrassed and deflated. My feet hurt in the platform shoes. There was still a soft breeze, and now a few clouds were puffing about. A lovely day if you could overlook the whole take-down aspect.

I looked at the guys. "What is going on? This is crazy." But they didn't seem at liberty to explain.

Dan re-emerged with the ring and the paperwork. I tried again.

"What's going on?"

"A woman reported a theft, and we keep an eye on Craigslist. Your ring was a near-perfect match." The tall woman was escorted out by what I guessed was an undercover guy, who must have been embedded in the jewelry store in case what? In case I made a run for it back *into* the store?

"Here." Dan handed me the ring and the paperwork.

The guys in black relaxed, meaning they exhaled stiffly, and then they dispersed, leaving me with Dan.

"I guess this means you're not going to buy the ring?" I was going for the laugh instead of expressing the outrage I probably should have been feeling. But I was disappointed that not only was Dan not going to be my new boyfriend, but I'd have to go back home with this stupid ring. And try again.

"We're sorry, but it was the only way we could confirm you weren't part of a jewelry-fencing operation."

"Yeah, I'm very scary."

He sort of smiled.

"So I just go now?" I asked.

"Yes. You're free to go."

"Great." I stumbled as I turned, after having been immobilized for a half-hour on the sidewalk. But I managed to keep walking until I got to the back of the store and went to my car. I looked around for a van or something, like "Ron's Flowers," where I imagined SWAT guys were now reconvening, guzzling water, and recuperating after a big stake-out and take-down. But there was nothing. No one.

I got into my car. Cried a little, felt stupid, and drove home.

Later that day, Dan sent me an email, again explaining the situation and apologizing. I asked him if he was really getting engaged.

"Married eighteen years, got two boys."

I had no further contact from Dan.

But a couple of months later, I emailed him.

"Hey, I'm selling a desk lamp on Craigslist. Can you maybe not send the SWAT team?"

He wrote back, "Noted."

25

Good Evening

Over the years, my phone calls with Warren reflected my growth. He may have seen a confident person who spoke her mind, whereas I felt I'd been passive and malleable. My early blind devotion was tied to a time when I was young and lost, and although I was no longer that young self, but now nearly sixty, I still tended to be careful about what I said so as not to appear too needy. I hadn't yet learned the full benefits of a long relationship: there's a presumed understanding the other person will stick around based on them having stayed around in the past. I didn't have much experience with that.

Now that I'd seen I could interrupt a sexy-talk phone call with reality ("I gotta go. *24* is on"), I settled into what was a strange friendship, a trust that longevity had provided. Although I may have been direct with Warren, I'd never gotten mad at him.

Then I did.

It was 2015. I was working on *Conan*, where I'd gotten into the habit of calling Warren every few months during lunch breaks, and we'd settled into a friendship where we talked politics, or how Hollywood had changed. Pointless, habitual, sexy banter was a thing of the past, and I was happy just chatting. I now experienced a different kind of dopamine hit when I called and he answered. Like *Look at me, I'm friends with Warren Beatty.*

One lunch break when I called him, he was busy and said to call him back at three if I could. We had a break in the afternoon, and I went into the voice-over booth where I had privacy, killed the mic, and called him back.

He answered. "Good evening." With that now-boring, sexy voice I knew so well.

I was confused. Then I was mad. I was way past the point of expecting any kind of physical contact with him—like a cup of coffee—so I was surprised by the implied sexuality of his well-worn greeting. He was doing what he'd always done, but this stunned me. We'd certainly had many conversations over the years that weren't about sex, so it wasn't that. We'd been through so much, and now we were back to this? How could we be friends if he couldn't even talk to me like a real person?

"Warren, for fuck's sake. It's three in the afternoon. Stop with that 'good evening' bullshit. The sun is shining. We're not going to have sex. Stop being all Warren Beatty."

And now it felt like a forty-year relationship was over with those two words: *Good Evening*.

I didn't worry that my being mad was too much for him or out of character for me. How could there be anything real if he couldn't start by acknowledging even the time of day?

I didn't worry if my burst of anger would mean it was over for him. It was over for me.

I wondered what had taken so long. Had I been trying to create some big story arc for my life that began with a fourteen-year-old girl's crush and ended—if not in romance—in some deep, long-lasting friendship? The fact that I saw it as a story made me wonder if I shared Warren's inability to be in the moment. I'd envisioned some satisfying endgame to compensate for the fact that I'd given this childhood obsession so much time and attention over the years. I thought I'd been honest in admitting I'd never be in the rarefied world of Isabel Adjani or Annette Bening, but I'd still felt special. Like I should get credit for knowing him the longest, dammit. But now, I was tired of tending to this subtle fabrication, of manipulating the truth to make it fit my idea of a good story. Maybe we were done. Maybe I was done. Maybe we weren't ever really anything.

I remembered a parable about relationships: If you think you are doing all the work, it's like being in a rowboat with someone. Stop rowing and see if the boat goes anywhere.

I stopped calling.

I went on with my life. As I always had. Warren had never stopped my life but was always an undercurrent. Or a perceived undercurrent. Or an abandoned undercurrent when I'd gotten involved with someone. The story with him was over. I wasn't worried that I'd need to explain to Warren why I'd stopped calling him because I didn't think—based on our history—he'd notice. If he had, we would have had a different relationship.

And as months passed, I felt an occasional sentimental pang for the times when I could just pick up the phone and call him. I reminded myself it was over, that this was an old habit, and eventually my habit of calling him turned into a habit of *not* calling him.

But.

Two years later I figured, what the hell. Or maybe I was bored. Or had just broken up with someone. Maybe it was simply that it was a warm mid-summer afternoon, and the days felt too long.

Or I simply missed talking to him.

I called.

He answered the phone: "Happy Halloween."

And all was forgiven.

26

Altered States

The needle pierced my skin, and I waited to feel the fluid hit my system. When it did, everything melted away. First, my shoulders relaxed, and then my body felt liquid, and I was happy and hopeful and in love with the feel of the light blanket on my skin. I closed my eyes and could see the dark colors of the opium den, which made no sense because I wasn't smoking opium, and I wasn't in an opium den. When I opened my eyes, I was looking up at a white ceiling with fluorescent lights. I was on a gurney in a hospital in Santa Monica, about to get a colonoscopy.

Which provided the only high I had left to me.

After Warren got married, we had less contact. Fortunately, by then, the mind-altering nature of my obsession had passed, and now we were friends who spoke only occasionally. Maturity and time had removed the need for the constant high I'd gotten from alcohol or cocaine. Or the quick blast of sedating stardust I used to get hearing Warren's voice. Although I still occasionally craved feeling swept away.

Lying on the gurney, I remembered a commercial from my childhood that promised overworked housewives a solution (to life, I guess?) with Calgon bath oil beads. The woman's plaintive cry: "Calgon, take me away." Sadly, the bath bombs of today don't take me anywhere, and I was still looking for an out. For a peaceful serenity. It had been suggested I try doing for others, doing good works, volunteering to be of service. You know, like charity work that would probably involve travel, but I prefer to experience my good feelings while lying down doing nothing.

I knew what to expect in the outpatient hospital, as I'd had a minor eye procedure many years before, and it had involved an IV drip and then anesthesia. I loved lying on that gurney with no responsibilities and a slow IV flow of relaxing Valium. I could have stayed there all day. Or the rest of my life. When it was time for the procedure, the anesthesiologist had me count backward from one hundred—as you see in the movies—but not only was I out in about three seconds, but I wondered later why—if it was going to be that fast—give the hundred-count business. Is that supposed to be calming? Anesthesiologists have done this before—they must know it takes three seconds. Why not give a ten count? Maybe some people experience fear going under (not gleeful anticipation like I do), so one hundred sounds far away and therefore doable; the potential actualization of their fear is far in the future and thus too far away to worry about. Like the difference between knowing you're going to die and knowing you're going to die Saturday.

And now, it was time for my colonoscopy. My doctor had explained the procedure and gave me a quick overview of the day, which would include the IV to relax me and a quick chat with the anesthesiologist. On the outside, I looked serious, nodding occasionally to acknowledge I understood what he was explaining. Inside I was all, "Can't wait!"

After the prep day, I was dropped off at the hospital by a friend and went in for the procedure. The nurse put me on a gurney, and I was worried my blood pressure might be a little high with the expectation of a Valium drip, but I was hoping she'd assume I was simply anxious about the procedure. The IV went into the top of my hand, and I was quite content to lie motionless and listen to other people showing up and nurses starting their shifts and the whoosh of privacy curtains opening and closing. I was part of this world. Happy to be a part of this world. I loved this world.

They rolled me into the procedure room. My doctor came in, patted my shoulder, and said the anesthesiologist would be in shortly to discuss things with me, which seemed odd because what was there to discuss? How to count backward from one hundred? Anticipating the visit from the anesthesiologist, I had time to think about this. And other things. And then nothing. Feeling good. Just enjoying the ceiling. I closed my eyes.

"Hi, I'm Dr. Winters, and I'll be your anesthesiologist." Like she was a server at a restaurant.

I looked over and saw a lovely woman standing there. Maybe in her forties, nice smile.

"Hi." I was relaxed from the IV. "Hi" seemed like enough at the moment. Like the whole world existed in that one word.

"Do you have any questions?"

This seemed like a hard question. I pondered. And finally said, "Oh! Yes."

"Go for it." She was fun. Everyone was fun on a Valium drip.

"Okay," I said. "I've been sober for a long time, and this is my only free ride, so could you give me a longer take-down than the three-second thing?"

She laughed. I figured she thought I was joking, which made me sad. All I was asking was for more than three seconds.

She said, "I've been in AA for fifteen years. I get it. I'll take you down slow."

And she did.

Heaven.

Admittedly, the lure of going under is a big draw for me. Maybe it's the absence of responsibility. I realize this may not be the case for a lot of people, but I also experience a similar strange calm when flying ("It's out of my hands; if we crash, we crash.") and with earthquakes ("Nothing I can do, guess I'll ride it out").

Maybe it isn't the Valium that provides such a profound and lovely peace, as much as my letting go of the belief that I'm in charge of everything on the planet, and therefore I'm due a rest. Even a narcotically-assisted rest.

When I was twelve, the only opportunity at that age for "out" was hyperventilating. I'm not sure who introduced me or my friends to this, but it became the fun thing to do at our little flat-chested, nightgowny slumber parties. It involved standing with someone behind you and breathing in and out as hard and fast as you can, and then the person behind you wraps her arms around your chest and squeezes until you black out. It was the coming-to that was fun. All disoriented and dreamy. This was standard slumber-party fare until one night in Kathy's den, Robin, who was taller than everyone, fell forward and hit her head on the coffee table. She was out for about a half-hour, and we didn't know what to do. Death vs. Getting In Trouble. Fortunately, she came to before we were forced to make a decision. We vowed to never do this again.

Until Terri's slumber party.

In my teens it was alcohol. Whether I was predisposed, as they say, or merely taking the edge off being alive, it became a pretty regular thing. My mom and Gramma Ruth both enjoyed an occasional cocktail—like every hour—so I may have come by it naturally.

I never saw my dad with a cocktail, but there was a reason he'd stopped drinking. He had been working on the Tennessee Ernie Ford radio show, and it was a new thing for guitar players to show up with small amplifiers. Jimmy Bryant sat right behind my dad and blasted his amp. Dad turned around several times and asked Jimmy nicely to turn it down. One day, Dad had had a few martinis at lunch, and Jimmy hadn't yet returned. A little buzzed, Dad took the small squirt bottle of water he used on the slide of this trombone, reached around, and sprayed the liquid into the back of the amp. When Jimmy sat down, he turned on his amp and it shorted out with a small explosive sound and maybe a few sparks, and no one was very happy with Dick Nash, the trombone player. He vowed that day to stop drinking. And he did. And from then on, he had no understanding of why others couldn't just stop.

Like my mom and her drinking or my brother and his heroin. Or me and whatever was available. He was the original "just say no" guy, which went along with his "shed a tear and move on" theory. As I got older, alcohol was my main outlet for rest and relaxation, although I was open-minded enough to try other modes of altered states.

Flotation tanks were a thing in the early '80s—for about seven months. The place I went was on Wilshire Boulevard, in a strip mall next to a tuxedo shop. I'd never been in a flotation tank. I was working on a TV production of *Ain't Misbehavin'*, and the producers gifted several of us with ten sessions after all the hard work we'd done. Once I'd recovered from several long and exhausting days on the show, I made an appointment at the flotation tank place. A pretty receptionist checked me in. Beyond the reception area was a changing room, showers, and then six private rooms, each with a flotation tank holding six inches of salt water. The idea was to get into the tank—which was like a semi-flooded coffin—close the lid, lie down, and float in the darkness. I remembered a grammar school science film about sensory deprivation and how the mind starts telling stories to compensate for the lack of physical input. I was expecting something like this: I'd float and experience nirvana, and along with nirvana, maybe the meaning of the universe. At the least, I'd get an hour's rest. However, anything worth doing was worth doing with cocaine, and knowing cocaine made me extra-thinky, I brought a pad and pencil and placed them on top of the tank so I could make notes of any valuable thoughts as they popped up. I got in the tank, settled in, and about thirty seconds later, I opened the half-lid to write something down. Then back in the tank. I did this in and out for the entire hour. I wrote many important things down, none of which were valuable, either for me or for my future biographers. I never went back. I sent a nice thank-you note to the producers, however.

When I eventually stopped drinking at twenty-eight, I did not want to feel how I was feeling. People in sobriety recommended prayer and meditation. Writing. Looking at my faults and making amends. Reaching out to people. Working with others. Some suggested that listening to Louise Hay's affirmation tapes at night would calm the rage. Help with the sadness. Heal the grief. I thought, too many moving parts.

Instead, I found gravity boots! I latched on to the idea that a few minutes upside down would cure everything. My dad had used a slant board in the '60s. The board was two feet off the ground at one end and on the floor at the other. He hooked his feet under a strap at the higher end and lay there. At the time, this was a mystery to me and just something Dad did, but it probably had to do with circulation. Or maybe it was his one excuse to lie down with impunity.

I was nearly thirty when I stumbled upon an ad for gravity boots. I read they would keep my skin young, my organs from compressing, and blood flowing to my brain (which I believe it does naturally, but whatever), and may even give the user a sense of mild euphoria—mild euphoria being the main objective in all activities, as I saw it. I looked in the Recycler every week, hoping to find someone selling gravity boots while overlooking the obvious: that if someone was selling them, they probably weren't the miracle cure they were hoping for and, by extension perhaps, not the magic answer I was hoping for. But I was on a mission. I knew the truth, and the truth was gravity boots.

I bought the boots, which were not boots at all but thick, padded ankle bands with metal hooks, and they came with a bar you attached to a doorway that looked secure enough to hold maybe a shower curtain. But I was ready for my new life to start if I didn't break my neck. Although maybe *that* would be my new life. I put on the "boots" and needed about ten minutes to figure out how to hook myself up without much upper body strength, so after getting a chair and hooking one foot on the bar, I dangled precariously for a moment but with a big swing got the other leg up there. Let my torso slowly hang, knocked the chair back like in an Old West hanging, and let my arms reach for the floor. I was sweating and had a headache. I hung there for about three minutes and said, *this is stupid*.

And resold the gravity boots in the Recycler.

After the initial grief of getting sober—regretting I'd never get to try Ecstasy, Propofol, or Zima (which came in 6-pack of cute little bottles, like for a picnic I'd never go to)—I settled into a sober life and thought, with a wistful surrender, all that was left for me was the occasional IV-and-anesthesia combo of a medical procedure.

I got my chance when I scheduled a face-laser thing with my dermatologist. I'd heard it was forty-five minutes of extreme pain, like a jackhammer of needles and hot lasers being dragged and pounded across one's face. Or, as the dermatologist put it: "There may be a slight stinging sensation."

When I mentioned I'd heard this was quite a painful a procedure, I was offered the option of anesthesia for another $500. I gave it a thought so as not to look too eager, and said yes. Anesthesia! Plus, I looked forward to having my pores look smaller.

Maybe not to the naked eye, but still.

The following week, I signed in, and was taken in a wheelchair to the operating room, which was cold and without charm. Someone efficient wearing a white lab coat inserted the preliminary IV into the top of my left hand. She said to relax and that the anesthesiologist would be in shortly.

I sat in the wheelchair and waited. Not for the anesthesiologist as much as for the slow flow of liquid relaxation. I was aware of a slight stinging sensation on the back of my hand where the needle had been inserted, but it bothered me less and less as I closed my eyes and felt the flow of Valium enter my bloodstream. My brain loosened its grip on things, and I felt my thighs relax. I opened my eyes and felt safe and warm in this beautiful room. Delighted by its simplicity, the multitude of many white things. I felt calm, like I'd been wrapped in a cozy blanket of "there, there." I felt pharmaceutically peaceful in a quiet, deep, and timeless way.

I was disappointed when my reverie was interrupted by the efficient woman in the white coat who took hold of the wheelchair and rolled me over to the gurney. I got up onto the hard bed, lay back, and felt the cool air on my cheek. I could smell a hint of lovely soap. It didn't take much to return to the euphoria of the senses. And now I was lying down.

But I was curious about something. I tried to act casual and avoid drooling.

"So what's in the IV?" I asked the non-speaking lady. Maybe there was some newfangled drug I hadn't yet heard of that had replaced Valium. It's good to keep up with these things.

"What?"

"What's in the IV?" Casual—like someone asking, "Is there dairy in the gazpacho?"

Maybe she wasn't allowed to discuss drugs with the patient. She responded, "Saline, to start the line."

"No Valium?"

"Just saline." (Like asked and answered.) And she left.

Saline? What? My high deflated as the room was restored to stark and ordinary. I was left alone again, staring up at the ceiling in a cold white room and I thought, this isn't right. I pay hundreds of dollars for a possibly useless procedure and I don't even get Valium?

This left me with one remaining option for getting any nice IV buzz: colonoscopies.

After that first colonoscopy, my doctor had recommended I get one every three years.

But to err on the side of caution, I'm thinking maybe every Friday.

27

Mulholland Drive

I was in Beverly Hills to get Botox. I rarely went into Beverly Hills except to do things to my face, and—driving past the Beverly Wilshire Hotel—I was flooded with memories of the Old World Restaurant, and therapy with Dr. Kastner, but mostly I was thinking of Warren and the last time I'd seen him: 1999—twenty years earlier—when we'd met up for lunch after discovering we both had dermatology appointments on the same day. After parking, I sat in my car and found it hard to believe so much time had passed since I'd last seen him. I was also surprised to think I'd been getting Botox for twenty years.

I felt sentimental and called him to tell him where I was and that I was thinking of him. He said to call him after my appointment. I knew how this would go: I'd call him after my appointment. He'd sound sexy and then say he was busy. He'd say, let's talk later. I'd say great, and I wouldn't call him. Or I would. Or he'd call me. Or a month would pass with no contact. Or a year. And if I was bored or lonely, I'd call him again and we'd go through this well-worn routine yet another time.

I called after my appointment as promised and he said, "I have a meeting in an hour but come on up."

What?

I figured the "meeting in an hour" meant he was fitting me in or laying the clear ground rules that this was not an amorous visit, in case that was on my mind. Which it wasn't. Not only was he married, but I was way past being interested in having sex with him. This was no date, but I was glad I was wearing a dress so I wouldn't feel like a total slob.

"Great," I said. And to acknowledge I'd inferred his meaning and that I'd understood the no-funny-business ground rules, I added, "We'll have a brief handshake and catch up. It'll be nice to see you again." Like making a plan with an accountant.

It was a cool fall day. GPS directed me up winding roads to his house at the top of the Hollywood Hills. I thought of the last time I'd been on Mulholland Drive with him. It was forty years before when he still lived at the Beverly Wilshire, and we'd go to Jack's house for parties or football. My mind was wandering, maybe as a distraction from the low-grade nervousness I had about seeing Warren again after all these years.

I turned onto a small drive, which led to a big metal gate, and after pressing the buzzer, the gate opened. I drove slowly up a steep driveway past some large, manicured hedges and saw five other cars parked along the drive.

I parked behind an old Toyota. I didn't need a mirror check, as I'd gotten Botox many times before, and I knew my face was pink and dotted from the injections, but I didn't want to be more anxious than I was. Seeing Warren—albeit infrequently—always triggered a Pavlovian response of giddy nervousness. It would pass. I got out of my car and walked along the drive past another large green hedge revealing the sprawling house. Warren was standing at the top of the front stairs, ready to greet me. He was smiling. He was still lean, wearing jeans, a white shirt, and a black windbreaker; his grey hair was thinning but perfectly in place. He put his arms out and I walked into his now platonic embrace and surrendered to the familiar fit. I inhaled and remembered his scent, which still reminded me of my childhood hamster cage.

He opened one of the big doors, and we went through to a tiled entryway revealing a large living room with a spectacular view of Los Angeles. The living room was filled with dark furniture and Persian rugs and—despite the light from the windows—looked gloomy. I followed him into the kitchen, which was not huge but more like a functional family kitchen. This was not a magazine showplace; it was home to a long-married couple who had raised four kids.

A big dog—a Newfoundland—wandered in, tail wagging.

"Be careful. He slobbers."

We remained standing as I said hi to the dog, giving him the back of my hand to smell. He wandered out, and Warren and I were alone. Although I imagined there were more people somewhere in the expansive house.

He gave me that smile.

"You look the same. Better," he said.

"Thanks. You look great."

Niceties out of the way, he seemed uncertain about what to do next. Maybe playing host didn't come naturally to him; it wasn't like the old days when he'd pick up the phone at the Beverly Wilshire and call room service and food would be delivered and then we'd have sex.

"Would you like anything to drink?" He seemed to catch himself as though he wasn't sure where the drinks were. "Water?"

I guess water was the option. "Water is fine," I said.

He handed me the glass of water and led us through the kitchen to the breakfast room. We sat at a big oval table that was too large for the room, covered with a green tablecloth that was too large for the table. Books and newspapers covered a lot of the available space, and as there were no coasters, I took a section from the paper and placed my water glass on it. Warren took the seat at the head of the table, and although I sat in the chair next to his, there was more than a foot between us, so it didn't feel awkwardly intimate. I had no idea how this visit would go—which was fun in itself—but with all the sexual stuff off the proverbial table, there would be room for a different kind of conversation, a different kind of interaction.

First, we covered all the familiar territory that comprised Warren's version of "kids today": how the movies weren't what they used to be with all the streaming platforms; there were no stars anymore; there was no mystery; it was all comic-book blockbusters, which led to a lot of "in my day" stuff. It was more of a monologue than a conversation, but I was still happy to be sitting with him, listening to him talk.

After running out of steam on the topic, he looked into my eyes like he was seeing me for the first time. I expected him to ask the same question he'd asked so many times over the years. *"How long have we known each other?"*

"How long have we known each other?" he asked. And it led to me recounting—yet again—many of our adventures. The Bob Altman party when I was still too young for him. The party at Robert Towne's, where he and Jack ate cheesecake out of the fridge. My brother teaching him how to play the sax for *Heaven Can Wait*. The trips to the Playboy Mansion. All the phone calls over the years. The "Good Evening" dust-up we'd had. He listened like I was telling him facts from someone else's life, and he was hearing them for the first time. I felt—once again—like a cross between Sisyphus and Scheherazade.

"Tell me again how we met," he said.

"The Old World," I said. I reminded him that I'd gotten the job there only so I could meet him. And that I'd waited a year and a half before he'd shown up.

"Really," he said, taking this in like it all finally made sense. As if my recounting of this childhood obsession, the job at the restaurant, and all the phone calls I'd made over the years was illuminating. Like something just occurred to him.

"You love me," he said.

Although dementia didn't seem to be an issue, his saying this reminded me of a story my friend Tom told about visiting his mother in the hospital. She had Alzheimer's, and although he saw her weekly, she was becoming less responsive to him. This particular—and heartbreaking—time, she looked up at Tom and said, "I don't know who you are, but I can tell you love me."

Maybe that's all it ultimately came down to. The ability to *feel* loved.

A young man quietly stepped into the breakfast room.

"Warren, you have that thing." Like a prearranged rescue.

"Cancel it. I'll call him tomorrow."

"Will do."

"Aaron, this is Nikki. A dear friend." A dear friend?

Aaron said, "Nice to meet you," and left.

Warren looked back at me and smiled. I looked at him warmly and waited for his words, considering I'd used a lot of them in the recounting of the past, and it was his turn.

"You are so beautiful," he said, which was sweet—and I believe he was sincere—but I was hoping to get past the superficial; I wanted to have a real conversation with him, and as it seemed he wanted to say something more, I let the silence remain, giving him space. I was moved to see him again after all these years, and maybe the time had come for summing things up. Based on our history and age—I was almost sixty-five and he was eighty-one—I thought this might be our last time together after all the years since we'd first met, and it was time to say nice things. Like wrapping-up things.

In his measured and thoughtful way, he told me how he'd been watching the *Golden Globes* and couldn't believe how "done" the women had looked.

"Here we are in the #MeToo movement," he launched, "and yet women continue to present themselves as fuckable commodities. The revealing outfits. The breasts. The immobilized faces."

I expected we'd now continue with a discussion of the #MeToo movement, and although women and sex were well-worn topics for him, I thought this new spin would offer up the possibility of a fresh take. Like a discussion about adornment, who does it satisfy and why? Or different types of adornment and its purpose for different genders. Adornment through the ages. Adornment as seduction or self-expression. Adornment as an antidote to boredom. I could warm up to this new topic. I was gathering my thoughts when he continued.

"When I see two women like that, standing together on the stage, you know what I think?"

Well, yeah, he'd just been telling me.

Instead I said, "You wonder if they all go to the same dermatologist?"

No laugh.

He said, "I think about *natural* beauty. You're so beautiful and you do nothing to your face."

"You know I just came from the dermatologist, right? For Botox?" I said. "In fact, over the years I've also had peels, cheek fillers, lasers, under-eye fat sac removal, and fifteen years ago I got a neck lift. So yeah, other than that, I've done nothing to my face."

He was staring at my face, when a woman about my age came in.

"Do you need anything else?" She was leaving for the day, which is when I realized the sun had gone down and the breakfast room was filled with a gloomy, diffused light.

"No, Rosie. Thank you."

She smiled in my general direction and left.

Warren must have run out of things to say because he asked me how I was. Figuring we'd covered enough of the old memories (again), I told him I was staying in a hotel room in Pasadena and had been for two months while I waited to move into a new condo.

"Like you at the Beverly Wilshire all those years ago," I said. "Except it's one room, and I have my cat Sophie with me, and she has a tumor and is dying. So I'm disoriented. Unsettled."

He didn't say anything but was looking at me intently as I spoke.

"It's a strange limbo, not having a home and not knowing how long I'll be there, but I'm really sad about my cat. Every time I come back to the hotel from work, I wonder if she's going to be lying on the bed, not breathing. It's a stressful time."

He looked at me warmly. He took my hand. I felt a wave of affection.

"Can I ask you something?"

Maybe he'd ask about my condo. Or Pasadena. Or work. Or even the cat.

"Have you ever had a threesome?"

"That's your question?"

"It's a good question."

"And my answer would be yes. Three times. All with you."

"Really." That smile. Like what, he'd invite Rosie back in and we'd get busy?

"Yes. As I've told you every time you've asked that same question over the years. We don't need to revisit that."

"What about erections?" He indicated his groin area as if to educate me as to where erections could be found. Was he having one? I didn't look, but I thought about erections generally, and with absolutely no neurological or biological research to back it up, and, based on my not-so-limited experience, I came to the conclusion that men liked to get sperm into things. Not that this was a big scientific breakthrough. But I didn't want to get into this discussion with him; I didn't want to encourage him. I didn't want to talk about erections.

Maybe I was frowning.

My reverie was broken by Warren's sultry voice.

"Is it off-limits to talk about erections?" Bantering, like I'd suddenly become prim and he'd tease me out of it.

"For fuck's sake, Warren. Can we not talk about sex stuff? I just told you that I'm living in a hotel, my cat has a tumor and is dying, that I'm sad, and you want to talk about erections?"

It was like he had sexual Tourette's. Or maybe he knew he could toss out anything he wanted because I was "safe." He was long-married; there'd been nothing physical between us since the early '90s, and even today's phone call confirmed this would be just a visit between two old friends and nothing more.

However, with each exchange, I felt more and more invisible. I could also see that my willingness in the past to banter sexually was the entrance fee I'd paid to hear his voice. To have him keep answering when I called. To get a dose of what was now a diminishing amount of collateral stardust.

"Jesus. I was thinking maybe even a question about my cat or something." I shook my head in resignation. I didn't know what else to say. It was time to go.

I stood. "Warren."

"Okay, tell me about your cat."

"Too late." I looked right into his eyes. "Here's the thing."

"Tell me." Smiling like this was going to be fun.

I sat back down.

"Stop being all WARREN BEATTY. It's me here with you. You don't need to fall back on the pointless sexy talk. Or is that just an old habit you can't let go of? We haven't had sex in decades, and we're obviously not going to now, or any time in the future. We both know that. You don't have to be all sexy. Just be a real person with me."

I realized that what I'd told him was the same lesson I'd been trying to learn my whole life: that I didn't have to do anything, except be myself. I didn't have to manipulate to be loved. I didn't have to fill the air with sexual innuendo or the promise of intrigue.

And yet, had I ever been myself with him? Maybe when I'd gotten mad at him for answering the phone "Good Evening" when it was three in the afternoon. So that's one time. But for the most part, I'd simply gone along with whatever he had to offer to keep our connection alive. Warren had always been kind; had never done anything to harm me. He was not in the least bit abusive or mean, and although I'd participated in this kind of sexual back-and-forth over the years, it seemed out of place now. Insincere. Habitual. Boring.

And like the bamboo stalk that collects more and more snow, causing it to bend until it's just barely off the ground, it only takes one final snowflake to make the stalk spring upward and throw all the snow off. Maybe it was something as benign as the mention of erections that made me say *enough*. Maybe it was the wrongness of the word, just after I'd mentioned my cat, or the superficial interest in the past we'd shared. Or maybe it was just one erection discussion too many.

I was done.

Warren was quiet. I finished my water.

Aaron came in, turned on a floor lamp—taking the room from gloomy to cozy—and left. If he noted a strange tension, he didn't let on. I felt like the mysterious woman who sat for hours in a director's chair when Warren was making *Bulworth*.

And, like back then, I was getting colder by the minute.

"I'm going to go."

"Why?"

"I'm cold."

"I can get you a jacket."

I stood again.

"Warren."

"Yes?"

"You are completely lovable doing nothing. We have a long history. Sex is an old reference point. You've been more than that to me. Do you understand? I'm sorry if I'm changing the rules out of the blue, but there has to be something else to talk about. I mean, fuck, my cat is dying."

My legs were stiff from sitting. From the cool air. The dog wandered in, maybe sensing it was time to walk the guest to the door.

"Don't go. Let's get married," he blurted out. Maybe he could feel me drifting away, and this was an attention-grabber. His flirty way of pulling a woman back in. I never wanted to marry him, and he never wanted to marry me, but maybe he just didn't want me to leave.

There was no need for a response. It was too little too late. It all felt very *Last Tango in Paris*, except instead of pulling out a gun and shooting him, I simply walked into the kitchen. I carried the empty water glass to the sink and had a dizzying flashback of fifteen-year-old me standing in the small kitchen at the Bob Altman party for *McCabe and Mrs. Miller* when I'd handed Warren Beatty a fresh glass from the cabinet. Then finally meeting Warren at the Old World, my broken finger in the glass of ice water. And now I was returning an empty glass to his sink. Like a full-circle hero's journey told through kitchenware.

"Thank you for always taking my calls." It was the only sincere thing I could say at the moment.

We hugged at the door, I patted the dog, said goodbye to Warren, turned, and walked into the cool evening air.

I felt shaky driving, first across Mulholland, then down Laurel Canyon and into the Valley. But it was a different shaky from when I'd driven up to his house several hours ago. I turned the heat up in my car and thought: Was this whole lifelong thing with Warren just some weird Wizard of Oz situation? If so, this had been an extremely long yellow brick road, only to find that the man behind the curtain wanted to talk about erections.

At the hotel room, I changed into my pajamas and sat on the bed, exhausted. Sophie jumped up and I put my hand on her chest to see how her breathing was. She seemed okay.

The afternoon on Mulholland Drive had left me feeling empty. Done. I would stop calling.

At fourteen, when I'd chosen Warren to give my life meaning, I'd chosen wisely, as Warren's apparent lack of actual investment gave me the freedom to get what I needed from him without the fear of rejection. Allowed me to get mad at him—with no fear of loss. It was like a nearly fifty-year course in becoming myself, made possible by someone whose self-involvement left me plenty of room to evolve on my own. Maybe if I'd thought it could have really mattered to him, I *wouldn't* have risked being myself. He cared just enough—although it may have been an illusory caring—and it had been all I needed. For a while. And although I was glad he'd always answered the phone when I called, I no longer needed to hear Warren's voice to confirm I existed.

I was sad, but I wasn't grieving the end of *him*, I was grieving because the end of him didn't matter that much. I can't even say I was "shedding a tear and moving on" because there was never much *there* there to move on from other than what I'd created with him—both in reality and in fantasy. Not only had the spell been broken, but I realized I had been the spell's creator and implementer. This path I'd created was supposed to free me from my past, where I'd felt lonely, but by virtue of being a path, it had kept me *connected* to my past.

Lying on the bed petting Sophie, I was flooded with analogies as I tried to make sense of these revelations.

It's like believing in Jesus. It feels like love. You believe he'll be there when you turn to him. But ultimately, he is an image created from the past to provide solace in the present or create a false hope for the future. Even if Jesus is an intangible, you still take Communion, just in case. Communion for me was all the phone calls I'd made over the years, ensuring there was still a connection that might ultimately lead to fulfillment.

Or like holding onto a child's blanket that becomes worn and ragged over the years, smaller with each washing, until it is no more than a piece of fluff which, like a dandelion, is taken by the wind and ultimately dissolves into nothing.

I was tired. I finally admitted this was never going to be a satisfying story with a happy ending and a credit roll, a story where Warren and I would have a heart-to-heart, I'd become friends with Annette, and we'd all have a good laugh and go play miniature golf.

THE NEXT MORNING, THERE WERE several messages on my phone. All from Warren. He loved me. He wanted me to meet Annette. He had a lunch thing that day with friends and wanted me to join them. He was so moved by our visit.

I didn't call back.

He called again while I was having coffee and reading the paper on my computer.

"I know I'm a narcissist."

"Your messages were very sweet," I said.

"You touched something in me. That was one of the most memorable encounters I've had in a long time. I was very affected by you. Can you come to lunch?"

"I can't. I have a hearing aid appointment."

"Which ones do you use? Do you like them?"

"I can show you, if I ever see you again."

"Why do you say it like that?"

Good lord, this was a new Warren. I took it for what it was. I was gracious.

The calls slowed down after that, as expected; his brief moment of awakening, if that's what it was, had passed. And it didn't matter. As a young girl, I'd chosen him as my salvation—my unexpected vehicle for healing—and now, after all this time, I'm glad he'd been there. He may not have been able to truly see me, but he'd never turned me away. I was no longer sad. Maybe wistful. But the overwhelming feeling was one of liberation.

And just as Kim discovered at the end of *Bye Bye Birdie*, it was time for me to say goodbye. Admittedly, Kim was sixteen when she grew up, and I was *way* past sixteen.

Baby steps.

28

Last Words

I am seventy now. I often think about dying, but not due to my age. When I get blood work done, I imagine the doctors will discover a rare blood disease, and I'll feel very special. I can take to my Victorian bed, and with the back of a delicate hand against my heated brow, I can contemplate my unfortunate and imminent demise. Friends will say I had so much more life to live. I was taken too soon— well, maybe not that soon. If I go now, it's not like I'm in my prime. I've lived a full life.

Plus, the blood work is always fine.

My brother Bill and I often talk about how relieved we are that those literal and/or figurative thoughts of suicide have receded, although we still occasionally check in on the phone about our amusing dark tendencies. We had this conversation recently:

"I was feeling low," Bill said, "and my doctor suggested Wellbutrin. I guess the law stipulates that he asks: Are you feeling suicidal? I said no. But I wanted to add: 'Although if the plane went down, I might not complain.'"

"You take Wellbutrin? *I* take Wellbutrin," I said. "And I got the same question: Are you feeling suicidal? And I was happy to report: 'Not at all. Just a little low.' But inside I was thinking: 'If someone just *happened* to shoot me in the head, not sure I'd complain.'"

My obsession with death began early. When I was eleven—and thinking deep and possibly precocious thoughts—I wrote this poem:

LIFE

You may step on a bug
Thinking of how useless it is.
While that same bug is suffering,
Disaster may be reaching out
And killing a member of our race.
A bug probably feels love.
Do you think Disaster feels love
While he is killing us?
If he can't feel love killing us,
We can't feel love grinding our
Heel into that useless bug.

Okay, a lot of problems with this "poem," like do bugs feel love? I have no idea. Is Disaster sentient? Or was I trying to sort out all the God stuff I'd heard people talk about? And if Disaster doesn't feel love, does that have any consequential bearing on what *we* feel, like it's some loveless quid pro quo? Maybe it was simply an ode to the love I felt for bugs. My first pet was a potato bug named Sylvia (we didn't have a lot of money back then), and after that, I enjoyed playing with the sowbugs in the mud, careful never to hurt them. They were my friends when I was little. Or maybe I was batting around the notion of "we kill things and other things kill us," which—although not the same as suicide—may have been the usual childhood fascination with dying. And how that all works.

General thoughts of dying aside, the concept of suicide has traveled alongside me as a parallel path, a road not taken.

When I was eighteen, I *was* thinking about suicide. But having no facility for poetry, I kept these thoughts to myself.

At twenty-eight I *tried* suicide. I took a bunch of Valium and sleeping pills, and obviously I woke up the next day. Tired. Instead of trying again, I did the next best thing and got sober. And although my suicide attempt isn't always the best story to tell at a dinner party, it always got a big laugh in the recovery rooms.

I think about death a lot. Not in an unhappy way. Maybe these thoughts are the natural response to aging, to considering purpose, to the fact that fewer years remain ahead on which to project hope for a different life, although I no longer *want* a different life. I love my life. I love my friends, I love myself, I love being outside in the wind, I love reading, sleeping, solving problems, laughing out loud, petting people's pets, and watching TV. I am content.

When I think of death—or rather memento mori (which is a fancier way of saying the same thing but in a way that won't get you committed)—I think of last words.

My mom died in 2009. I was there in the hospital with her, so I heard her last words. She was never a typical Toll House cookie mom, so I never expected her last words to be mushy. I no longer expected *anything* mushy from her. Although I secretly held out hope for an unexpected turn-around and an effusive outpouring of love, I can finally accept that she did do her best—as the cliche goes. I learned so much from her: grammar, logic, how to sew, how to look things up and to not wear gold and silver jewelry at the same time. She was irreverent and funny and a solid friend to her girlfriends. And as Bill said, she had a keen bullshit detector.

Bill and I were reminiscing after she died, and he recounted one of his favorite Mom exchanges, which took place when Mom and Dad went to an auto dealership to look into getting a new car.

Car Dealer: "Nice to meet you."

Mom: "I don't see how you could know that."

Although I had learned over the years not to expect much, I still longed for something. Years before—long before she'd gotten sick—I gave it the "old one-year-of-college try" to see if we could have a better relationship, or, at least, better for me. I called her one day, got the machine, but kept talking, hoping she'd pick up the phone.

"Hi, Mom. It's Tuesday and I'm calling to say hello and it's a little windy, and I'm having some coffee and also—"

I talked long enough for her to get her drink and cigarettes and carry them to the counter in the kitchen where the phone was.

"Hi. What's up?" Sounding a little breathless. A little annoyed.

"I wondered if you might want to get together for lunch. Just the two of us."

"Jesus! Christmas is coming."

It was August.

Maybe it was all harder for her than I'd known. Doing life. When she died, I no longer had to carry around the hope that she would one day be happy and, by extension, would have room to love me. I've found many parallels in our personalities, and had I been born a generation earlier, I may have had her life. Her seemingly caged life, her unexpressed intelligence, and thwarted singing possibilities. Her alcoholism. Her ambivalence about children. She once confessed something to me when she was drunk at a party.

"If I had to do it all over again, I don't think I would have had children."

If nothing else, I appreciated her candor. And maybe not surprisingly, I never had kids.

But now, years after her death, something has cracked open in me, and what I find is empathy for my mother. She experienced depression, as did her mother, as do I, which makes me think it could be genetic, and makes it easier to accept than to always look to blame. It wasn't easy for her. Her father, Frank, died when she was fourteen. Gramma Ruth admitted to me years ago she no longer wanted to live when her husband died—wanted to walk into the ocean—but had to stay alive for my mother. That couldn't have been a happy or nurturing environment for my mom, and I can imagine how alone she must have felt growing up without her beloved father.

But along comes Dick Nash. Voted Most Popular and Most Handsome, president of his class at Arlington High, where they'd both gone to school. They barely knew one another and had crossed paths only a few times, and when Handsome Dick Nash returned from Korea, they met on a trolley car and he said to her, "How do you think you'll like California?"

They got married, and not long after, they drove across the country where it must have occurred to her that something was wrong, that she'd married a man she didn't know and with whom she had little in common except music, which worked out well for him. She'd wanted to be a singer, but after getting married, she learned she had polyps on her throat, ending any hope of her musical career, and although she was intelligent and funny, she was eclipsed by the bright star of charm and talent that was my father. She became *Barbaranashdicknashswife*.

She got pregnant at twenty, and my impending birth was a topic of scripted conversation on Tennessee Ernie Ford's radio show—where my dad had gotten a job when he had only five dollars left in his account—and my birth was announced on the radio. Going through my father's old folders and datebooks, I found a typed script from the show, which was telling in that it was not only pre-scripted—even seemingly impromptu chit-chat planned out ahead—but it relegated my mother even further to her place in the world. Which was common for most women in the '50s. Be pretty and have a baby.

TEF: You know, it's been about eight days since Dick Nash, our trombone player, and his pretty wife had their little baby girl. Yes, Dick just got himself a new little Nash Rambler! Dick, how is everything going with that 2 o'clock feeding? We haven't heard much out of you for the last week about the baby.

DN: Well, I've been too tired to talk about it.

TEF: Have you changed your first diaper yet?

DN: No I really haven't, Ernie. I made a little deal with my wife. She doesn't play the trombone and I don't change any diapers.

There were occasional pockets when her depression lifted, and she seemed okay. Lighthearted. And I appreciate the efforts she made when she may not have felt up to it. When we were little, she put food coloring in our dinner on St. Patrick's Day so everything was green: milk, mashed potatoes, scrambled eggs. Same for Valentine's Day when everything was red.

As my brothers and I got older, Mom focused on social injustices. One time she wrote a letter to the Crayola company, chastising them for having a crayon called "flesh."

"Not everyone's flesh is beige," she admonished them.

I loved that she took me to meet Ann-Margret, even if that meant witnessing my father's flirtations.

Or that she could solve problems. One night, I was in total despair because I couldn't finish a suit I was making for my high school graduation. I'd bit off more than I could sew, and I went to bed not knowing what I would do. She stayed up all night and finished the suit for me.

She had a wicked sense of humor, which occasionally veered into silliness. I had a Halloween party, and, on the invitations, as a joke, I'd attached one-inch square barcode stickers to use for entry. When she showed up, she WAS the bar code. She had sewn black strips of varying widths on a big square of fabric and wore it like a kaftan. Another time, for Christmas, I'd given her a keychain for her car keys that had a mini-camera attached. The following Christmas, she gave me a small photo album. I opened it and there were maybe ten photos, all of the interior of her car. The brake pedal, the steering wheel shaft, the ashtray, the handle to roll the window down. She was playing the part of a dimwitted someone (she called them The Stupids) who took pictures while the keys were in the ignition. And she'd waited a year for the joke to pay off.

She was funny and creative and astute, and her ability to love may have been more indirect than I was able to discern at the time.

But she wasn't forthcoming on an emotional front.

In 1994 my dad called me. "It's your old man. Your mother is in the hospital with throat cancer. We've known for two years. She's having surgery tomorrow. Wanted to let you know. Talk later."

It sounded like he was about to hang up. I stopped him to get more details, but he was trying to keep it together, so I didn't push. Although she and I communicated occasionally—mostly via fax when she sent me articles and jokes—nothing was ever said about cancer, and I realized maybe it was physically hard for her to talk. I asked my dad what hospital, and he said UCLA, but he made it clear she didn't want any visitors the night before the surgery. That night I bought a card, wishing her well, sending her love, and drove to the hospital. I found the nurse's station on the appropriate floor and asked the nurse if she'd give the card to my mother. The nurse seemed confused by this.

"She's just over there in that room," she said, indicating an open door about twenty feet away.

But I knew my mother; if she hadn't wanted visitors, she would have been enraged to see me. I left the card with the nurse, and I left the hospital.

The next day at the hospital I stayed with Dad and held him when he broke down and cried. The day after the surgery we visited her in the ICU. She was stable after a remarkable thirteen-hour, ground-breaking (and jaw-breaking) surgery. The ICU was bustling with machine sounds and people sounds and gurney sounds, and the air felt chaotic, with harsh lights and nurses in and out and things beeping and jarring announcements on the PA system. Mom's face was as big and round as a basketball. Her eyes were nearly shut with the fluid surrounding them. She wouldn't be able to speak for weeks.

She was groggy but awake, and indicated she wanted the writing pad, which I then handed to her. She wrote something on the pad. I was expecting a revelatory admission, like she was glad we were there. Or glad to be alive. When she finished writing, she turned the pad around and waved a hand toward the ICU. In a barely legible scrawl, she had written: IT'S PARTY TIME!

Fifteen hard years later, in 2009, the throat cancer returned, and my mother was dying. Since her initial surgery, she'd spent the intervening years with a scarred face and an inability to eat solid food, her only comfort being the vodka and ice cream shakes she made in a blender. She was hospitalized for the last time, and after several weeks of bedside visits—of my reading to her and putting lotion on her feet, of my dad's ritual of dropping the mail off at the foot of her bed—we were informed by the doctor there was nothing more to be done. My mother was refusing further treatment. Her feeding tube kept getting infected, and all the meds were making her feel worse. She didn't have it in her for yet another invasive procedure, which must have seemed pointless by then. She was done.

It was New Year's Eve. I called my brothers and said they should fly out as soon as they could, and they both got on planes. Bill from Seattle and Ted from New York. Ted would arrive the next day, but Bill arrived at the hospital at 11 p.m. and held Mom's hand a few minutes before she died.

Earlier in the day, when my dad was in the cafeteria, I sat with my mother, and the nurses began the slow increase of morphine after explaining the process and the possible death rattle at the end. On the walls were pictures of my cats, which I had taped up weeks before at her request. She was more comfortable with photos of animals than with photos of her kids. Which was fine, and not a surprise. I did what I could. I like cats, too.

She was still lucid. I held her small, dry hand, but not for long, as she didn't like much physical contact. She was thin and frail at this point and looked tiny in her hospital bed. How could she ever have been so scary to me? She was somewhat alert, the TV was on, and there was a lot of New Year's Eve banter in the background. Shots of the sparkly ball in Times Square. Revelers already excited—drinking and tooting horns.

She whispered something.

I couldn't hear her. I leaned in, thinking these could be her last words before the next round of morphine quieted her even further. I needed to pay attention. For my dad and my brothers. She was raspy and I asked her to repeat what she'd said.

She swallowed and did her best to gather some energy. She

whispered again, what would indeed be her last words: "I love Kathy Griffin."

Years later, while re-watching the last episode of *Six Feet Under*, I couldn't stop crying. *Six Feet Under* didn't end with only the matriarch dying, but with each character getting older—sons and daughters and lovers and grandchildren—and each had a deathbed scene until we were years and years into the future. It was brilliant. And beautiful. And devastating. And maybe my tears were a delayed reaction to my mother's death.

As my dad is still alive, I can only guess what his last words will be, but I have an idea. He is ninety-six and still going strongish, although he is hard of hearing, and losing his memory. He has a great girlfriend, Melinda, with whom he either did or did not have an affair fifty years ago. I'm happy he's happy, and I am glad she is with him now, particularly as he slowly loses touch with things. Dad doesn't say much, but when he says something, it's always with kindness.

"How is the writing coming?"

"Fine. Thanks for asking, Dad."

"I'm just so proud of you kids."

"We couldn't have done it without you."

We've had this exact exchange maybe fifteen times in the last year, and I'm happy every time for his thoughtfulness. He lost his parents when he was a child, ended up in a boys' home, and somehow came through it with a good attitude and a trombone.

Ten years ago, he lost his leg to a misdiagnosed aneurysm. Ted, Bill, and my sister-in-law Michelle all flew in, and we took turns at his bedside. It was three months of infection and surgeries and ultimately a rehab facility, where he was fitted for a prosthetic leg and started physical therapy. And flirted with the nurses.

After he was out of the woods and the dust had cleared, Bill and I launched into our usual gallows humor about how it would be when Dad got out of the hospital.

Bill: He's not going to have a leg to stand on.

Me: He'll be fine once he gets back on his foot.

Bill: It's like he already has one foot in the grave.

Me: We shouldn't joke until we've walked a mile in his shoe.

Our brother Ted was rarely in on these irreverent exchanges. Maybe he's nicer than we are. Or busier, but I made sure to give him updates. Recently, Dad and Melinda had been over for dinner, and I'd given Dad a small bowl of cat treats to entice my shy kitties. He said thanks and ate a few treats. The next day I texted both Ted and Bill to give them my weekly Dad update.

Me: He said he was so proud of us kids. And then he ate some cat food.

Ted: Cat food?

Me: Well, it was just kibble.

Bill: Ted, you remember when he found a half-eaten can of cat food in Melinda's fridge and polished it off with a Coke for lunch?

Ted: Oh, my god.

Bill: Maybe he has hairballs.

Me: Seriously though guys. It sounds like time for some kind of assisted living.

Ted: Or a kennel.

When I imagine my dad's last words, it's a toss-up. Either "I'm so proud of you kids" or "Hand me my trombone." The latter isn't out of the realm of possibility. He was in the hospital recently with a heart thing and asked Melinda to go home and get his trombone. She did. And lying in the hospital bed—trombone in hand—he tooted out a few licks, which provided the desired effect of having a couple of nurses come in and *ooh* and *ahh*. He sure loved nurses.

MY THOUGHTS ON DEATH HAVE taken many forms, although sometimes it's hard to take myself seriously. One day, in my thirties, I was consumed with self-loathing and the desire to no longer be alive—triggered by the attendant chemical reactions of depression—and I typed a long (and boring) entry in my computer journal about why I wanted to die; why life was no longer worth living. How I didn't even have enough of a spark of life, or a desire to live, or to get on with my day, or to even get up out of the chair. Then I used Spell Check to catch any mistakes I might have made. I couldn't stop laughing, and the laughter obviated the need to kill myself. Or distracted me long enough for the feeling to dissipate. I've learned that any passing thought of suicide now indicates that *something* has to die, just not me. That "ending it" is often my knee-jerk reaction to mitigate the fear of impending change, when what must die is usually an old idea, an outdated way of looking at something. When I have those thoughts, I pause and wonder: what am I afraid to let go of? The idea of fame? The need to be smarter than everyone? That I have to be perfect? That I should be attractive? That I must have a partner to be happy? It's those *ideas* that must go for me to find freedom. My thoughts of death have evolved from being a possible solution to pain to the acceptance of all our eventualities and thus to an acceptance of what is. Amor Fati.

By letting go of my imagined ideas for the future, I am left with a lot of room for the sensual now. The feel of my bare feet on a fluffy bath mat. The lingering scent of someone's cologne as they walk past me. Getting warm when I've been cold.

And yet, despite all my yap about the sensual now, I occasionally ponder death.

There is a book, *Famous Last Words,* and this is one of my favorites: Oscar Wilde was looking around the room from his deathbed and said, "This wallpaper and I are fighting a duel to the death. Either it goes or I go." And he died.

And so, after a lifetime in the rock tumbler, softened by all my encounters, I think of my last words.

I'm in a clean bed in a quiet hospital room, with subdued lighting and the low hum of equipment, a nurse or two nearby, and I hope my brothers are with me.

Just before dying—mostly to make Bill laugh—I'll say: "Can I get anyone anything?"

Enjoy more about
Collateral Stardust
Meet the Author
Check out author appearances
Explore special features

About the Author

Growing up in Hollywood, Nash studied acting, took piano lessons, and wore a nun's habit to buy alcohol so she wouldn't get carded.

She began working in TV as a gofer on *Mary Hartman, Mary Hartman,* and ended up as an associate director on a variety of shows including *Soul Train, Love Connection, Jimmy Kimmel, The Kennedy Center Honors, Ellen, Jeopardy,* and twelve years with Conan O'Brien.

When she wasn't working or napping, she tried skydiving, playwriting, screenwriting, standup comedy, swing dancing, poker, and painting.

She likes eating toast and still watches a lot of TV.

Acknowledgments

For help with the book, huge thanks to:

Nancy Montgomery, who read every chapter, flagging spots where she encountered incoherence or boredom. She was fantastically encouraging, and yet never patted me on the head.

LP Mitchell, for her help with tone and POV, as well as for her friendship that started on a boat in Costa Rica. "...some have entertained angels unawares."

Bobbi and Don Vandervort, my pandemic bubble (and beyond) friends, who heard stories every week and said, "You should write a book."

Kristen Lee Sergeant, for all our back-and-forth texting about art.

Lisa Rosenberg, for our weekly mutual-cheering-on lunch dates.

Kelly Coty, who lived through many of these stories and often remembers more than I do.

Tracy Mazuer and Marin Zielinski, for all the support over the years.

Marilyn Kentz, who pushed my little sailboat until the wind picked up.

Jill Mullikin-Bates, for her continued enthusiasm and help in getting the book out there.

Bob Bates, for taking my author photo and making the process delightful.

Lex Passaris, for his insightful feedback and continued good ideas.

Steve "Sailor Pants" Grody and Bob "Pretty Cards" Claster, for their impeccable typo-finding skills.

Bob Sipchen, for his incessant* help and weekly poker games.

Paul Vandeventer, who paid me to mention him in glowing terms. But I ran out of room. (*He also told me to add "incessant" to Bob's thing.)

Neal Pollack, who introduced me to my agent when I had only a handful of stories.

Murray Weiss—said agent—who made great suggestions from the start, and then kept me grounded with his reality checks during the rest of the process.

Mitch Laurance and Shari Stauch for putting me on the map in South Carolina. (Note to self: Locate South Carolina on map.)

Alicia Feltman, for making the book beautiful, Julia Park Tracey, for making it better, and Vicki DeArmon, for making it public. And all at Sibylline Press.

Jonathan Kirsch, for his legal acumen, as well as his fun voice on the phone.

Kim Dower, for her tireless and enchanting PR work on getting the book out there.

Dr. Susan Krevoy, for keeping me alive during the rough times.

Connie Kaplan, a self-involved, overly-opinionated, sartorially-confused, "Nikki-obsessed whore" (her words—I'd never call anyone a whore), who brings invaluable and unwavering delight to my life. And I to hers—or so she says.

And to my beloved cat Basil, who accepts any invitation to sit on my lap. (Unlike that selfish whore-of-a-friend, Connie.)

Sibylline Press is proud to publish the brilliant work of women authors over 50. We are a woman-owned publishing company and, like our authors, represent women of a certain age.

ALSO AVAILABLE FROM
Sibylline Press

Other People's Kids: A Novel
By Kim Culbertson

FICTION
392 PAGES, TRADE PAPER, $22
ISBN: 9781960573438
ALSO AVAILABLE AS AN EBOOK AND AUDIOBOOK

After a violent incident at her prestigious Bay Area school, English teacher Chelsea Garden returns to her rural hometown seeking refuge and a fresh start. There, she reconnects with a burned-out principal and an old flame, both working at the local high school. *Other People's Kids* follows three educators at different stages of their careers as they navigate second chances, personal crossroads, and the risks of starting over.

Seeds of the Pomegranate: A Novel
By Suzanne Samuels

HISTORICAL FICTION
416 PAGES, TRADE PAPER, $22
ISBN: 9781960573445
ALSO AVAILABLE AS AN EBOOK and audiobook

After illness derails her dreams of becoming a painter in Sicily, Mimi Inglese immigrates to New York, only to be dragged into her father's criminal underworld. When he's imprisoned, she turns to counterfeiting to survive, using her artistic gift to forge a path through Gangland chaos. As violence closes in, Mimi must risk everything to escape a life built on desperation and reclaim the future she once imagined.

You Could Be Happy Here: A Novel
By Erin Van Rheenen

FICTION
280 PAGES, TRADE PAPER, $19
ISBN: 9781960573476
ALSO AVAILABLE AS AN EBOOK and audiobook

When Lucy loses her mother and discovers her real father may be a man from her childhood summers in Costa Rica, she sets out to find him—and herself. But the village she returns to is no longer the paradise she remembers, and her search raises more questions than answers. *You Could be Happy Here* is a story of identity, belonging, and redefining home in a world that no longer fits the past.

The House of Cavanaugh: A Novel
By Polly Dugan

FICTION
248 PAGES, TRADE PAPER, $18
ISBN: 9781960573469
ALSO AVAILABLE AS AN EBOOK and audiobook

In 1964, Joan Cavanaugh has a secret affair that leads to the birth of a daughter whose true paternity she takes to the grave. Fifty years later, a Thanksgiving reunion unearths the buried truth, shaking the foundations of two tightly connected families. *The House of Cavanaugh* is a gripping story of hidden pasts, unraveling loyalties, and what it really means to be family.

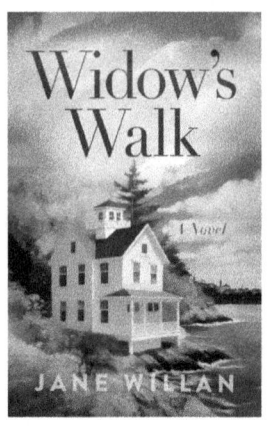

Widow's Walk: A Novel

By Jane Willan

FICTION
336 PAGES, TRADE PAPER, $20
ISBN: 9781960573452
ALSO AVAILABLE AS AN EBOOK and audiobook

When new Reverend Miranda McCurdy brings progressive change to a tradition-bound coastal church in Maine, her efforts spark fierce resistance—especially after she challenges the town's beloved Thanksgiving pageant. As the congregation splinters and a woman seeking sanctuary raises the stakes, Miranda must choose between fleeing back to her old life or staying to fight for the community she's slowly come to love. A stray dog and a mysterious stranger may tip the scales in this story of conviction, belonging, and second chances.

Reviving Artemis: The Making of a Huntress

By Deborah Lee Luskin

MEMOIR
280 PAGES, TRADE PAPER, $19
ISBN: 9781960573759
ALSO AVAILABLE AS AN EBOOK and audiobook

At sixty, longtime writer, gardener, and teacher Luskin feels a wild new calling: to leave the safety of her garden and learn to hunt deer. *Reviving Artemis* follows her late-in-life transformation as she confronts fear, embraces the forest, and reclaims a primal connection to nature. Blending humor, vulnerability, and myth, it's the story of a woman choosing to age on her own fierce terms.

 For more books from **Sibylline Press**, please visit our website at **sibyllinepress.com**

www.ingramcontent.com/pod-product-compliance
Lightning Source LLC
Chambersburg PA
CBHW031314160426
43196CB00007B/533